Straight A's at Stanford and Harvard.
How to learn faster and think better.
By Peter Rogers MD. Copyright August, 2014

Table of Contents
- 1. Intro   2. Magic Bathroom   3. PreRead   4. Stanford
- 5. Transformation   6. Condensed notes   7. Music   8. SAT
- 9. MCAT   10. Interviews   11. Midterms   12. Evol of mind
- 13. Phases learning   14. Intelligence   15. Genius   16. Sleep
- 17. Stress   18. Future Jobs   19. Feynman method
- 20. Brain speed   21. Speed read   22. How read book   23. Cone of Learning
- 24. Apprentice   25. Vision   26. East Genius   27. Instant Smarts
- 28. Word Assoc   29. Time Mgmt   30. Hilite   31. Peak
- 32. Dress Success   33. Puzzle   34. Mirror   35. Incremental
- 36. Meals   37. DVR   38. Mindset   39. Edge   40. Textbook
- 41. Q book   42. Sport   43. Extracurric   44. High School   45. Concepts
- 46. Neurogenesis   47. Shadow   48. WBL   49. Build Brain
- 50. WBL Two   51. Method   52. Educ Future   53. de Bono
- 54. FIQ   55. Metaphor   56. FC's & Leitner   57. Kasparov

- 58. Fast Learn 59. Kuhn 60. Shower 61. **Periph** Brain 62. Boyd
- 63. DKM 64. Puccio 65. Molloy 66. **Master**y 67. NeuroSci

68. 3P Brain 69. L Body 70. Maltz 71. Expertise 72. Idle 73. Speeds 74. How much? 75. KMS 76. Fail 77. Flow 78. Overspeed 79. Overlearn 80. Bio 81. Early 82. Car

- 83. Wit 84. Wisdom 85. Words 86. Jokes 87. Writing
- 88. Gram 89. Oratory 90. Cram 91. RipRead 92. Tape 93. History 94. Bloom 95. Mastery 96. OCD 97. Habit 98. Purpose
- 99. Stigler 100. Zeigarnik 101. Checklist
- 102. Summer 103. Focus 104. Research 105. Class
- 106. Wozniak 107. Ebbinghaus 108. FC 109. more FC
- 110. Anki 111. Room 112. When 113. What 114. Win
- 115. Class 116. TA 117. Mult Ways 118. LN alphabet
- 119. # system 120. AutoBio 121. Loci 122. Cards
- 123. Mnemonics 124. Maps 125. Standing 126. Poster
- 127. Always 128. Notes 129. Web 130. Bkpk 131. Secret
- 132. Andragog 133. Age 134. Outside 135. Happy

136. Social 137. Parents 138. EIQ 139. **Pharm** 140. Marriage 141. Mentor 142. Gr Teach 143. **Motive** 144. Calib 145. Sched 146. Decide 147. Attn 148. W&T

- 149. CHO 150. Fat 151. Plants 153. Caffeine 154. WM

- 155. Teeth 156. Trauma 157. Yin Yang 158. Goals
- 159. Toxins 160. Exiles 161. Math 164.Med Appendices …Music..About author

Chapter 1.

How to use this book.

TRAIN YOUR BRAIN TO GAIN. This book will help you learn faster, think better and become smarter.

You can read it in continuity or skip to whatever interests you.

Story information is included because the context of an insight helps show its importance.

Chapters on learning, thinking, creating, speaking, remembering, IQ, Stanford, Harvard, Northwestern and U. Illinois are mixed together for variety.

Life is a race to learn what you need to know before a challenge.

Dr. Rogers is an expert mentor to help you prepare for your learning, thinking and speaking endeavors.

Chapter 2.

About the cover – the Magic Bathroom.

Ok, I know this is a crazy looking picture, but it will soon make sense.

The mystery of the "Magic Bathroom" will be revealed unto thee.

The pictures taped to the shower door and wall were put there when studying for a neuroradiology boards exam because visual memory is the best.

The **bathroom is a great place to tape pictures to the wall, because we go there so often.**

The pictures near the mirror are persons who inspire me.

The table next to the sink is for flashcards. I saw a Monty Python skit called, "every sperm is sacred" and it gave me the idea that **"every piss is "sacred." Meaning, why not look at flashcards while voiding?**

Mozart liked to write letters while on the loo. He wrote, "I think it only fitting to write while shitting." This gave me the idea of, **"I think it only fitting to read while..."**

Who says, "men can't multitask?"

Lots of people read on the loo, but I figured it would be easier if there was a table. The **table had to be portable**, so I just stacked two plastic crates, that you can slide over, in front of the loo by pushing them with your foot.

As a matter of fact, the loo is a great place to read difficult stuff.

If knowledge is money, and money is gold, then this is **modern day Alchemy.**

Feces (wasted time) is turned into gold (knowledge).

Who says, "you can't polish a turd?"

There is a CD player by the entrance door for listening to audiobooks while flossing, brushing and shaving.

This creates an extra 2 hours of "learning-studying" per day from 60 min reading, 30 min audiobooks and 30 min flashcards.

People often ask, where do you find time to read so much? How can you remember so well?

Well, there's your answer, the Magic Bathroom.

Chapter 3.

Prereading.

This is a game changer.

It changed my life.

Every student knows what it is like to be overwhelmed by a lecture. This happened to me in biochemistry. I'm sitting there, in the front row, like a good boy, and 10 minutes in, the professor starts picking up the pace, getting more and more complex.

Soon, I'm like Hansel and Gretel in the forest with no bread crumbs. I try to take notes, but it's no use. I'm lost. Ouch, ouch, ouch.

This means, I'm gonna have to study this stuff all evening and all weekend. I'm mad at the teacher for going so fast and I'm mad at myself for being so clueless. Another weekend chasing biochemistry facts instead of girls.

I call my friend, the great Charles (Chuck) Kinder, a cardiologist in Chicago. I knew he was the best student in his medical school class at the university of Illinois.

I said, "Chuck, it's like drinking water from a firehose. I can't keep up. What should I do?"

Chuck said, **"get the co-ops from last year."**

Me, "what's a co-op?"

Chuck, "The students get together and each makes a typed copy of the lecture notes from one class. You can buy last year's version.

The lectures are about the same each year. **Everybody is smarter when they have seen the material before. You will be too."**

The clouds parted, and the sun shone brightly.

Eureka! is an understatement.

The night before a biochemistry class, I read the last year's coop notes. I look at the pictures in the book. I read some of the book. Now, I've got the general concept. Sure,... There's a couple of details to fill in and a few things to memorize. But that's no big deal. I've got the big picture, and that's all I need.

Bring it on professor, I'm ready.

That's right.

The next day, **I'm a goalie sitting in the front row.**

"Nothin gets past me."

I try to anticipate and catch every word the professor says.

If the professor gets a fact past me, that's a goal for him.

If I can follow just about everything in the lecture, then that's a win for me.

My ability to comprehend a biochemistry lecture just went from 30% to 95%.

I went on to score 780 out of a possible 800 on the medical school, national boards exam in biochemistry. Given that the 99th percentile began at around 690, this was one of the highest scores in the USA, perhaps the highest.

Chapter 4.

Getting started at Stanford.

At Stanford, the average SAT score is 99th percentile. Ie. the average student is in the top 1% of college students. The premed classes tend to be some of the toughest classes at any university. In a Stanford premed science class, the "average" SAT score is in the upper half of the 99th percentile.

Stanford is on the quarter system instead of the semester system. At the beginning of my first, freshman quarter, it was a safe bet, that I was one of the worst students in the room for all my classes.

Stanford is the land of "California Valedictorians." The majority of the students are from California and the west coast. A large number are from fancy, east coast prep schools with names like "Groton."

There were lots of parties. All these good looking California guys with nice cars. Everybody talking about social life in California and their high school sports teams and their plans at Stanford.

I was a total nobody. I did not know anyone in my dorm. There was one other guy from my high school in Illinois, but we were not allowed to live together because the school wanted people to meet new people.

During a warm day in September, in order to get in shape for wrestling, I went for a run in my usual black stocking knit hat, sweatshirt and sweatpants. Well, wrestling isn't exactly the most popular sport in California. The other kids in the dorm looked at me like I was crazy.

The black hat seemed to be the thing that flipped the switch. I had told one of them I was from Chicago. They yelled out, "look it's the Chicago Hood." "Hey, do you know Al Capone?"

Don't ask me why, but whenever I'm in California, people ask me that. The "Chicago Hood" became my freshman dorm nickname. My roommate was a punk rocker, and even he thought this "Chicago Hood" "Al Capone" stuff was funny.

I was in over my head and I knew it. I had been recruited on an athletic scholarship because Stanford was trying to build up it's wrestling team. I had wanted to go to Iowa because I used to be a good wrestler, but an injury had put an end to all that.

In high school, junior year, scholastic style, I had been 39-1, 3rd in state despite virtually no coaching. I felt that I could become really good with some coaching. Then I fractured the growth plate in my collar bone, and it would not heal. My physique began to disappear. Kids at the high school kept asking me, "what happened? You used to be strong."

I could not wrestle my senior year of high school, and I wanted to drop out of school and come back the next year and win state. My father wouldn't let me drop out of high school. I wanted to run away from home. I didn't know anything about Stanford. It was like "a million miles away" from Illinois. I had never even taken an honors class in high school except for senior English which was a joke. I had never even heard of an "AP test."

The Stanford coach somehow had heard of me, and he called. He said, "Pete, we think you have the potential to help our team and we are gonna offer you a one third scholarship. Dave and Mark Schultz, national champions, are gonna be assistant coaches. Are you willing to sign a letter of intent to "commit yourself" to Stanford?"

At that moment, I was desperate. I wanted to escape from my life. I was so sick and tired of people asking me, "what happened to you?" I wanted to reinvent myself. I wanted to create a new identity. I wanted to be far away from the people who tied me to my past.

Then, in a moment reminiscent of Kent Dorfman, "Flounder" in the "Animal House" movie, I said, "I'll do it! I'll do it! I'll do it!"

This was a chance to reinvent myself as a student far away. This was a chance to be coached by the Schultz brothers who were the best in the west and would later go on to world and Olympic gold medals. Dave Schultz was the "Bruce Lee" of wrestling and Mark Schultz was "Superman." There is a movie about them called, "Foxcatcher" that opened in November 2014.

Sitting in my dorm room, all alone, day after day, with no friends, "commit yourself" seemed like the right choice of words. My girlfriend, Carol, the hometown honey, a senior in high school, was far away, back in Illinois. She called me up.

Carol, "Pete, would it be ok with you if I went to Homecoming with Mike Lynch? I mean, it's my senior year. I just want to go to the dance. All my friends are going. I promise not to do anything with him in a sexual way."

Me, "that's a great #*#*!!! idea!"

Then I got injured again while wrestling, and it looked like I was out for the season.

I called my mom.

Mom, "How's it going Peter?"

Me, "Great Mom. I have no friends. I don't know anyone here except the coach. The coach is mad at me because I got injured, and he told someone that he is sorry he "wasted a scholarship" on me. My girlfriend is fooling around with some other guy. And I'm the worst student in the room in all my classes. I think I'm going to flunk out. But other than that, everything is going well."

I started crying. "Mom, I want to come home. I don't belong here. I want to transfer to a school in Illinois. I'm so lonely."

Mom, "Peter. I want you to listen to me. I love you more than anything in the world. I want you to do something for me. I want you to try as hard as you can for one year at Stanford. Just do your best for one year. If, at the end of the year, you want to transfer back to a college close to home, then it's ok. You can call me every day."

"Thanks Mom."

I loved my mother more than anything in the world.

"Ok, Mom. I'll do it for you. One year. But then, I'm coming home."

That moment, I finalized the decision.

I decided that I was going to become the best student I could be. I was going to study until I dropped.

I didn't know if I could make it, but I knew I could push myself. Wrestling had taught me that. When I was a freshman in high school, lots of guys were better than me. But I worked harder than them and got better faster. Junior year of high school, I had pinned my way through the Spring freestyle tournament of Schoolboy State.

I said to myself, "I'm gonna make academics my new sport."

"I'm gonna take all my sadness, frustration, anger and energy and channel it into becoming the best possible student."

"I AM GOING TO BECOME A LEARNING MACHINE."

I looked out the window of my dorm room. There was vomit on the sidewalk. Some guy had gotten drunk last night and puked.

I smiled and thought to myself,

"Good. Go ahead, get drunk."

"Go ahead, go to all your parties. Go ahead and go home to your families and friends every weekend. You are probably smarter than me. But it doesn't matter. While you are goofing around, I'm gonna be studying, and I'm gonna catch you."

Chapter 5.

<u>Personal Transformation at Stanford.</u>

I took a class called, "How to College" for substandard students like me. They told us stuff like, "you need to take good notes," "you need to study every day," "you need to be organized and turn in all of your assignments on time."

My grandmother could've told me that. But I still liked the class. It was nice to see a bunch of clueless jocks and miscellaneous, loser, musician types in the same room. I no longer felt like I was the worst student on campus.

On the weekends, I studied and studied until I couldn't take it anymore, and then I would eat or go workout. Then in the afternoon and evening I would study some more. Lonely is an understatement.

I wasn't sure I was gonna make it with a real course load, but I knew that if I failed, it wouldn't be for lack of effort. I would study until I dropped. Life had taken away my friends, my family, my girlfriend and my athletic ability but it could not take away the fire that burned inside of me.

I had a purpose and I was gonna pursue it.

In order to be successful at something really challenging, you have to devote yourself. It has to be a top priority. You have to concentrate your powers. You should write down your goal, write out a plan to achieve it, and then get to work.

I only took one real science class the first quarter. With this brilliant strategy of "just study a lot" and "do what the teacher says," I got all B's the first quarter. I was just happy that I didn't flunk anything.

Through trial and error, I was slowly improving my study methods, and the 2nd semester, I got all B's and one A-. That meant a lot to me. It was proof I was capable of getting an A at Stanford.

It is very helpful to have mentors, and luckily I found one midway thru first year when I met up with my old, high school classmate, Jay Rehm. Jay told me that he was getting straight A's in all his science classes. He had gotten A+'s in math, physics and engineering type classes.

I was like, "Holy crap Batman, how did you pull that off?"

Chapter 6

Condensed notes.

Jay said, "Condensed notes."

Me, "Is that like condensed milk?"

Jay, "No. **Condensed notes means that you make your own set of summary notes** for all the important stuff covered in the class. You just put it into an 8" x 11" spiral notebook. This includes information from lectures, the text and practice problems."

Me, "why does it work?"

Jay, "Because **in the process of making the condensed notes, you are learning the material and reviewing the material. It gets you to study in an active way.** This deeper level of processing leads to a deeper level of understanding and to a better retention of the information."

Me, "But isn't that a lot of extra work?"

Jay, "No. Because, **it makes you more efficient.** I just keep refining my condensed notes. Before the exams, I just go over my notes. I don't need to to look at the textbook. It actually saves time, in that way."

Me, "sounds good. Do you want to take some classes with me so I could copy your notes?"

Jay, "No. **You have to make your own notes. You learn from the process of MAKING the condensed notes. A lot of thinking goes into deciding what to include and exclude.** You develop your own system of abbreviations and memory methods to remember the information."

Me, "Is that it?"

Jay, "It also helps to draw stuff out. I like to draw out chemical structures to better understand them. I like to draw out what is actually happening in a physics problem, such as the objects in motion or the electrical circuit, so that I can better picture it and better understand it."

Me, "But Jay, you're a genius. Will that work for me? I'm just a stupid jock."

Jay, "Pete, these things are universal to all mankind. Everyone learns better when they write stuff out, analyze the material and draw pictures of it."

Me, "Thanks, Jay! You've given me hope. Maybe, I could get an A in a real science class at Stanford."

3rd quarter, freshman year at Stanford, using Jay's method of condensed notes and my own little bag of tricks, I got straight A's.

That summer, in calculus, an A+.

From there on out, I got straight A's in every premed class as far as I can remember including A+'s in organic chemistry and biology, and in the weed out classes where the California Valedictorians were dropping like flies.

From my freshman dorm, there were 12 premed students. Only 4 of us got into med school.

In college, I just used spiral notebooks (eg. organic chemistry) and class syllabus (biology) for condensed notes.

Chapter 7

<u>Music and Ear Protectors.</u>

Sophomore year at Stanford I lived in the trailer apartments with Jay Rehm, Martin and a guy we'll call East Coast Genius. Given that Jay had better social skills than me, these guys were his friends. Jay allowed me to live with them out of pity. His mom probably forced him to let me live with them.

I had my own bedroom which was an improvement over the dorms. I studied in my bedroom on a big desk. I liked to listen to baroque music which also matched my bank account, "brrroke."

The baroque music that I liked for studying had no words. The reason baroque music is thought to be good for studying is that it has a cadence and organizational structure that seems to help the mind.

The best music for studying is Bach, Vivaldi (4 seasons), Teleman, Handel and Arcangelo Corelli.

In college I listened to baroque music routinely when studying at home. In medical school and residency I just wanted the room to be quiet.

Now I have a new approach. It's called EAR PROTECTORS."

I love them. I wear 3M Peltor, NRR 31 Db, over the head Earmuffs.

Here's why. Think of your brain's processing power as being like a cable internet connection with a limited amount of bandwidth. You gonna hear the noises around you, especially if the noises contain words.

Perhaps this occupies 5-10% of your intellectual bandwidth.

By wearing earmuffs you acoustically isolate yourself. That intellectual bandwidth can now be focused on the desired task. Sounds like a great deal. Just put on some earmuffs and you get 5-10% smarter.

Just a few more thoughts on music. **Music speaks directly to our emotions just as comedy speaks to our minds.**

It reminds me of the Jack Lalanne quote, **"Exercise is the king and nutrition the queen and together they make a kingdom of health."**

Comedy is the king and music is the queen and together they make a kingdom of happiness.

As I have gotten older, I have come to believe that the academic world overemphasizes the logical mind, and underestimates the emotional mind. The emotional mind is very powerful. It is good to try to learn about it in order to enjoy it, to control it better and to harness its power for your benefit.

I sometimes like to watch the highlights films of my favorite athletes because they inspire me. For example, for Cristiano Ronaldo the soccer player you can check out the You Tube video "Cristiano Ronaldo – remember MU." Ilya is name of guy who made the video.

For Michael Jordan the basketball player, check out You Tube video "Michael Jordan Highlights" from Chicago Bulls 92, with Kayne West, "Amazing" as well as CIU, "Put it on the line" soundtrack.

For college wrestling fans, some of my favorite wrestlers to watch were Wade Schalles, Gene Mills, Randy Lewis, Rob Koll, John Smith, Mark and Dave Schultz. Favorite match was Mark Schultz versus Ed Banach in the NCAA finals.

When you see human achievement raised to this level of greatness, it inspires you to also strive for excellence.

In the **appendices** to this book there are some music suggestions for different situations.

Chapter 8.

The SAT.

Junior year of high school, I went out on Friday night before the SAT test, the next day. At that time, my plan for my life was to be a wrestler at Iowa, a national champion, an Olympic champion and then a wrestling coach and a college professor or something like that.

I couldn't have cared less about some, silly test that I was being forced to take. I didn't realize that the SAT test and the ACT test are really opportunities.

I did reasonably well on the SAT, but lots of kids at my high school scored higher than I did.
The real question is why did I do as well as I did.

Here's the reason. Reading.

Personal reading builds the mind.

The vocabulary in a nonfiction books is an order of magnitude greater than the vocabulary in routine conversation.

The vocabulary in novels and science textbooks is another order of magnitude greater.

The more you read, the more your vocabulary grows. The bigger your vocabulary, the more you can understand, the more you can say, the more precisely you can express yourself.

Also, the more precisely you can think your way into someone else's head. Ie. The better grades you will get on written papers because you can provide in writing what the teacher wants.

Also, the better your scores will be on an SAT like test that covers vocabulary and reading comprehension.

My father grew up in a house with a dirt floor, next door to a beer factory. Most of the boys in his town ended up working in the factory.

His mother read a lot, and my dad imitated her. I imitated him. Growing up, I seldom had a chance to talk to my dad. He was working all the time. At night, he would read in his bed and listen to classical music. It was understood by the family that he was tired and to leave him alone.

His older brother was a physicist and his younger brother, uncle Jon, a doctor, like my father. They would argue about books all the time.

Uncle Jon was a real pain in the butt. He would read a book the previous weekend and then act like he was the world's expert on the subject. He would then ask me questions, that you could only know, if you had just read the book.

He would try to make my dad and me look stupid. I couldn't understand how my dad could like him, and I said to my mom, "why do you invite that guy over. He is so obnoxious."

My mother said, "your father loves to talk to him about books. Everyone knows that uncle Jon is a pain in the butt. We don't take him seriously."

I was offended that he was calling my dad names. I was offended that he made fun of me. Uncle Jon would say things like, "what would you know about the war in Nam, you are just a young idiot." "Oh look, the son is as stupid as the father."

That pissed me off. I would read and read. If I knew uncle Jon was coming over, I wanted to have a fresh stack of books that I had read so that I could turn the tables and ask him questions.

As a kid, in junior high and high school, I didn't know enough to be able to effectively discuss books with uncle Jon, but I still benefited from his visits because they motivated me.

I wanted to be well read like my dad. I wanted to be able to defend my self in open debate against obnoxious people like uncle Jon. In retrospect, uncle Jon probably knew this and was just having fun teasing me.

My father was my hero. It was a big deal for me every couple of months to go to the bookstore with him. There was no internet in those days. This was our time together to talk about books and other things. My dad would buy about 10 books for himself and 5 for me.

I had a big bookshelf in my room and was proud of having read every book on those shelves.

The point is that any type of reading develops the mind.

Reading builds a scaffold of vocabulary and word associations that facilitates learning new information. It improves your brain processing speed for text because you have better, more rapid comprehension.

I think that this is why, even though I was not in honors classes in high school, and did not care much about school until my athletic career got sidetracked, I did well on vocabulary tests, the spelling bee and writing assignments.

Now that I have kids of my own, I have noticed that my daughter reads a lot more than my sons. Even though she is a lot younger than them, she has a much better vocabulary.

Senior year, because of my injury, I could not wrestle. I was able to run and joined the cross country team. The cross country team at my high school was kind of "Nerd Headquarters." These guys were the best students in the school.

I heard them talking about their SAT scores and they had done a lot better than me. Jay Rehm was on the team, and he had crushed the SAT's.

I hate losing. I had lost my athletic career to an injury. Now I wanted to start a "career" as a student, so I decided to take the SAT test again.

I bought one of those SAT preparation books and studied on my own. My score went up a lot. About 200 points. At that time the SAT had only two parts "math and verbal."

I still felt like I could do better. So I decided to take the SAT test a third time. My scores went up even more. Altogether, my scores improved about 220 to 250 points. I do not remember the exact numbers. But I do remember that this was a big deal at the time.

I realized that **one can tremendously improve their scores by preparing for a standardized exam**. This was significant because at that time the "word on the street" was that the SAT was like an IQ test, an "aptitude" test, and that you couldn't prepare for it.

The truth is that it is actually an **"achievement" test.** Ie. The more you study and know, the better you do.

Chapter 9.

The MCAT.

The MCAT (Medical College Admission Test) is the big test for premeds and it's taken late in the course of college.

By this time, as a junior, I felt like I was a "big dog" at Stanford. I had joined Delta Tau Delta fraternity. The Delts. This was THE athletic fraternity of Stanford.

The great quarterbacks, Jim Plunkett and John Elway were Delts. John Elway was a few years older than me. He and the other football players used to travel around campus on golf carts. He was very nice, and was well liked by the Delts and other people at school.

My shoulder had healed up and I was able to return to wrestling. I had set the school record for most victories in a season and earned the Student Athlete of the Year Award at Stanford (called the "Block "S" award for outstanding academic and athletic achievement). I had grown from being an insecure freshman to being an arrogant frat boy.

Don't get me wrong. I was still a loser with the ladies at Stanford. As a matter of fact I never had a girlfriend that was actually from Stanford. I asked out this one girl named Patricia. We were in Econ 101 together and I used to help her with her homework.

She was about half as pretty as my hometown honey from high school, but the dating situation at Stanford was different. As a matter of fact, Trish pretty much laughed in my face because she probably had 100 guys chasing her.

It was difficult to attract a girlfriend at Stanford in those days. There were lots of good looking, athletic guys in comparison with the girls. The old joke was "9 out of 10 California girls are pretty and the 10th one goes to Stanford." "What do you call a pretty girl at Stanford? A visitor." "Having trouble finding a spouse for your daughter? Send her to Stanford and the men will fight over her."

There was even an article in the paper by someone from USC who wrote, "so what if you guys are smarter than us. We are beautiful and you are ugly." At the USC versus Stanford football game, the USC crowd had some taunt song similar to this. The Stanford crowd responded with something like, "that's alright, that's ok, you'll all work for us some day."

My hometown honey, one year younger than me, was a musician and she went to USC. USC has a great music school. For grad school she went on to Juilliard for music. I realize that readers of this book could care less about the hometown honey, but she will return to the story in an interesting way later.

Anyways, back at the frat, little did I know what was about to happen. The other premeds were gearing up for MCAT's (Medical College Admission Test). They invited me to join their study group. I declined.

At that time, I felt like the MCAT was a joke. My attitude was, "what should I care about the MCAT? I'm one of the best premed students at Stanford, if not the best. I felt that it was beneath me to study for the MCAT. I'll just end up babysitting that study group." Well, you've heard it before, "pride goeth before the fall." In all my arrogance at that time I had forgotten the lessons of the SAT.

They all did better than me on the MCAT. It was quite embarrassing. Studying makes a big difference on standardized tests.

But that was only the beginning of my embarrassments.

Chapter 10.

Medical School Interviews.

Ok, ok, ok. I know that many of you could care less about med school interviews.

However, there are valuable lessons here for any type of interview situation and for social intelligence in general.

Jack from the frat got into Yale.

Owen got into Harvard.

There was this other football player, from a different frat, whose name I can't remember that got into Stanford. He was doing a research project with a professor at the Stanford medical school. I remember thinking that he was a butt kisser. I figured, "I'm a much better student than him. Surely they'll take me before him."

Wrong again. I was rejected by Stanford.

Lesson learned. Butt kissing is a very useful skill in life. There ought to be a class called, "butt kissing 101" or something like that.

If it isn't obvious already, let me put it into writing, "I was the poster child for good academic skills and lousy social skills" and this caused me a lot of problems in life.

I interviewed at Northwestern. One of the persons who interviewed me was this woman who seemed a wimpy, wallflower, boring sort of person. She asked me how I liked Stanford. In retrospect, she probably wanted to hear about the beautiful sunset and the red roofs and the sandstone buildings.

However, at the time, being the self absorbed, bonehead that I was, I felt obligated to talk about beloved Delta Tau Delta, the animal house, athlete fraternity and some of the wild parties.

Well, judging by the look on her face, it was pretty obvious that the only thing she hated more than frat boys was jocks.

Needless to say, I was rejected by Northwestern.

After all these mistakes, the interview went better at the University of Illinois.

One always rationalizes their situation and I was no exception. U. of I was a state school so I saved money on tuition. For example, yearly tuition at that time for U of I was $8,000 per year versus $24,000 at Northwestern.

U of I provides an excellent education. It is affiliated with very good, private, public and VA hospitals for student and resident training. Lots of the best students in Illinois make U of I their first choice for these and other reasons.

U of I was close to my parent's house, so I saved money on laundry and could coach wrestling at the local high school and college.

Lessons learned. When interviewing don't rely too much on your credentials. It is good to be respected, but it is more important to be liked.

A college and a medical school are different than a sports team or a business where success is measured in victories and dollars.

Colleges, medical schools and hospitals will any day of the week take a likable person with minimal qualifications over a highly qualified person that they don't like.

It is important to try to make yourself more likable.

The Dale Carnegie book about "How to win friends and influence people" is worth reading.

Chapter 11.

Midterm exams at the University of Illinois medical school.

My freshman year of medical school, I was very confident going into the first set of midterms. I figured, "I'm the big dog from Stanford. This is going to be a walk in the park."

Wrong again.

I was expecting to get the highest grade in the class. Instead, my test scores averaged around the tenth percentile.

No way! How could this have happened?! I felt like I had been mugged in an alley. After all the studying I've done these past years, this was an outrage.

How did so many other students do better than me? I brooded on this for quite some time.

Then one day at the lunch table, in casual conversation, some med students were talking about what classes they took in college. One of them said, "well that semester I took anatomy and physiology and histology."

Holy crap! That's it!

The reason so many students did better than me was because they had already taken these classes. In college they had majored in real, premed biology that emphasized humans.

Meanwhile, back at the ranch, at Stanford, I had majored in evolutionary biology that emphasized animals. Instead of learning human anatomy, I had been counting the number of mitochondria in a bug's ass.

It's a big advantage to have seen the material before.

With this new found understanding I no longer felt so bad. I knew that I just had to learn the material better, and that would happen with time. I wanted to go into orthopedic surgery and I figured, that I should try to be in the top 5% of the class to guarantee a good residency position in ortho.

I went on to get 99% on the medical school, national boards exam part one (now called USMLE 1), the highest score in the entire U. of Illinois class of 333 students.

Chapter 12.

Evolution of the human mind.

"For our own species, evolution occurs mostly through our behavior. We innovate new behavior to adapt." - Michael Crichton.

Most other animals have evolved by developing superior physical abilities suited to their niche. The fish swims, the antelope runs, the bird flies.

There is a theory that the human mind evolved so that man could be better at making tools and hunting.

There is a newer theory that the mind evolved for social reasons, to be able to get along better in larger groups.

It is a lot easier to understand a science book than a wife or one's teenage kid.
There are also other theories.

"We have reason to believe that the first man walked upright fo free his hands for masturbation."
- Lily Tomlin.

Chapter 13.

The Three Phases of Learning.

Alfred North Whitehead was a famous mathematician who wrote that there are three phases of learning.

Romance is the first phase.
Everything is new and exciting. Progress is rapid. There is a wonderful feeling of unlimited potential. This is like starting out in a foreign language where you learn the beginner vocabulary quickly, and you see the beautiful music and culture that you can't wait to experience.

The **second phase** is **the "long grind,"** learning the nuts and bolts of the field. This phase tends to last longer. All the dry stuff like the technical vocabulary of a complex field. You hit a plateau. This is where people sometimes give up.

The ones who push through make it to the **third phase of generalized expertise** where things become a lot **more fun**. This phase can last the rest of your life.

You have accumulated enough knowledge to start getting paid well. With your newly developed expertise, you can do **creative** things.

"The Paper Chase" is a movie starring John Houseman, about going to law school at Harvard from the perspective of a freshman student.

This is a good movie. It captures the initial frightened uncertainty and how different students cope with it, how some figure out how to do well and others don't.

Chapter 14.

<u>Definitions of Intelligence.</u>

"Intelligence is quickness to apprehend." - Alfred North Whitehead

"Intelligence is the ability solve problems." - Robert Kiyosaki.

"Intelligence is the ability to make finer distinctions." - Robert Kiyosaki's dad (the "poor" dad).

"Intelligence is behaving in a way that helps you achieve your goals." - Brian Tracy.

"The true sign of intelligence is not knowledge, but imagination."
- Albert Einstein.

"There are multiple different types of intelligence including verbal, mathematical, musical-rhythmic, kinesthetic-athletic, interpersonal, intrapersonal." - Howard Gardner.
"Intelligence is a potential. Thinking is the skill with which we use that potential." - Edward De Bono.

"Common sense is not so common." - Voltaire

"Common sense is a euphemism for intelligent behavior." - unknown

"I'm not offended by dumb blond jokes, because I know I'm not dumb, and I know I'm not blond." - Dolly Parton

Curiosity is a sign of intelligence. A good vocabulary is a sign of verbal intelligence. Ability to make jokes and puns is a sign of verbal intelligence.

Verbal intelligence is the most important intelligence for school. Reading for pleasure in one's free time, is the most effective way to increase verbal intelligence.

However, social intelligence, which can also be referred to as emotional intelligence is the most important type for making and keeping friends and for getting promoted at a job.

Persons with high social intelligence and entrepreneurial intelligence often are a lot wealthier than persons with high academic intelligence. When I drive around the rich, housing subdivisions in the suburbs, there are a lot more business people living there than doctors.

According to the famous psychologist, Howard Gardner, a person's academic intelligence has a significant effect on the extent of their academic achievements (this also of course depends on opportunity and teaching), whereas their social intelligence effects how far they will rise in that field.

Eg. a lot of persons who were C student level academic performers in medical school, have A level social and financial intelligence and end up owning their own medical clinics or imaging centers. Then the A student doctors like me, go work for them.

Mr. Robert Kiyosaki, author of "Rich Dad, Poor Dad" was a C student in the high school world, but an A student in the real world of entrepreneurship, finance, sales and social intelligence.

I am the poster child for high academic skills and low social skills and low financial skills. I basically dominated almost all of my academic challenges from 19 years old onward, but screwed up most of my financial and social opportunities the first time around.

I am not the only one. In fact medical doctors are routinely mocked as "HENRY's" which means High Earners Not Rich Yet because they are so poor at managing their money. (HENRY is a term first found in a June 2003 article in Fortune magazine called "Taxpayer Beware" by Shawn Tully).

The good news is that all of these things are improvable. You can greatly develop social and financial intelligence just by being aware of it and making an effort by reading about it and talking about it with persons who have more experience.

In many ways, life is like the movie, **"Groundhog Day"** starring Bill Murray. You get up and go out into the world and you do well on a few things, but then screw up on others. Lets say you did 3 out of 5 things well that day, 1 so-so and 1 screw up. Initially you are embarrassed, frustrated, angry or all of the above.

Then you talk about it with a friend and perhaps read about it and then think about it. The next day, you go out and try to do better. For example to do well on 4 out of 5 and so-so.

It's just part of life. In order to grow as a person, you have to keep doing new things and learning new things. This means you are going to constantly go thru those phases of being a beginner again, making stupid beginner mistakes and improving yourself in these new areas.

If you "play it safe" and do not do new things and learn new things, then you will soon make yourself obsolete. The following is a quote from the Red Queen in the book, "Through the Looking Glass" by Lewis Carrol;

Alice is running and running but not seeming to get anywhere. Alice says, **"one generally gets somewhere if they run."**

The Queen says, **"Here you see, you have to run just to stay in the same place. If you want to get somewhere, you must run at least twice as fast as that!"**

"A business is either growing or shrinking. Your job is to keep it growing." - Robert Kiyosaki from the "Midas Touch."

Fluid intelligence is considered to represent the ability to solve new problems and in a sense relates to how fast a person can think their way thru a complex situation. It is often said, and probably is true that young adults tend to be able to think faster than older adults.

Does that mean that younger adults are smarter than older adults? The answer is that it depends.

Older adults tend to have more **crystallized intelligence**. Crystallized intelligence is how much you know, your knowledge. This can keep increasing throughout life.

For example, my high school son thinks he is smarter than me. If we had a competition, who would win?

If the competition task was to figure out some new cell phone app, to get to the next level on Xbox or to run an obstacle course, he would kick my butt.

On the other hand, if the topic was history, I would win because I have already read lots of history books from Greeks to Romans, philosophical, scientific, artistic etc.

If the subject were psychology, I would win because I've already experienced almost all the basic stuff, moving away from childhood home, love, rejection, marriage, parenthood, mother dying of cancer etc.

If the task was to treat a collapsed lung with a chest tube or to drain an abdominal abscess, the patient would be better off with me.

Although the high school student has a faster brain than I do, he has read little, experienced little, and has not had medical training.

That is why education and training is so important. **For knowledge intensive tasks, accumulated learning is far more important than brain speed.**

This is why a lot of doctors in cognitive based medical fields such as internal medicine, psychiatry and diagnostic radiology can keep practicing at 75 years of age. Because it's based more on "brain knowledge" than brain speed or hand dexterity.

An abdominal surgeon finds it more difficult to continue doing surgery after 75 years of age.

I said to a friend of mine, "Wow, it must be difficult for orthopedic surgeons to continue practicing after 60 years of age. Doing a hip replacement requires a lot of physical work."

My friend laughed, and said, "My wife is a physician assistant. She works with an older orthopedic surgeon. He plans the operation, but she is the one who actually hammers in the artificial, hip prosthesis."

It is a lot harder to get into medical school than it is to finish medical school.

You have to be a really good student to get into medical school. However, to make it thru medical school, you just have to show up for everything, do as you are told and study a lot. Most schools try to help the students along once they are accepted.

All this academic competition stuff like the MCAT serves as a barrier to entry. Nowadays, there are more and more opportunities in health care in the USA for jobs such as "nurse practitioner" and "physician assistant."

I took a look into my "crystal ball" to try to figure out what was happening and I think that I now understand it. Health care in the USA is becoming too expensive. The pharmaceutical companies want their medications to be available. The solution has been to carry out more and more research studies to standardize medical practice. This is called "evidence based medicine." The goal is to use research to establish algorithms for patient management where possible.

Once there is a standard algorithm, the problem can usually be managed by a nurse practitioner instead of a physician. When the problem is more complex and requires more "fuzzy thinking" and "more educational training" it gets sent to a physician.

That's why it is good for a physician or anybody in almost any field to try to develop a wider and deeper range of skills. The more you know and the more you can do, the less likely you are to be replaced.

Bruce Lee perhaps said it best with his advice, **"the best defense is to be like water. Water can adapt to anything. You cannot break it."**

It is usually not good to be a "one trick pony." If you are going to be a one trick pony, then try to be a very good one trick pony in a highly specialized field.

Academic intelligence quotient (IQ) has been described as a Gaussian curve with the mean IQ at 100. It has been written that the average IQ of a 4 year college graduate is 110, a law school graduate 115, a medical school graduate 125 and an Ivy league college graduate 140.

For this system of IQ measurement, one **standard deviation** is approximately 15 points. Therefore an IQ of 115 would be one standard deviation above the mean.

If one takes the range for IQ's from 2 standard deviations below and above the mean, 70 to 130, that would include approximately 95% of persons such that 2.5% would be below and 2.5% above. This corresponds to an IQ of 130 being the 97.5 percentile.

The following are some approximate correlations between IQ and percentile are the following;

100, 50%
105, 65%
110, 75%
115, 85%
120, 90%
125, 95%
130, 98%
135, 99%
140, 99.5%
145, 99.9%
150, 99.95%
155, 99.99%

Now, I don't know how true or useful this is.

However, the idea of putting a numerical value on IQ makes it quantitative, and this can be helpful to you for planning an academic skill optimization strategy.

The key point is that I think these tests should be called "Achievement" or "Assessment" tests and not "Aptitude" tests. It has been clearly proven that careful study can lead to dramatic improvement on all of the above tests.

Students who study more and have more training, and better training score higher. There are a lot of things a student can do to improve their scores.

Here's another little **secret**. The tests are often intentionally designed to have "too many" questions. This is done to make the tests more difficult on purpose.

The theory is that a "smarter" person, which means "better prepared" person will be able to solve the problems more quickly such that **it's really a test of more than problem solving ability. It's a test of SPEED at problem solving.**

The more you familiarize yourself with the test format and the types of questions on the test, the faster you will get thru it and the better will be your score. You become more efficient at it.

Just as a well trained athlete can greatly outperform others of similar ability who are less well coached, optimal coaching of a student makes a big difference.

"It is not your aptitude, but your attitude that determines your altitude." - Zig Ziglar, American writer and speaker.

Let's say we start out with an average IQ of 100.

Well if we eat a healthy diet, our IQ will go up a couple of points. Let's call it 105. If you eat better foods, your brain cells will have better raw materials out of which to make neurons. Healthy neurons conduct action potentials faster so that you can think faster.

Now if we exercise, it goes up a little more, let's say 110 because of;

- Improved brain glycogen (energy storage),
- More mitochondria (mitochondrial biogenesis for energy production),
- Better blood supply (angiogenesis for improved oxygenation and nutrient delivery),
- BDNF (Brain Derived Neurotrophic growth Factor),
- Neurogenesis (production of new neurons),
- Improved attention.

Now if we optimize our sleep 115 because of improved memory consolidation and attention.

If we study from the best textbook and practice questions book, 120.

If we have a good teacher 125.

If we have a great teacher 130.

If we learn a couple of study skills from this book 135.

If we learn most of the study skills in this book 140.

If we study every day and manage our time well 145.

There it is. **The key concept of this book is that just like an athlete can be trained to optimize their performance in many ways, a student can likewise improve their performance in many ways.**

It is important to remember that IQ is typically discussed in the context of academic IQ. **Lots of persons with high academic IQ's have low social, emotional and financial IQ's.**

This is part of why lots of high IQ persons are not wealthy.

Another criticism of IQ tests is that like other academic tests there is a single correct answer. For example, 2 + 2 = 4. On an academic test, all the information is right there. You just need to use logic to solve it.

However, in the real world, we routinely have to make decisions based on incomplete information. In this setting, it is a combination of our knowledge, our perception and our judgment that we use to make a decision.

In the real world, you can have an academically smart person who has poor social perception and they will make some stupid decisions, because their logic was working with a very limited data set due to their poor perception. This is a big part of why academically smart persons do a lot of foolish stuff in the real world.

Chapter 15.

Genius.

"**Nearly all eminent people were voracious readers.**" - D. K. Simonton.

"**The sole job and responsibility of a genius is to create and to contribute value.**" - Piotr Wozniak, inventor of Super Memo.

"**Talent hits a target no one else can hit. Genius hits a target no one else can see.**" - Arthur Schopenhauer.

"**Mediocrity knows nothing higher than itself, but talent instantly recognizes genius.**" - Sir Arthur Conan Doyle.

A great illustration of this is when Salieri talks about "Serenade for the Winds" by Mozart in the movie Amadeus.

"**On the page, it looked nothing. The beginning simple, almost comic, just a pulse, basoons, basset horns, like a rusty squeeze box. And then….suddenly!…..High above it; an oboe. A single note, hanging there, unwavering, until a clarinet took it over. Sweetened to a phrase of such delight. This was no composition by a performing monkey. This was a music I'd never heard……**"
- Salieri in the movie "Amadeus."

"Amadeus" is one of the greatest movies of all time.

"People err who think my art comes easy to me. I can assure you, dear friend, that no one has devoted as much time and thought to composition as I. I have studied diligently, the works of all the famous composers, many times." - Wolfgang Amadeus Mozart.

"When a true genius appears, you can know him by this sign. There will be a confederacy of dunces aligned against him." - Jonathan Swift.

A lot of academic genius types become physicists or research scientists and make around 70,000 to 90,000 dollars a year. Meanwhile, lots of other persons with perhaps less academic skills, but more financial intelligence go into business, law or medicine and make a lot more money.

What these research guys will tell you is that they chose to pursue their interests despite knowing that they would make less money.

"Talent does what it can. Genius does what it must." - Owen Meredith.

"Genius is one percent inspiration and ninety-nine percent perspiration." - Thomas Edison.

"If Edison had to find a needle in a haystack, he would not stop to reason where it was most likely to be, but would proceed at once with the feverish diligence of a bee, to examine straw after straw until he found the object of his search.....Just a little theory and calculation would have saved him ninety percent of his labor." - Nikola Tesla.

I have seen many scientists that are very happy. They do research in something that fascinates them, they have a new crop of graduate student trainees coming thru every year that are fun to teach and their kids get a discount for going to the professor's college. Their main stressors are getting funding for their research and getting tenure. All in all, it's a good life.

In fact, if I could do it over again, being a doctor at a rural state university would be a good choice. The doctors are well paid. The cost of living is low. The commute is brief. The public grade schools and high schools near a university are usually very good. Your kids get a discount on college tuition, because you work there.

The university community tends to have lots of entertainment events from sports to movies to music. Young people do a lot of stuff and the college environment reflects that.

"Genius is always impatient of its harness; its wild blood makes it hard to train." - Oliver Wendell Holmes.

Chapter 16

<u>**Sleep.**</u>

Sleep is very important for learning and memory.

We spend about one third of our lives, asleep. It must be very important to have been evolutionarily conserved all this time.

Our immune system surveils our body during sleep to heal our injuries, to cure infections and to help prevent cancer, Sleep decreases your risk of cancer.

During sleep we "recharge our mental batteries."

When we wake up in the morning we are fresher, our brains sharper, with faster processing speed.

During sleep, short term memories are either discarded by the brain or converted to long term memories, ie. **consolidated**.

Most things don't need to be remembered. Ie. We don't need to remember irrelevant, mundane things. It would be a waste of time to do so.

Myelination of brain neurons, which makes them faster, also occurs to a large degree during sleep.

For something that is important to you, eg. a review list of information for a test tomorrow, it is **helpful to go over it just before going to sleep** so that your mind will focus more on it, when you sleep that night.

Here are some ways to help you to sleep better.

The **key is to mimic natural processes** and optimize them.

Exercise during the daytime, helps you to sleep better that night.

Make your **bedroom dark**. Humans are diurnal creatures and it is normal to sleep at night.

Get **opaque curtains**. Cover up the light from the house alarm system etc.

Make your bedroom **cool**. It is normally cooler at night.

Minimize the amount of electronic stuff in your room. Ie. Do not have a TV or cordless phone in the bedroom.

The bedroom should be for **sleeping and sex only**.

Have a comfortable bed, pillow and blanket.

Going from an awake state to a sleep state is largely a transition from sympathetic autonomic system (**SANS**) dominance to parasympathetic autonomic system (**PANS**) dominance.

Therefore **avoid stressful things** in the last few hours before bed.

Eg. if you like to watch the news, then watch the 6:00 news and not the 9:00 news.

Melatonin, a sleep inducing substance produced in the pineal gland is made in larger amounts in relative darkness, rather than in daylight.

Therefore it is wise to **avoid bright lights** several hours before bedtime. Keep your office dark at night. Put a lower wattage light bulb, eg. 15 to 25 watts, in the hallway, your bathroom, and your bedroom.

The color blue, perhaps because it mimics the sky can especially block melatonin. Consider spend less time on your computer in the last few hours before bed.

The process of **transitioning from awake to asleep** also includes **decreasing sensory input** to your brain. Your body does this automatically while you are asleep, but you can add to it by wearing **ear plugs**. But make sure you can still hear the phone ring. I have 5 dogs and they wake me up if there is anything else going on.

I like silicone ear plugs that you "smush" with your fingers so that they fit into your ears.

What about naps? Naps can be beneficial. They can break the day in half and recharge your brain. For example, if I plan to study a lot on a given day, after studying from 7 am until 1 pm, my brain will tend to be tired and no longer capable of complex work.

Then I will eat a box of cereal, eg. Mesa Sunrise, and chase it down with some organic almonds and organic carrots and water. A half hour later, I'm sleeping like a baby.

Wake up 1.5 hours later and the brain feels like it is morning again, is fresh and ready for complex work.

The major pitfall of naps is that they can give you insomnia at night.

There seems to be a benefit from going to bed earlier, rather than later. In high school, my wrestling coach told me, "the sleep hours before midnight count for more than those after midnight." This might be because people tend to wake up at about the same time every morning and if they go to bed earlier, then they get more time in bed that night.

Professor Arguelles says that he needs less sleep when he goes to bed early eg. if he goes to bed at 8 pm.

It is good if possible, to go to bed and wake up at about the same time everyday.

"The student rested, does bested, when tested." - Peter Rogers MD.

Chapter 17.

Emotion, stress and memory.

Emotion and normal, low level stress are key ways to enhance memory.

Professor James McGaugh summarizes this nicely in his book, "Memory and Emotion," where he writes that nature was able to come up a **double duty system** in the **acute stress response**.

Things that are important are often associated with a little bit of stress. The acute stress response in severe examples is called "fight or flight." However, there are normal mildly stressful events all day long.

Eg. if you are walking down a path in a forest and you see a large animal move, at first it might be a stressful. "Lions and tigers and bears, oh my."

Then you realize it's just the breeze or perhaps a deer and you relax.

Now, let's say it was a wolf. You would remember that moment well for the rest of your life.

Why?

You will need a lot of energy to climb a tree or get ready to fight.

Your adrenal medulla releases a burst of **epinephrine and cortisol.** This triggers a release of glucose from your liver to provide more energy. The blood vessels to your muscles dilate.

The epinephrine causes increased **norepinephrine** activity in the memory centers of your brain. The **cortisol** also activates the memory centers of your brain, eg. it stimulates the hippocampus.

Nature is brilliant! This **same hormonal cascade gives you** the **energy** you need, to do what you have to do physically, and it simultaneously carries out **double duty** by **activating your brain to remember** the event so that you will be able to recognize and react to a similar situation in the future, even more quickly.

The manifestations of the acute stress response have been likened to **being chased by a tiger in the dark** whereby the pupils dilate, blood clots a little faster (to prevent you from bleeding), blood flow to muscles increases, and blood flow to the gut decreases.

In the more common daily setting, of minor stresses, less epinephrine (adrenalin) and cortisol are released from the adrenal gland.

For example, the **Socratic method of teaching** is to, verbally ask a student a question, in person, typically in the presence of other students. Asking a medical student or residents questions in this way is called "pimping."

This is a little stressful for the student who is asked. They want to look good in front of the teacher and their peers.

This makes you remember better. Eg. radiology residents are routinely called up to sit at the front of a conference room and describe the findings on a CAT (computerized axial tomography) scan or MRI (magnetic resonance image). They have to answer the question in front of a group of their peers. This motivates them to study a lot.

The low level stress response associated with Socratic questioning causes the epinephrine and cortisol to "tell the hippocampus memory center in the brain" that something is important and that it should be learned, and placed into long term memory storage, ie. consolidation during sleep.

Too much stress, eg. post traumatic stress disorder (**PTSD**) can cause too much cortisol release. This can overstimulate a hippocampal neuron. This overstimulated hippocampal neuron can be depleted of its neurotransmitters and be damaged by the process. This is called excitotoxicity.

It is wise to try to avoid negative, rude and hostile people as they cause unnecessary stress. Try to find jobs and social environments where people are nice to you, or at least fair to you.

Emotions are also often associated with stress.

For example, fear is one of the most primitive emotions and plays a major role in memory. The amygdala (means "almond" in another language) is located just in front of the hippocampus.

The **amygdala "tags" memories with emotional labels**. Ie. in a metaphorical sense, the amygdala says, "this event is important because it could be helpful or dangerous. Put it into long term storage."

This is the reason why, when making **word association "stories"** to facilitate memory **it is good to try to add an emotion, motion, sex, taboo, humor or violence to make it more salient** to your amygdala so that the item will be placed on the "high priority list" for long term consolidation.

This combination of emotional input and stressful input along with amygdala and hippocampal postprocessing of the information to determine if it is worthy of consolidation is a highly efficient way that the brain effectively remembers important stuff, and conserves energy by not wasting neuron "memory storage space on irrelevant stuff."

In other words, **emotion and stress provide signals to your brain to label information or events as important, as worthy of long term storage in memory.**

Chapter 18

Future jobs.

"The best way to predict your future, is to create it." - Peter Drucker, Austrian-american author who wrote about business.

"Bill Hewlett and I were brought up in the great depression. We weren't interested in the idea of making any money. Our idea was if you couldn't find a job, you'd make one for yourself." - David Packard, cofounder of Hewlett and Packard company.

"I find out what the world needs. Then I go ahead and try to invent it." - Thomas Edison.

"We are like tenant farmers chopping down the fence around our house for fuel when we should be using nature's inexhaustible sources of energy, sun wind, tide. I'd put my money on the sun and solar energy. What a source of power? I hope we don't have to wait until oil and coal run out before we tackle that." - Thomas Edison.

"The only way to be truly satisfied is to do what you believe is great work. And the only way to do great work is to love what you do. If you haven't found it yet, keep looking. Don't settle. As with all matters of the heart, you'll know when you find it." - Steve Jobs.

"Study hard whatever interests you, the most in the most undisciplined, irreverent and original manner possible." - Richard Feynman, American scientist and author.

"In times of change, learners inherit the earth, while the learned find themselves beautifully equipped to deal with a world that no longer exists." - Eric Hoffer, author and philosopher, 1902-1983.

"For the best return on your money, pour your purse into your head." - Ben Franklin.

The following observations might help you.

It is easier to keep doing a job when you are over fifty years old if the main tasks are reading, writing and talking.

For example, administrators, business people, history professors, cognitive physicians and lawyers are doing fine in their seventies.

"I talk for a living." - Professor Allitt, British-American, history professor at greatcourses.com.

Sounds like a rough job. You could do that when you are 85 years old.

Alexis De Toqueville wrote that, **"Lawyers are the aristocracy of the USA."**

"Extrapolating from the statistical growth of the legal profession, by the year 2035, every person in the United States will be a lawyer including new born infants." - Michael Crichton.

Law can be a great career choice, but it is also very competitive. If you go into something like that, you don't want to be a one trick pony.

It is good to have two skills. For example, if you also have experience in construction and real estate, then be a real estate lawyer.

Medicine is a good field, but a long grind. To be a doctor, the key is to make up your mind that that it is what you want to do, and then make it the number one priority in your life for about 10 years, from 20 – 30. After 30 you can then gradually expand your focus to include other things like marriage, family and hobbies.

Nursing is a good field, but you have to be careful as there are both good and bad jobs in nursing. The nurses with advanced degrees do best. They often are able to secure nice, administrative jobs with good hours and good pay.

The ICU is a fascinating place where one learns a lot. It is difficult to do ICU nursing for an entire career. It is a good place to work for a decade or two and then move on to something less exhausting.

Nurse anesthetists and nurse practitioners are doing very well and these fields are likely to grow a tremendous amount.

"Round up the usual suspects." - line from the movie, Casablanca.

Once something is in an algorithm the trend is to have it more and more be managed by nurse practitioners, instead of doctors. This is likely to increase over time. This is why more and more doctors are going into specialized fields.

Currently in the USA, internal medicine doctors are undervalued. A good internist can save your life in many ways.

For example, when a patient is sent to a specialist or hospitalized, they benefit from having an internist that knows them and knows the specialist and the hospital systems. In other words, the patient benefits from having a knowledgeable internist who is "watching the store."

The USA population has more and more elderly people, and they have a lot more medical problems than younger persons. That is why there will continue to be a lot of jobs in healthcare.

If you want to do physical work primarily, after fifty to sixty years of age, then it is very important to maintain your fitness.

A lot of guys that do physical work have a hard time after fifty-five years of age due to arthritis, obesity, poor eating habits, tobacco etc.

It is good to have a family business. You are less likely to get fired if you work for the family business. It is good to grow your knowledge over the years so that you can be in charge of the business and supervising younger persons who are doing the difficult physical component, while you mostly do the part that relies on experience and knowledge.

It will be more and more useful to speak Spanish in the future in the USA. Farming might make a comeback because hardly anyone goes into it anymore.

Lots and lots of persons are getting MBA's which is devaluing that degree. I think that an MBA will carry a lot more weight if it comes from a prestigious school or is combined with some other highly developed skill.

An argument can also be made that college is overrated. Many highly successful entrepreneurs never finished college such as Bill Gates, Michael Dell, "rich Dad (from book by Kiyosaki)."

While the college students were sitting around taking required classes, and accumulating tuition debt, the entrepreneurs were building businesses.

When you get to be over thirty years old, life often becomes more complicated. People often have a house and kids and lots of bills to pay, so they have to keep that "secure job."

In contrast, when you are twenty years old and living with your parents, you have no bills or hardly any. What a great time to start a business! So what if it fails. Mom and Dad will keep you fed and sheltered.

In life, there is so much to learn. It is more than any young adult can imagine.

That is why being able to learn quickly and well, is such an important skill. Also things change. They change a lot.

You have to keep learning in order to be able to adapt to these changes. In my life I have seen the onset of color TV, cable TV, fax machines, personal computers, cellphones, internet, email etc.

"It is not the strongest of the species who survives.....It is the one most able to adapt to change." - Charles Darwin.

In fact the most important skills in life are learning how to learn, how to get along with other people, how to build up one's social network, how to be happy, how to make money, how to maintain one's health and how to understand oneself, which helps you to do the other things.

The internet and globalization have changed the workplace in a big way. Factory jobs are now handled, more and more, overseas, Eg. in China and elsewhere.

More and more stuff is done by robots and computers. As more manufacturing is done by robots, the advantage of lower cost for labor overseas is decreased, such that a company might return a factory to the USA.

For engineering students, there will likely be lots of jobs in robot design and maintenance.

It still sounds like there will be a lot of unemployment, which leads to a lot of alcoholism. This will create jobs in liquor stores, Alcoholics Anonymous, alcohol rehabilitation centers, addiction psychology and psychiatry.

The internet has led to intranets in individual companies that are able to track individual worker "productivity" more closely than in the past. The net effect is that people in the white collar world-so called professional world of the USA, are working harder than before.

Things might be more efficient from the company's perspective, but they are more competitive and laborious from the individual worker's perspective.

It is like the industrial age assembly line transformation of the blue collar worker in the USA in the 1900's is now happening to the white collar worker.

Machines are taking over more and more jobs. It used to be just manual labor jobs, like plowing a field.

Then rote tasks like phone answering machines became possible. But now machines are doing more and more "knowledge" types of jobs like a "talking" GPS etc.

There are good opportunities in electrical engineering and some other engineering fields.

To some extent, one can categorize fields of study into three major groups. This includes the humanities such as history, literature, art and philosophy, then the biological sciences and the physical sciences.

Currently hot fields of study are often those that combine fields from the other categories, such as 1. the humanities, 2. the biological sciences and 3. the physical sciences. For example, psychology can be a bridge between all three as it utilizes functional MRI to study the human mind.

When you decide what you want to do, try to choose something that is unlikely to be replaced by a machine.

"Continuous learning is a requirement for high level jobs.......Brain power is more important than muscle power." - Brian Tracy.

Another point of view, is that in the future, there will be less oil and gas available, such that there will be more manual labor jobs in things like farming. There will be more demand for solar and wind power.

Fracking has produced a tremendous amount of natural gas and there might be opportunities in that, including overseas.

Practical skills will remain highly valuable such as auto repair, air conditioning, home maintenance, bilingualism, computer programming, website design, sales, and others.

Chapter 19.

The Feynman learning method.

I never used this method for school. I had used a variant of this method for years as an adult in my thirties, before I found out what it was called. I like it for when I am trying to learn about something in the real world, more so than in the academic world, because that is where I have experience with it.

For example when I am considering buying something and need to learn more about it, I will take an 8 x 11" piece of paper and start writing on it whatever I can learn about that thing such as suntan lotion, milk, water filtration, an audio CD player, a car etc.

Richard Feynman was a Nobel prize winning, physicist genius in the USA who was also a great teacher and writer.

I heard this method described by Scott Young in a You Tube video. As I remember it, **you just take a few sheets of paper and write on them everything you know about a subject. Then you keep adding to it as you learn more.**
Eventually, the goal is that you will master whatever it is that you need to know about it.

Why does this work?

My guess is that as usual, it is multifactorial. Writing stuff down helps you to remember it. Your working memory can only hold about 7 things in it at a time.

Putting all the information down on paper lets your working memory work with more variables simultaneously. In other words, this makes you smarter.

Having the material written down in front of you and going over it as you decide where to add more info is a also form of SIRS (Spaced Interval Recognition System).

Deciding how to categorize the information as you add new information is a form of deeper level processing and this leads to increased memory and can lead to deeper insight.

Chapter 20.

<u>Brain processing speed.</u>

Brain processing speed is used here to mean **speed of thinking.**

Can it be increased?

Yes of course! When you first learn to hit a tennis ball, let's say from a coach or a ball machine, the ball comes at you slowly and it is a challenge to react correctly. With practice you are able to react more quickly and to hit a faster ball.

Why?

The neural pathway for the thinking and motor components are being reinforced over time by myelination of the neuron (conducts faster) and synaptic strength augmentation by formation of increased number of synapses and/or increased neurotransmitter release.

Is that just for motor activities, or does it also occur for cognitive function as well?

Cognitive speed can also be increased. For example, as you get better at learning L2 (second language), you get faster at recognizing words in L2.

The same thing occurs in English, but is less noticeable. When I listen to English audiobooks and then discuss related topics with friends, the vocabulary just comes more quickly and precisely. The brain has been trained to handle the words more quickly.

Any medical student can tell you that during freshman year there is a significant mental shift in going from studying biochemistry to studying anatomy. However, by late in the second year, while preparing for boards, it becomes a lot easier to fluidly transition from one subject to another.

Well, does that just relate to "time on task" for a specific activity, or is the brain becoming smarter overall for everything?

One definitely gets faster at the specific activity. There is some general carryover to other categories. For example, when you get faster with words from reading in one domain, you also to a variable extent, become faster with words for other domains.

As one gets older, you realize how precious time is. **One way to get more out of time is to "speed up the world."**

This can be done by listening to audiobooks on a variable speed CD player. This can be done by watching DVD's and streaming videos on a variable speed video player such as VLC media player.

VLC media player allows you to watch lecture videos speeded up 1.5, 2, and even 2.5x. I like speeding up science and medical lectures to about 1.7x routinely and faster when the speaker is clear, the content straightforward and there is minimal motion.

Excess motion is the pitfall. Even though the brain can handle speeded up audio well, it does not like excessively speeded up motion. This can cause a headache and should be avoided. If the video has motion, ie. is a movie with some action, rather than a lecture, then I usually limit the speed to 2x or less.

This seems to be a way to help maintain fast, brain processing speed.

Why live your movie watching life at 1.0 when you could enjoy it at 1.5 or 2.0. With clear speakers, and good audio, 2.5 or even 3.0 is possible.

That is such a cool concept, the ability to speed things up!

There are also several computer programs for "brain training" that claim to improve brain processing speed. I don't have any experience with them. I have been impressed by some things that I read by Michael Merzenich PhD, who is an expert on cochlear implants and has done research on auditory processing speed, in autism as well as during learning.

Chapter 21.

Speed Reading.

"I just got out of the hospital. I was in a speed reading accident. I hit a bookmark." - Steve Wright (comedian from the United Kingdom)

Is it for real?

Yes!

Teddy Roosevelt used to read a book a day. He was an interesting guy, kind of like the Simpson's cartoon character Ned Flanders on steroids.

What is the story about Evelyn Wood?

She was trying to learn about ways to read faster and in frustration she tossed a book on the ground. When she picked it up and then **began to dust the cover off, by moving her fingertips from side to side** down the page, she noticed something.

Her eyes automatically tracked her fingers, even as she went faster and faster.

Voila! You've got chocolate in my peanut butter! (annotation for the youngsters; famous commercial for Reese's peanut butter cups in the 1980's).

That is the big discovery that got things going with speed reading. There is a whole lot more to speed reading than that, but this is still the key point.

Average adult readers read somewhere around 150 to 200 words per minute (wpm).

According to Peter Kump, "less than 1% of Americans can read faster than 400 wpm."

With just the finger tracking method, it is easy to get up to 400 wpm. Instead of using your index finger, you can just track the lines of the page with a pen. Keep moving forward, forward.

That is what I do. **I prefer the pen, because I can circle key phrases. I also fold over the upper, outer corner of the page to mark a page that I want to go back to.**

Abby Marks Beale calls the pen a "**pacer**." It is like greyhounds at the racetrack chasing the mechanical rabbit.

Why do people read so "slow?"

Because they hang on to grade school habits of reading one word at a time. Remember how you were taught? Sound it out. C-A-T, cat! D-O-G, dog!

Our eyes can see a lot more than one word at a time. Take a look out the window, you can see a panoramic view.

With speed reading, you are retraining your eyes to look at more than one word at a time. In a glance, you can take in two words, three words, a third of a line, half a line or more at a time.

Really good speed readers apparently can see an entire line of text at a time.

A famous, champion speed reader, Howard Stephen Berg wrote that **he uses speed reading to find information and then later goes back and memorizes the key parts.** I think it is a great approach.

Basically you blow thru the book or article quickly and circle the key points. Then you go back to just the stuff you circled and decide if you want to memorize it.

When I track with a pen, I start at the junction of the first third and the middle third of the line of text. Then I jump to the junction of the middle third and the last third of the line of text. You can draw vertical lines down the page at these junctions as part of training yourself to do this.

The combination of looking over the table of contents of the book and the covers and the pictures (preliminary overview of the book) as well as the pen pacer, enable me to routinely read at about 450 to 500 wpm. I must admit, that I still do often subvocalize which is a major no-no for speed readers.

In order to speed read at the higher rates like 1,000 wpm and above, you need to overcome subvocalization. Subvocalization is reading out loud or saying the words in your head.

People are able to visually recognize things faster than they can say them. For example, you can look at a painting and instantly know more about it than you could describe in 10 seconds.

High level, speed readers are able to read by looking at the text without subvocalizing. This takes a lot of training, probably about six months to a year.

I had heard that speed reading was fake, so I never looked into it until I was forty-nine years old. You can learn how to preview a book and pen track the text in one day.

It's a great deal! One day of studying speed reading training and you double your reading speed for life. That will save you a lot of time. Just being aware that increased speed is possible will speed you up with all kinds of reading tasks. No one could run the mile in under 4 minutes until Roger Bannister did it. Then lots of people did it.

Now of course, you will be able to go faster with some texts than others. **It is easier to speed thru narrow columns of text** such as in newspapers. The narrow column of text also makes it faster to speed thru mass market, small page size, paperbacks than thru larger books.

I used to routinely prefer the bigger, hardcover version of a book. Now, I often go for the smaller, paperback version so that I can blow thru it quickly while walking.

Speed reading benefits from an assertive attitude like, "I'm gonna plow thru this text fast and scoop up the meaning quickly."

What is the big picture?

"Nothing is so difficult to see as that which is right before our faces." - Goethe.

What these speed reading pioneers have done is to analyze a routine thing like reading, break it into individual parts and then figure out how to improve each one. It's like an athlete going over all the components of their sport. Like a triathlete studying the mechanics of running, bicycling and swimming.

These pioneers have made reading into a sport. It was a lot of fun to read their books. I recommend that you do it as part of your speed reading training. They have a contagious enthusiasm. You will catch it with your mirror neurons.

Peter Kump, **"Reading is an intellectual sport."**

Why walk thru a book when you can run thru it?

Some may say, "well, I just want to enjoy the book." Well, fine. I enjoy books just as much when I go thru them fast.

The main reason I want to blow thru books fast is because I always have five more stacked up that I want to read. I am eager to get to the next book. Once you start speed reading, you will blow thru a lot of books.

On average, I read about 5 books a week, if all sources are included, audio and print (including journals). This would be based on a generic definition of a book being something like 250 pages of paperback size pages, such that a 1,000 page, book would count as 4 by this definition. This is mostly from audiobooks, "walk and talk" and reading on the loo, etc.

My high school son loves to challenge me, and tell me that I don't know anything. One day I said to him, "I have been reading about 5 books a week for the past 32 years. That is 260 books a year x 32 years or 8,320 books."

Then, "given the fact that I have read probably 10,000 books more than you, isn't it likely that I know more than you?"

That shut him up for about 5 minutes.

Then he said, "But a lot of what you learned is obsolete!"

"Now I know why tigers eat their young." - Rodney Dangerfield (from the movie Caddyshack) and Dr. Peter Marshall (title of his book).

Another key point about speed reading is level of comprehension. For some things you need higher levels of comprehension. Focusing on higher level comprehension can slow you down. When you hear claims of very fast reading rates, it is relevant to ask, "at what level of comprehension."

I like to keep my level of comprehension around 100%

If I could do it all over again, I would definitely try to become good at speed reading. I might even take a try at moving up to the 1000 wpm range if I can free up some time later this summer.

Over the course of a lifetime you will save tons of time if you learn how to speed read, even if only with the pen pacer.

"I have always imagined that Paradise will be a kind of library."
- Jorge Luis Borges, Argentinian writer.

There are some websites that allow you to practice online speed reading for free. There are lots of You Tube videos on speed reading. There are some in person speed reading courses.

There is a software program called, "Ace Reader" by Stepware, Inc., that I have used a little bit and found it quite good. It times you, tells you your speed and helps you to progress in a good way. When I restart my speed reading training, I am going to use this program again.

There are a lot of books on speed reading. Three that I found helpful are "Ten days to faster reading" by Abby Marks Beale, "Super Reading Secrets" by Howard Stephen Berg and Breakthrough Rapid Reading" by Peter Kump.

Howard Stephen Berg was the worlds fastest reader and was featured in the Guiness book of world records.

Another helpful reading trick is to make sure you capture any especially interesting key points by writing them down on the inside back cover of the book. That way, all you have to is look at the inside back cover and you will recall the key stuff.

Chapter 22.

How to read a book.

A book is a tool to help you learn. A student's goal is usually to learn well and to learn fast.

The following description is of how to read a paperback book that that you own and intend to keep. If you plan to sell the book back to the store, then you don't want to do these things.

The "first pages" are usually a title page, copyright page, acknowledgments and preface. I usually **rip these out and throw them in the garbage.**

When I open a book, **I want to go directly to the table of contents.** I don't want to waste time flipping thru that irrelevant stuff.

The only exception is when I intend to use the book as a picture atlas, in which case, I will cut out pictures from other books and tape them over those "first pages."

Science books are read in a different way than literature books. For science books, I am usually going directly to a specific topic such as looking up an anatomical region or a disease and thus the book is used like a reference.

For literature or nonfiction books that I intend to read cover to cover, **I "speed read" with a pen "pacer."** In most books, the majority of the content is background material and "fluff." I just blow thru that stuff quickly.

When I come to something interesting, I **circle it with the pen and fold over the upper right (reader's right side) page corner.** This is a marker to go back to that page later. If the item is especially interesting, I make an asterisk in the margin next to it.

The purpose of the initial speed reading is **to find the information.** The reason for going back to it later is to memorize the important stuff.

I had been doing this for many years, often reading at a relatively slow pace. The speed reading book by Howard Berg motivated me to do the same thing at a faster pace.

If a book is worth reading, there will usually be around one to five great things in it, things that definitely should be memorized. These are **AO's.**

For these, I will often write a brief note on the inside back cover and list the page number. These are so important that the extra effort is worth it. They are the reason for reading the book. By writing them on the inside back cover, I make sure that they won't accidentally be later skipped over.

Upon completion, I put the book onto a pile of completed books next to my desk. I read about 5 books a week. If it's an audiobook, the information will be written on a notepad with those pages then torn out and put into the same "completed reading pile."

The next time I sit down at the desk, I go thru the books and decide if the information is really worth memorizing. Most of it is not. If it is, then I put it onto flash cards or enter it into some other form of long term storage.

For example, a good new joke is added to the joke file. A new insight about neck anatomy or diseases to the neck book. About the brain to the brain book, etc.

For a literature or nonfiction paperback book of 300 pages it is routine that I will only find 3 to 30 sentences worth memorizing. The other pages were read to set the background, and because I had to, in order to find the good stuff. That means it can take reading 100 pages to find one good sentence in a low yield book.

Chapter 23.

The Cone of Learning, visual learning.

I first saw the cone of learning diagram in a book by Robert Kiyosaki (author of Rich Dad, Poor Dad, and lots of other books) with the diagram labeled as adapted from Dale 1969. The cone of learning was developed by Bruce Hyland based on Edgar Dale's "Cone of Experience" created in 1946.

It points downward, like an upside down pyramid.

The teaching concept of the "cone of learning" is that, the more visual, active and participatory a learning experience is, the more the student remembers.

You can just type into any internet search engine, "Robert Kiyosaki, cone of learning" and you will see it.

I cut out the picture out of the book and taped it to the wall near my bathroom mirror so that I would see it everyday, to help me optimize my learning methods.

As one goes from reading alone, reading with pictures, reading with audio, video, observing the activity live, discussing the activity, to participating in an imitation scenario, to participating in a live scenario, the level of learning and retention increases.

This is one of the reasons that immersion is a great way to learn a language.

"That which we learn, we learn by doing." - Aristotle.

Which is faster way to learn to ride a bicycle? Watch someone, and then do it yourself or read about it and then figure it out yourself?

Mirror neurons are the key of course. These mirror neurons enable us to "mirror" other persons. Someone smiles and we smile. We see someone ride a bike and now we see how we could do it.

Mirror neurons are very important for many types of learning including and perhaps especially for the development of social intelligence.

"We learn by example and by direct experience because there are real limits to the adequacy of verbal instruction." - Malcom Gladwell.

Chapter 24.

Medical Apprenticeship.

Apprenticeship is a great way to learn. I have been amazed to see how much people learn in apprenticeships.

Medical residency training is an apprenticeship. Medical school in the USA is 4 years in duration. A fourth year medical student has a lot of "book knowledge," but typically, little, real world, clinical knowledge.

When medical students observe me doing a procedure, I routinely ask them, "how does prep (skin antiseptic) work?"

They never know. Both of the common skin preps require time to dry as they sanitize the skin bacteria by desiccation.

That's the joke. The 4th year med students have memorized thousands of rare and complex diseases. From college thru med school, they have jumped thru more academic hoops than a dolphin at Sea World.

After prepping the patient, I then ask them, "where do you think I learned to prep like that?"
They say things like, "in the OR (operating room) etc."

My reply, "in prep school."

These same 4th year med students then do a residency. The first year of residency is called "internship year". In one year they routinely go from being little greenhorns who ask lots of cute, innocent, clueless questions to managing complex patients, and they do it well.

They learn fast. Real fast. This is because they are actively managing these patients while tagging along with senior residents and attending physicians. They are learning from hands-on, real world participation.

So whenever you have a choice, seek out the most active, the most participatory option for learning. Seek out the best mentors.

A good mentor can save you years of time by guiding you to the "good stuff" to high yield areas. They can help you pick a good clinical field or research field to work in. They can really improve your life.

For example, here is the advice of one of my mentors.

"I don't recommend proctology. You start out at the bottom and you stay there." - Rodney Dangerfield.

"Why are infectious disease doctors the best to date? They are the most cultured and sensitive." (they send every specimen for C & S which is culture and sensitivity (to antibiotics) – Peter Rogers MD.

"Why are nephrologists the worst to date? They are always getting pissed off." - Peter Rogers MD.

"What is the difference between a hematologist and a urologist? A hematologist pricks your finger." - Old medical school joke, source unknown, unable to find source on internet.

Chapter 25.

<u>Vision.</u>

Vision is the most important of all the senses.

There are far more brain neurons devoted to vision and visual processing than any of the other senses. This is a good indicator of how important vision is to humans. It is energetically expensive to maintain human brain tissue.

The reason, nature gives us lots of brain real estate for visual processing is because it is very important for learning, communication and survival. Therefore, whenever possible try to add a visual component to your studying.

It's true, "a picture is worth a thousand words." Our memory retains a mental image of a picture a lot easier than it retains text. Eg. Just think of watching a TV show or a movie. It is relatively easy to remember the sequence of events. Or think of someone showing you a series of pictures. Again this is easier to remember than it would be to remember the text used to describe those things.

Humans only developed written language about 5,000 years ago, for the purpose of keeping track of agricultural stuff. The point is that **visual communication through body language and gestures has been around a lot longer than text and reading.**

Just the other day, I was driving to work and somebody honked. I looked up and there was a deer crossing the road. A few days later, somebody honked at me. Oops! I looked up and the traffic light had turned green, time to go. We have all seen people honk car horns to tell someone they've arrived at the house, to give someone a ride, that they are not happy about being cut off, and other reasons.

The point is that this single sound, a car horn beeping can convey a lot of meaning. You don't need a lot of fancy words. What it really does, is get you to look up, and then your visual glance tells you what is going on.

In analogous fashion, a cavewoman could probably communicate effectively in some similar manner such as throwing a rock at her husband. This would get him to look up.

If he sees the kids making a mess next to momma, that means, "help me with these damn kids!" If he sees her pointing to the apple tree "orchard" in the valley, that means "go out and forage you lazy bastard. My girlfriend never has to ask her husband to forage. Why can't you be more like him."

Videos are a very good way to learn. I was talking to a lovely, Cuban surgery resident in ENT (Ear, Nose and Throat surgery) who shared her experience about learning neck surgery.

She said, "It was Sunday, and I had a big case on Monday. I had read about the operation all weekend, and I just did not understand it. I could not get clear the sequential rationale of the recommended steps. I was afraid that my attending (senior physician) would think I was incompetent."

"Then I found a video on You Tube about how to perform this operation. It was amazing. All of a sudden, all the steps in the operation made sense. I could clearly see the rationale for proceding from one anatomical neck space to the next in the recommended sequential order. I understood better how to protect the nerves coursing thru the surgical field."

"The key was the video. The reading helped, but it was the video that gave me the confidence that I could be the lead surgeon for the entire operation. The case went great."

The human eye is a miracle of evolution. Even Darwin (in the early phase of evolutionary science) was impressed by it's complexity.

"To suppose that the eye with all its inimitable contrivances for adjusting the focus to different distances, for admitting different amounts of light, and for the correction of spherical and chromatic aberration could have been formed by natural selection seems, I freely confess, absurd in the highest degree." - Charles Darwin, "The origin of species", (1859).

Charles Darwin did then go on to put forth explanations for how the eye likely evolved and the updated information on how the eye evolved has been more recently explained by Richard Dawkins and others.

The human eye only has 20:20 vision in the fovea. The fovea is located near the posterior center of the eyeball and has lots of cones which are photoreceptor neurons for high acuity, color vision. You need adequate light for the cones to function effectively. This is why putting more light on something can make it easier to see the details of the object.

Also, up to a certain point, increased light can also be beneficial by decreasing the size of the pupil and sharpening focus. This is why in the operating room surgeons will often say, "we need more light here."

The periphery of the eye has rods which are for black and white vision. They are very sensitive to small amounts of light. Try to avoid putting on too many bright lights first thing in the morning. Never look at the sun. These things are not good for your rod photoreceptor cells.

It is rather surprising how little light one needs to be able to walk around at night. In effort to save on the electric bill, and to optimize my melatonin for sleep, I decided one month to try walking around the house without turning on any lights.

I could navigate with just the smoke detector and surge protector lights. Everything was going great until I fell down.

The rods are also good for tracking motion. This attracts our interest. For example, a stand up comedian can make themselves more interesting just by walking around on the stage.

Chapter 26.

Old tests, Martin and the East Coast Genius Guy.

Old tests are very helpful if you can get a hold of them.

Some college classes actually make them available in the library or online. You need to ask!

This is like taking candy from a baby.

If old tests are available, then study them diligently.

Sometimes the previous class of students will, after a test, write down the questions. These are called "recalls." These can also be very helpful.

Make sure that you are not breaking the rules. Never cheat on anything in high school, college or med school. I have seen good people accused of cheating on one thing get suspended and even kicked out of school. Don't even do anything that appears remotely suspicious of cheating.

As Bluto said in the movie Animal House, "Seven years of college down the drain."

Now it's time for the story of Martin and the East Coast Genius.

Jay Rehm, Martin, East Coast Genius and me were roomates in the trailer apartments.

Let's flashback to sophomore year at Stanford and listen in on Martin's monologue one Saturday night after a few too many.

"I don't even know why I'm at Stanford. I don't belong here. I'm a dumb motherf___r. I don't belong at the same school as guys like Jay. Jay is a motherf____g genius. I wish I was back in Florida. All I want is to get into law school. All I want is to join my daddy's law practice in Florida. I don't know if I'm gonna make it, but I'm gonna study my ass off."

Now, by Stanford's standards, Martin was kind of a fat hillbilly. He had a folksy accent and he swore a lot. No one in a million years would mistake him for an Ivy Leaguer.

He always looked exhausted. He studied all the time.

Jay said that Martin studied more than anyone he knew. I lived in the same 4 person trailer apartment with Martin and hardly ever saw him. He was always studying. But Martin made it. He did well at Stanford and as far as I know, went on to law school and probably joined his dad's law practice.

Now, the East Coast Genius was another story. Jay Rehm is a genius, but he said that Mr. East Coast was smarter than him.

So obviously Mr. East Coast was the best student? No! Mr. East Coast was the worst student. The problem was that Mr. East Coast was the least motivated. He could not make up his mind what he wanted to do. He didn't know what he wanted to major in.

He didn't know if he really wanted to be at Stanford. If you saw this guy you would be impressed. He was tall, handsome and brilliant. He was easily the most erudite out of all of us. We all liked him. He always seemed sad. I know he flunked several classes. I felt sorry for him.

I think he dropped out. I hardly ever saw him.

The point is that the most important thing is to be a hard worker. East Coast was twice as smart as Martin, but Martin was twice as hard a worker.

In the end, Martin was more successful than East Coast.

People sometimes ask me "how is it possible that some medical doctors seem kind of stupid?"

The answer is that it is possible to make it through med school if you are not that smart. However, it is impossible to make it through med school if you are lazy.

There is no such thing as a lazy medical doctor in the USA.

The most important thing in school is to be a hard worker and to learn as you go along. If you do this, other people will respect you, and you will get better at the "game of school" as you go along.

Chapter 27.

Instant smarts on the ACLS test

ACLS stands for Advanced Cardiac Life Support test.

This chapter shows you how to quickly memorize stuff and make yourself seem to know a lot more than you actually do. You don't need any medical knowledge to read this chapter or this book.

ACLS is a requirement for physicians every 5 years or so. In actual practice, I never have to run codes (manage code blues, cardiopulmonary resuscitation), so I get quite rusty on this stuff.

The ACLS classroom was full of people who run codes all the time, like ER and ICU doctors and nurses. It is a fair statement to say that I knew less about EKG's and cardiac drugs than anyone in the room.

I raise my hand to ask the teacher a question, "Can this be an open book test?"

Her, "Are you going to have time to open a book in the middle of a code?"

Me, "Maybe."

Her, "No."

Well, what to do? I've gotta figure out a way to memorize these drugs and EKG's quickly.

First drug, amiodarone 300 mg. How to memorize that?

The "m" has three downstrokes (learned this trick from the letter number alphabet system as taught by Harry Lorayne and discussed later in this book). Mentally, just rotate it 90 degrees clockwise into the "sky" and it looks like a number "3".

The mental visualization of the letter "m" rotating up in the sky and turning into a letter "3" is helpful for locking it into memory.

The word a"m"ni"o"dar"o"ne contains its dosage. **Just take those letter "O's"** and mentally visualize them, there, pulled up into the "sky" after the "m made into a 3" and voila! You've got it, "300."

Next drug, adenosine 6 mg. Just think of it as adenoSEX and then adenoSIX, Six mg. Walk in the park. Like taking candy from a baby.

Next drug, atropine .5 mg. A little more challenging, but still, one needn't break a sweat. AtroPentagon, 5 sides, .5 mg dose. You could also use "pentagram" a 5 pointed star. The key point is taking something relatively intangible, like a number, and turning it into something concrete like a shape, like a a pentagram.

And so it goes for the other drugs. Likewise for the EKG's. I couldn't read an EKG to save my life. But for a test, you just memorize the distinguishing feature of the common rhythms and you're "in like Flynn."

Test time. I was first in the room to finish the test. Crushed it like a bug. How could that be?

The real code blue experts were probably over analyzing the exam and thinking about real world scenarios. I just asked myself, **what does the examiner want me to know for this test.**

This strategy of focusing on a the high yield information makes for quick progress. The use of word associations greatly aids memory. These two methods in combination, help you to perform "smarter" than you really are. Sometimes "you gotta fake it, til you make it."

Chapter 28.

How to make word associations.

"Combinatory play seems to be the essential feature of productive thought." - Albert Einstein.

Word association techniques are super important. I used them all the time as a student, and I still use them routinely. What you are doing is **encoding information** in a way that will be easy to understand and remember.

In order to remember something, **it is helpful to intentionally associate with something you already know.** Understanding what your brain likes, helps you to form more memorable word associations. These are sometimes called, memory "handles," "tricks," "wordplay," etc.

Your **brain prefers concrete over abstract.** For example a noun is easier to remember than an abstract adjective.

Your **brain is primarily visual.** There are far more neurons devoted to visual processing than any other sense. Therefore it is very helpful to make your word association into something you can visualize.

Your **brain loves novelty**. Novelty is memorable. We remember our first kiss, our first sexual intercourse, our first fist fight etc.

Your brain is good at **looking for patterns** and categorizing things.

Your brain needs to conserve energy. It is very expensive from an energy point of view to have a big brain. That's why other animals do not have such big brains.

In order to save energy, the brain focuses on things that are relevant to survival and reproduction. It does not want to waste neuronal, storage space on the mundane. There is no reason to remember what you had for dinner 3 months ago.

However, there is a lot of reason to try to understand things like, "why did that lady give me an unusual look? Was that an IOI (indicator of interest) or an IOD (indicator of disinterest)?"

"Your brain is a survival machine." - Sam Wang, PhD. Author of Everyday Neuroscience.

Your brain pays attention to things that might affect survival, like violence, motion (someone or some animal may be attacking you), social taboo (you may be beaten or ostracized if you violate this). The "forbidden fruit" aspect of social taboos also makes them more memorable.

When it comes to making word associations, short and vulgar is better than long and polite.

"I am a vulgar man, but my music is not vulgar." - Wolfgang Amadeus Mozart in the movie, Amadeus.

Large things are potentially more dangerous eg. a big rock, big dog, big tiger.

This is why **it is helpful to add concreteness, motion, violence, exaggerated size, sex and taboo to your word associations. Making up a funny story for a word is helpful.** The wilder the better as this helps to make it more interesting and "memorable."

To make word associations you **look at the word or phrase and see if it yields any immediate clues.** Does it contain anything that reminds you of sex, violence, motion, taboo, excitement? Does it rhyme with anything? Does it mean something in a different language?

You can also do **"word substitution."** This means to substitute another word for the word in question because the substitute word is easier to remember.

For example, the word adenosine in the last chapter was substituted with adenoSex and then adenoSix.

"Train your brain to gain." - Peter Rogers MD.

"Hip, hip hooray! Word play saves the day." - Peter Rogers MD.

"Visualize and picturize to memorize." - Peter Rogers MD.

Rhyming increases memory. For example, in high school, I had to memorize and recite the poem, "Annabel Lee" by Edgar Allen Poe. Because of the rhyme, it was relatively easy to memorize and difficult to forget.

"I was a child and she was a child, in this kingdom by the sea; but we loved with a love that was more than love, I and my Annabel Lee."

The concept of opposites can be helpful to memory. For example, the following line is one of the most memorable from the first page of any book.

"It was the best of times and it was the worst of times..." - Charles Dickens.

Making a joke about a word or phrase can help you to remember it. Sometimes someone has already made the joke for you.

For example, what is the word for wife in Spanish? Esposa.

What is the word for handcuffs in Spanish? Esposas.

If only it were always that easy.

You have to really pay **attention** and think about that word. This leads to a **deeper level of processing,** more **familiarity** with the word, more contact with the word. Then you get a dopamine rush when you come up with a way to memorize the word.

Using word associations and other memory tricks will make you more confident. You know that you can generate the information at will. This makes you feel better about the learning process and decreases test anxiety.

Going into exams, I typically felt very good about my knowledge. I knew that I knew the material well. I did realize that the test might be difficult, but all the students were in the same boat, so I knew that even if my preliminary score on an exam was not that high per se, it would be high when graded on a curve.

Chapter 29.

<u>Time Management.</u>

"Dost thou love life? Then do not squander time; for that's the stuff life is made of." - Benjamin Franklin.

In 8th grade, I read an article about Dan Gable, the great Iowa wrestler, and it inspired me.

I took out a piece of paper and wrote at the top of it, "How to get good at wrestling." Then #1. build strength. Do push ups and pullups. #2. Improve flexibility. Do stretching.

#3. Improve technique. So I bought the book, "The Making of a Champion. The Takedown" by Bobby Douglas (great wrestling coach).

As a college freshman, my new goal was to become a better student. So I took out two pieces of paper. On the first one, I wrote, "How to become a better student".

On the second piece of paper, "Time Management."

I wrote down each hour of the day 8 am, 9 am, 10 am etc. Then I analyzed how I was using my time.

Look for areas where time is wasted.

Look for areas where you can do two things at once. Ie. Tandem processing as engineers are wont to say.

For additional advice on time management I also like the Stephen Covey book, "Seven Habits of Highly Successful People" and the Brian Tracy book, "Time Management."

Chapter 30.

Highlighters, underlining and margin notes.

Highlighters can be helpful, but should be used sparingly. It's only a "highlight" if used occasionally. The typical rookie highlights too many things and basically paints the page yellow.

In order to make something "unique" there must be exclusivity. It can be helpful to highlight key words and key concepts.

In college and med school, I did use yellow, orange, red, green and light blue highlighters, and called this the "rainbow method of highlighting." This process of categorizing information is helpful.

Eventually, I came to prefer reading with a blue pen. I would circle key stuff more often than underline it.

In the margins I would sometimes make an "asterisk" or draw an arrow to point out that a text item was important.

Margin notes can be very helpful. Eg. I would read a paragraph, and then try to paraphrase it in my head, and then write "my own" paraphrase in the margin.

This is a form of **"self test"** that is helpful because it gets you to actively study, to process the material and gets you to write it out. All of these things improve understanding and retention. It is a good to be an "active studier."

Now, to clarify the above paragraphs, in this chapter were written about how to read textbooks.

There are other types of reading. Eg. There is the reading of literature, of history of general nonfiction and of foreign languages. There is also the concept of speed reading and the concept of "takeover condensed notes." Each one of these is best done with a different approach. We will come back to these topics later.

Chapter 31.

<u>Peaking for standardized tests.</u>

Timing is important. You want to peak for the most important tests. This is typically final exams for a given class and standardized exams overall.

Standardized exams are important because they provide a means for schools and residency programs to compare you. Other things being equal, when applying for graduate school, an ivy league student has an advantage over someone from a less prestigious school.

However, if the student from the less prestigious school does well on a standardized exam, they can leap frog ahead of the ivy.

Peaking means long term preparation geared towards that exam, and extra time dedicated to preparation in the preceding 6 months, 2 months and 2 weeks.

It is good to begin with the end in mind. Eg. the first semester class of med school is part of the preparation for the boards exam at the end of the second year. By staying organized all along, you will be better prepared.

This includes things like keeping all your books and study materials for a given subject on the same bookshelf.

Sometimes taking a review course can be helpful.

Chapter 32.

Dress for success and John Molloy.

John Molloy wrote a famous book called, "Dress for Success." He did research on which types of clothes tend be associated with financial "success." The book focused on how to dress for the job world, especially the business world.

Now I realize this is probably the farthest thing from the minds of teenagers. In college, I routinely wore T-shirts. In college I had a couple of minimum wage jobs like washing dishes. My freshman year at medical school, I was still often wearing T-shirts.

Notice I wore T-shirts when I was working at minimum wage jobs. In general, the higher paying the job, the better you are expected to dress, until you become the boss and then you can wear a T-shirt again.

As described in painful detail earlier, I never had a girlfriend from Stanford. Part of the reason was the competition, but there is another reason. I noticed that the guys from the "pretty boy" frats seemed to have a lot more girlfriends.

These guys looked rich. They usually wore shirts with collars, "real shoes" (not gym shoes) and they just had a more refined look to them than the guys I hung around with at the animal house, athlete fraternity.

So, I don't completely understand it, but I think that women just found those guys more attractive and trustworthy because they dressed better, looked richer, and had more sophisticated manners. Dressing well seems to immediately generate more trust.

Try it yourself. When you are dressed nice at the grocery store or any public place, you tend to get treated better, and people are more willing to talk to you.

At 23 years of age, I spent a summer at the University of Wisconsin hanging around with the wrestlers. My brother was on the varsity wrestling team there, and the summer wrestling camps were in session.

Now if you have any experience with college wrestlers, you know that they are very high on themselves. For a lot of young guys the idea of being "tough" seems important, and wrestlers think that they are pound for pound the toughest guys on campus.

We all wore T-shirts, often with the names of wrestling tournaments on them. One fine summer day, we were driving thru downtown Madison in a convertible full of wrestlers. We were in love with ourselves, enjoying the day and hoping to meet some girls that night at a local bar. Everything was good.

Our car pulled up to a street corner and there was several, nicely dressed, middle aged people standing there. They looked at us like we were low lifes, pieces of crap. The contrast between what we thought of ourselves and how they viewed us was extraordinary.

I thought, "how could they not like us?" The radio was on, but it wasn't that loud. Our hair was a little long, but it was summer. Our conversation was usually about wrestling or girls, and filled with the usual juvenile stuff about physical prowess and sexual conquest, but nothing to offend bystanders.

I came to the conclusion that to them we just seemed like a bunch of vulgar, young jerks. That was one of those beginning moments where I started to realize that it might be time to start dressing better. Maybe they were just thinking, "these are the kind of guys our daughters talk to in those bars?"

John Molloy makes the point that **people make judgments about other people to a large extent based on their clothes, and that they just do this without telling you.**

For example, when you spill food on your shirt, who tells you? Usually it is a friend. In the same way, a knowledgeable friend tells you when you are dressed in an inappropriate way for a given situation. Other people just look at you and say to themselves, "oh, that person doesn't know how to dress."

The point of this chapter is that **it is good to be aware of the effect that clothes have on people and to dress accordingly.**

Part of the reason for writing this book is to help young nerds going thru what I went thru. I had no clue about clothes until I was about 23 years old, minimal competence by 27 and finally a good understanding by about 46.

To rich, sophisticated people, the following is obvious, but to lots of young guys, it wasn't, and part of it is that teenagers just don't care about certain things.

Basic rules for guys include, a shirt with a collar is dressier than a T-shirt. Jeans are less dressy than most other types of pants. Nongym shoes are dressier than gym shoes. Button down collars are good when you are not wearing a tie. Nonbutton collars are better when you are wearing a tie. Simple, elegant ties are dressier than flashy ties.

Life is easier when you know the rules. It is a "rule of life" that if you dress better, people treat you better, and we all want to be treated better.

When at work, it is good to follow the old rule, "when in Rome, do as the Romans do."

Chapter 33.

<u>Problem solving like a puzzle.</u>

Complex problems are often multifactorial. There is no single book or person that can tell you how to solve them.

The key to solving problems like this is to think of them as being like a puzzle. Your job is find the pieces and put the puzzle together.

Some knowledge is so far out in the open, you practically trip over it.

Other knowledge is more hidden and obscure and sometimes scorned. You have to look for it.

Sometimes key parts of the puzzle are in a book written by someone 40 years ago. Sometimes a key part of the puzzle is in a book written by someone from another country that is more open minded on the topic or approaches it in a different way.

For example, if you want to understand American democracy, you can learn a lot from the French guy, Alexis De Toqueville who wrote about it in 1835. If you want to learn about nutrition in the USA, you can learn a lot from the Irish Dr. Denis Burkitt.

The key is to recognize that the pieces of the puzzle come from all over the place. Some from books, some from people, internet, personal observation and experimentation.

You may have the puzzle three quarters solved, and then not find a key piece until years later, that allows you to instantly figure out all the rest.

The key is to understand how it works and to have respect for information from wherever it may come. Give it a chance.

Sometimes people who seem kooky actually have a helpful insight. Sometimes the so called expert is really just a paid off fraud.

Be willing to consider information from seemingly conflicted points of view.

Take what is useful from old theories and add to them.

Chapter 34.

<u>Mirror neurons.</u>

"Monkey see, monkey do." - unknown.

"See one, do one, teach one." - standard teaching of procedures in USA medical schools.

"Just watch me do one IV, and then try it yourself. You are gonna screw up at first. You're gonna hurt a few people. That's just the way it is. That's how you learn." - OB resident telling me to go start an IV on a pregnant lady when I was a third year medical student. (This sounded so crazy, that I have remembered it for the rest of my life).

"C'mon man. There's really not much to say. You just need to strap on some balls and do the case." - Senior radiology resident telling me to go do a procedure that I didn't know how to do, because he was busy.

A word of advice. If you ever are asked to do a medical procedure, try to make sure at least one person in the room knows what they are doing. Unless of course it's an emergency in which case you can probably read about it on the internet (that was a joke).

Mirror neurons are another gift from evolution. We talked a little about these before. When someone smiles, we smile, etc. This is automatic and instinctual.

Basically, **a lot of physical things are learned better by imitation** than by reading.

We learn to ride a bike by watching someone else and then trying ourselves. The ideal situation is when there is some intermediate step like training wheels. Unfortunately, often there is not. Often one must take a "leap of faith" from the theoretical to the physical and just go for it.

We learn tennis strokes, golf strokes, swimming strokes, etc. from watching other folks.

It has been shown that the same groups of neurons are activated by watching a sports activity as performing it. This is why an athlete can get physical benefit from mental practice.

Also of related interest is that when we learn a new skill in the daytime a pattern of neurons in our brains is activated. **Then at night, when sleeping, this same type of pattern is "replayed" as the brain is consolidating the memory, converting it to long term memory.**

It is obviously a little more complicated than that, but those are the main principles that hold and give you a useful working model of reality.

In other words, the way to learn is, watch the expert, imitate the expert, get feedback from the expert and then get some sleep.

Mirror neurons are also important for social interaction. We can read another persons emotions by looking at their faces. We can to some extent "experience their emotions" and feel empathy. We can't know their thoughts, but we can know something about their emotions.

For example, is their body language one of the two standard types, open or closed. Open (interested, open to conversation, friendly) or closed (untrusting, distant, cold).

I have noticed a third type of body language that tends to occur whenever I try to flirt. It's called, "the pretzel," ultraclosed, with multiple simultaneous IOD's (indicators of disinterest).

When an Eastern European or Russian woman displays this type of body language, I call it the "Siberian Pretzel" sign.

Mirror neurons help us to think our way into the thoughts of other people. For example, when I was dating the woman who would become my wife, we went to a Mexican restaurant where the Mariachis sang, "Besame Mucho."

My date said, "oh what a nice song. Do you know the words?"

I said, "Yes. They are saying, "Besamay, besamay culo. They love it when you sing along with them."

So my date sang to the mariachis, "Besamay culo."

When they started smiling and laughing, my date's mirror neurons told her something was up.

The look on her face activated my mirror neurons to turn my legs away so that I was not injured when she kicked me under the table.

Mirroring is also a normal conversational method, typically subconscious. We tend to mirror the body language of the other person when we are in an enjoyable conversation.

There was a Greek general named Alcibiades who was famous for being able to mirror other persons in conversation. He was full of mischief and a very interesting character.

Edgar Allen Poe also said something along the lines of, **"when I want to get a sense of another person, I imitate their facial expression and then thoughts come into my head that help me to understand them."**

Mirror neurons help us to quickly recognize whether another person is friendly or hostile. This is obviously very important from an evolutionary point of view.

Chapter 35.

Incrementalism.

Incrementalism is defined here as doing a little bit of the task each day until it is finished.

For example, breaking it down into smaller manageable parts and finishing them one by one. Brian Tracy has called this the **"Swiss Cheese method"** whereby you keep punching holes in it until it is all gone. In actual practice this usually means **reading a book**.

Eg. I'll read that book at breakfast, on the loo, at dinner and perhaps even while walking for exercise (if the book is not too heavy). I'll read it in the car if someone else is driving.

The point is to keep chipping away at it. 10 minutes here, 15 minutes there and pretty soon this adds up to a lot of reading. Keep nickel and diming it until you finish.

I have used this technique many times to read big books that would otherwise be too cumbersome to read, cover to cover, such as neuroradiology textbooks that are over 1,000 pages.

Using this method you can easily read several books every week.

Chapter 36.

Meal time learning.

It is fun to talk to other people while enjoying a meal.

However, the reality for most people is that we eat most of our breakfasts alone and likely quite a few dinners even if we have a significant other or kids.

This is because in modern families people are often quite busy with different schedules.

Whenever I eat a meal seated and alone, I read a book or journal.

Quite often, when alone, I eat breakfast and dinner while walking. I am always trying to get more walking into the day.

The time of walking and eating is also good for listening to audio CD books or courses.

Chapter 37.

Digital Voice Recorders.

DVR's are digital voice recorders. They typically have a USB connection to add audio files to a computer.

The audio file can be an L2 song or audiobook.

You can also dictate into your computer or directly into your DVR. This can be a way to capture random interesting thoughts or to summarize recently learned material.

For example, if you just studied a topic for a couple of hours, you could **verbally summarize it** into the DVR. There are two keys to this.

The first is to make the summary immediately after mastering the material so that your summary will be good.

The second is to have a planned time to listen to the summary. For example, you could listen to the summary while doing a walk and talk. Or you could listen to the summary as you walk from your car to your school or job.

DVR's have some nice features. One of my favorites is **slow play for learning a second language (L2).** Slowing down the rate of speech can be very helpful for learning L2.

Speeding up the rate of speech can make material in L1 more interesting. For example, it can be boring to listen to review material in L1 at a normal speed. However, the same review, when speeded up is more of a challenge to listen to and this can make it more interesting.

You can also share your DVR recording with someone else.

You can listen to it when waiting in line etc. Being the old, codger that I am, I originally tried to do this listening thing in public with a miniature, portable CD player. However, people looked at me kind of funny. In comparison, the small, handheld DVR's are convenient, because they resemble cell phones.

Chapter 38.

Mindset of C, B and A students.

In the book, "Midas Touch", Robert Kiyosaki wrote about his mindset in high school.

He said, "**I was a "C" student. I was not that interested in school. I would rather go surfing. I just wanted to make sure there were some kids in the class that were worse students than me. Then, I just tried to focus on what the teacher said was important.**"

A couple of observations. Just doing enough to get by tends to lead to grades of "C" in school (in a system of A, B, C, D, F). Lack of interest lessens performance. While it is important to follow the emphasis of the teacher, it is also important to have a self directed component to one's learning.

A **typical B student** is more motivated, studies more, turns in all the homework and basically does everything that the teacher expects of an average student for that particular class. A typical B student will often say things like, "I did what I was supposed to, how come I didn't get an A?"

A "B" student is a good student, but they are somehow doing less in the mind of the teacher than the A students. A first step is to try to really understand the teacher. This is especially important if the class is graded in a subjective way. Eg. in most so called "creative" writing classes, what is really rewarded is conformity. It is good to write the way the teacher wants you to.

Listen closely to the teacher's **intonations**. That is a common way to **show emphasis,** to show how students will be graded. Try to talk to older students who have taken the class before, to provide you with insights. Check if old class notes are available in printed form or from an older student so that you can preread the night before lectures.

Check if the lectures are available on line and can be watched in advance. Check if the same lecture topic is available in some other way. Check if there are free online videos of the topic. Consider buying a course from the "Great Courses.com" and go thru that before you take the regular college class. Consider taking a free online class on the subject before you take the class.

Try to get along well with the teacher. By this I mean, be nice and do not do anything that annoys the teacher. For example, if the teacher thinks that wearing hats in class is disrespectful, then do not wear a hat.

You may say, "why should I have to play the game?"

My reply, "because that is the way life is. It is difficult to change the world. It is a lot easier to adapt yourself to the world. The only thing that you are guaranteed to be able to change is yourself. It is simply a fact that teachers are human and they are gonna look more favorably on people who follow their expectations."

"We are emotional creatures who think, rather than thinking creatures who have emotions." - Jill Bolte Taylor, PhD, author of "My Stroke of Insight".

This is an extraordinarily profound and important insight. I heard her say this during a Ted talk.

So many vague, as yet unanswered ponderings in my mind about social interactions became clear and moved into that happy, "situation now understood" part of the mind.

The teaching point is that young people, ie. less than 40 years old, tend to overemphasize logic.

Yes, it's true that scientific research depends on objective, logical truth. It is equally true that writing to ask for grant money for a research project depends a lot on the emotions of the donors. Also, the grading of multiple choice test tends to be a lot more objective than of an essay test.

The wise move is to have a lot of respect for both. You will be more successful in academics and in your social life if you remember that both are important.

Here is a related quote that I wish I had known about 20 years ago.

"Logic makes people think. Emotion makes them act." - Zig Ziglar.

Let's get back to how to become an A student.

It is good to think of school as being a sport. A "B" student is an above average, academic "athlete." An "A" student is a really good to great academic athlete, for that level of competition.

Chapter 39.

Getting the Edge.

Winning in sports is all about "getting the edge." David Lee, my roomate at Stanford, was an All American and National Champion college wrestler. He said to me. **"You've got to get the edge.**

The guy who has the edge wins. It doesn't matter if he wins by only one point, he still wins. The guy with the edge figures out how to win. It's like he has a bag of tricks on how to make sure he comes out a winner.

Even if he usually wins with leg attacks, in a big match, when it's crunch time, he'll do whatever it takes. He'll hit a throw or score with a turn. He has a an extra reserve that he can draw from when he needs it."

The point is that, **if you want to become a better student, an "A" student, then you have to do more self directed stuff.** For example, do more practice problems.

In a science class, there will be "problems" on the test, so make sure you are good at solving them. Consider buying an extra workbook of practice problems. Develop a system to memorize the key information. Use mnemonics, wordplay and other strategies.

The bottom line is **be proactive**.

In a competitive academic environment, if you just go along with the crowd, you will probably get "B" or "B plus" grades. That is good.

However, if you want to get "A" and "A plus" grades, you have to figure out how to get the edge.

Chapter 40.

How to select a textbook.

You usually should buy the textbook recommended by the teacher. It does depend on the class. If there is a single textbook that the class is going to follow all semester, then you have to buy it.

On the other hand, in medical school, some professors just recommend several textbooks, seemingly out of a sense of obligation, to avoid being asked what they recommend etc., and never mention the book such that it could be a waste of money.

The point here goes back to our "A" versus "B" student. You typically buy the recommended textbook as a step towards "B" level work. However, you should usually also buy another book to help propel yourself to "A" level work.

Diagrams, illustrations and photos are of tremendous benefit. Try to find the best illustrated book in your subject. One glance at a good illustration can sometimes be as good as hours of study.

"And what is the use of a book," thought Alice, "without pictures or conversation." - Lewis Carroll.

Areas of **bold print in the text and photo captions as well as summary boxes of key points** are good signs that the authors are making an extra effort to help you. When feasible, single author texts tend to be more consistent. For example, if it's the same author, and you like chapter one, then probably all the chapters are good. With multiauthor texts, it is worthwhile to skim a few chapters before making up your mind.

I prefer **short chapters with lots of subheadings**. The author is helping you by having already subcategorized the information. Sometimes, I will copy key parts of the chapter outline subheadings and then "self test" to see if I can say out loud or write out the key points of each.

Reputation can be helpful. Ask older students which book is best for the class. However, be careful who you ask. C students are often poorly informed about what is going on in a class and will inadvertently recommend the wrong books.

In addition to interviewing the top students in medical schools, I also worked for years as a tutor for students who were not doing well. A poor performing medical student would say things like, "oh, anatomy is my best class", and they would be about 60% in that subject." While the best students in the class would say something like, "oh anatomy is my worst subject. I have to work harder in that class." Meanwhile, they are like 90% in anatomy.

Does the book have the correct emphasis for your class? Eg. Biochemistry books for college students and medical students are the usually the same. However, neuroanatomy books for medical students and neuroradiologists are very different.

Big print is a positive. I just find it easier to read, even when I was a young whipper snapper like yourself.

Size. If you have to carry multiple books in your backpack every day, then a really big textbook might be cumbersome. If the book is great, you might want to buy two of them with one at home for writing your margin notes, and one at school or work for looking up stuff on the spot.

Brevity is a good thing. A concise textbook tends to provide a good overall summary of a field and usually contains a higher return on investment. Ie. more useful information obtained per hour spent studying from that book.

Typically, I would study primarily from a smaller, concise textbook, and then only use a big, bulky textbook for looking up stuff, not explained in the smaller textbook.

Format. In general, outline format books are more precisely organized and make better "foundations" for "condensed notes."

In other words, for many subjects, I like to buy a medium length outline book and then just add additional information into the margins to personalize it and add value to that book. This combination of the baseline outline format book, plus my margin notes then serves as my "condensed notes" for that subject.

Prose format books can be good, if the author is good. I like it when the author is highly opinionated. Even if you disagree, it's memorable.

Prose gives the author more opportunity to explain things, to develop a theme, to make "quirky comments." I love it when an author makes "quirky comments."

Why?

Because it means they are trying extra hard to please you. They know that someone is going to criticize them for being quirky. Someone is going to say, "that is unprofessional, immature, etc." Yada, yada, yada.

However, these quirky comments are remarkably memorable and often seem to lock the subject into your memory in a good way. I can remember quirky comments from over thirty years ago. It goes back to what differentiates a good teacher from a great teacher.

A little bit of theatrical flair improves memory. A lot of big shot professors are very busy and very much in demand. They get publicity for writing research papers. For them, writing a textbook is kind of beneath them. I have seen entire textbooks which were ghost written.

For example, big shot professors typically have several graduate students under their supervision. It is not uncommon that fellowship trainees in the medical world will be the ones to actually write the textbook chapters. The fellow will often have a less than enthusiastic attitude. They want to learn their field, publish some papers and promote their own career. They are being forced to write the book chapters because they don't want to annoy their boss, upon whom they are dependent for recommendation letters.

Well, back to quirky comments. Fellows don't write quirky comments. **Experts write quirky comments.** You can't joke about something or make deep insights about it until you know it pretty well. A junior person like a fellow does not typically have the experience or the interest to be making quirky, insightful, potentially socially embarrassing comments. They want to write the chapter fast and to get on with their lives.

Quirky comments can be embarrassing because there is often is a component of sex or taboo or other silliness involved. For example, when memorizing the segments of the anterior cerebral artery (ACA), I was having a hard time conceptualizing the A3 segment. So I asked myself, "what is unique about it? What is the difference between A3 versus A2 or A4?"

Well, A3 goes around the anterior genu (bend) of the corpus callosum (white matter fiber tract that connects the right and left brains). The anterior genu projects forward like a breast. The letter 3 is shaped like a bra. That's it! The A3 segment can be memorized by thinking about a "bra" on the anterior genu of the corpus callosum."

I care about it because thinking about this reminds me to check this area for aneurysms and vasculitis on CT angiograms (CTA) and MRI angiograms (MRA).

The same thing that makes a comment seem "unusual" is often what makes it memorable. **Our brain cares about sex, taboo, novelty, emotion, motion, violence etc.** Therefore, within the limits of reasonably good taste, I have found these sort of comments helpful.

Mnemonics. It is a good sign if the author includes some of these. It means that they are trying hard to please you.

Margin space. Wide margins provide space for your notes.

Detailed table of contents. Sometimes I like to highlight or check off each table of contents listing as I go thru a book. This adds to a sense of achievement. A detailed table of contents facilitates this.

Index. This is important in a textbook, because you are going to be looking stuff up. The more extensive the better. I will often cross reference directly to the index of my main study book-condensed notes for a subject.

For example, let's say it's a bird biology book without any information on blue jay behavior. Then I read an interesting article on blue jays in a magazine. I will reference the magazine article into the index of the main book. My ornithology teacher at Stanford loved to point out that "blue jays were the assholes of the bird world."

Author expertise. The more the author knows, the more the author can potentially teach you. For example, there are lots of great anatomy books. However, my favorite atlas is the Netter atlas. Frank Netter was a surgeon as well as an artist. I think he does a great job of drawing anatomy in an accurate, clinically relevant way.

Practice questions. Practice questions are helpful if they are at the end of chapters and the answers are in the book.

To buy or not to buy? In general, I prefer to buy my books. However, sometimes you need to save money.

You could buy used books at your school bookstore or online. You could borrow a book and then put the key info into your condensed notes and then return the book. You could buy ebooks or kindle books as they both tend to cost less than paper books and then you could use them as references to add to your condensed notes.

You could just buy an outline format review book and then go online to see pictures and drawings of relevant topics.

Another pet peeve I have is when people over emphasize typos. Well, so what? If a book is good, communicates useful information and is entertaining, then I'm happy. I see these book reviews on Amazon.com where people write stuff like, "There were ten typos. This book needs a new editor." And they never comment on the book. Unless it's a grammar book, then big whup, who cares?

Chapter 41.

Question books.

Sometimes it is good to buy several additional books. For example, an atlas of illustrations and a book of practice problems. For practice problems, I always want the answers in the book. With practice problems **I focus on memorizing the answers.**

Now I know that a lot of people will say that, "you should test yourself first." that is all well and good, but I simply found it faster and more effective to look at the answers in the back of the book, then circle the correct answers at the end of the chapter.

Then I would **analyze why the correct answer was correct**. It is helpful to try to think your way into the mind of the person who wrote the test question.

For example, "what is the key point they are trying to emphasize?, is there a pitfall that they are teaching me to avoid?, are they trying to trick me by juxtaposing things that sound similar but are different?"

When **you get a little, happy, warm feeling, that means you have understood the point of the question and your brain has rewarded you by releasing a little bit of dopamine neurotransmitter.**

Our brain rewards us for solving problems because solving problems is an important part of life. We are designed to solve problems walking down a path in a forest, but the same neurotransmitter reward system is also activated when solving academic practice problems.

Understanding the question is important because it enables you to memorize it. Understanding comes first, then lasting memory.

The first time around, the questions will often seem difficult. They are usually designed to be that way. Don't worry. This is normal.

That's another reason I don't like to use these books to "test myself," because it is both misleading and demoralizing.

On the other hand, circling the answers and then analyzing them to the point of understanding and memorizing them is uplifting. One says to oneself, "Good. Now I know the kind of questions that are asked about this subject."

A lot of students say, "I don't have time for question books." That is often because they spend too much time trying to test themselves and then to "figure out" the answers.

My way is faster and better. **Just circle the answers, understand them and memorize them.**

It is good to go thru the practice questions immediately after studying a subject. This provides both a review and new learning.

There is a sort of background, penumbra of limbo land material floating around in our heads after we study a subject and this material may be remembered or forgotten.

It seems that going to practice questions immediately after studying a subject helps us clarify some of these concepts, and to capture them into our long term memory.

These newly learned "tidbits" of information can then be added to your condensed notes. It is important to put the key info into your condense notes. This is where you will review it later.

You can also put it onto flash cards for SIRS.

If you go thru the practice questions when you are studying the subject initially, then review it for midterms and final exams, you will be quite familiar with them when it is time to prepare for a standardized test.

It is a lot better to have used the question book during your regular class, than to buy it at the last minute and try to use it for a standardized exam like the MCAT or USMLE part one.

Chapter 42.

Choosing a sport.

Exercise belongs in this book because it is proven to make you smarter which is discussed in detail in later chapters along with neurogenesis.

Golf and tennis are great sports because you can play them all your life and significant injuries are uncommon.

Wrestling helped me a lot for academics in the following ways; self discipline, strenuous workouts increased brain glycogen and number of mitochondria, increased number of brain capillaries, increased intellectual stamina, the complex task of learning technique, self reliance etc.

If you are considering wrestling there are a couple of things you need to know. Focus on technique, not on weight loss. Starvation is a bad thing for teenagers.

I never cut weight in high school. In college it was easy to sweat off 5 to 7 lbs, but I never starved myself. Starvation is bad for your brain and can stunt your growth.

I think that wrestling would benefit from promotion of a more intellectual image. For example, when I talk about wrestling with my friends at the hospital or with the teenage friends of my kids, they talk about not wanting to lose weight and things like that.

I think the martial arts Bruce Lee role model is a great thing. A guy who uses technique to overcome bigger opponents.

This type of wrestler like Wade Schalles, Dave Schultz, Gene Mills, Randy Lewis, John Smith etc. has wide appeal and promotion of it can generate more interest in wrestling. It gives hope to anyone that they can dramatically increase their physical power.

The folkstyle wrestling scoring system should be changed to place more benefit on scoring points and less on control as this will make it more fun to watch, and draw more fans.

Wrestling should also promote its stars more. For example, Stanford coach and Olympic Champion, Mark Schultz was the most intense person that I ever met in my life.

He was like a combination of Superman and Conan the barbarian. It was so much fun hang around with him and listen to stories about the Oklahoma team, NCAA's, the Russians etc.

I can't wait to see the Foxcatcher movie and to read Mark's Foxcatcher book which are both scheduled for release in November 2014.

Wrestlers are known for their loyalty and honesty. When I was having a difficult time at Stanford, Mark Schultz took me aside and told me, "Pete, your problem is that you are hanging around with the wrong people. You need to spend more time with the wrestlers and other positive people."

I was very lucky to have him for a friend.

He got me to run stadium stairs on a routine schedule, and to practice with more intensity. He put a lot of time into teaching me and helping me compete at a higher level.

He encouraged the wrestlers to live at the Delta Tau Delta athlete fraternity where we could more effectively stick together as a group outside of the official team stuff.

This led to the wrestling team getting a lot better and my own performance improving a lot. I then went on to set the school record for wins and become the Stanford student athlete of the year.

Chapter 43.

Extracurricular activities.

Some of the best activities are those you can enjoy for life.

Playing a musical instrument is great.

Guitar and piano are great.

If you want to get better at math, then join the math team.

If you want to get better at public speaking or go to law school, then join the debate team.

For Spanish, join the Spanish club.

The high school newspaper can be a lot of fun. This could be an opportunity to learn photography including sports photography.

Computer programming is a good thing to know.

Car mechanic skills are valuable.

Drawing is a great skill.

Someday, when you are an adult applying for a job, it will be impressive on your resume that you play a musical instrument, speak L2, know photography or drawing, automechanic skills etc.

Usually, no one will care that you were on sport teams.

Chapter 44.

Super High School.

"The most necessary task of civilization is to teach people how to think. It should be the primary purpose of our public schools." - Thomas Edison, American inventor.

As of 2014, in America, high schools teach a lot of information and then students take standardized tests like ACT, SAT and AP tests.

I would implement focused exercise programs like the one at Naperville high school that improved math test scores so much, by 20%. I would let some students opt out of this, because I believe more in recommendations than requirements. Also some kids already have sport practice after school.

I would recommend that high schools should include in their curriculums, study skills, memory techniques, SIRS, speed reading, drawing, etc.

I could walk into any high school in the USA and dramatically improve its performance on standardized tests by teaching these things to students.

The students would benefit from this training for the rest of their lives.

Chapter 45.

<u>**Thinking – General concepts.**</u>

To get 90 to 95% on a college or med school test you usually just need to write out the answers that you memorized.

However, to score higher on tests you often need to think your way into the mind of the person who wrote the test question. Ask yourself, "What are they trying to make sure I know? Are they trying to trick me?

These chapters on thinking will help you in school and even more so in your professional and **personal** lives.

"Since the quality of your thinking determines the quality of your life, you need to become a skilled thinker if you sincerely desire to fulfill your potential." - Brian Tracy from "Maximum Achievement."

"In every work of genius, we recognize our own rejected thoughts; they come back to us with a certain alienated majesty."
- Ralph Waldo Emerson.

"It is the first duty of a thinker to follow his intellect to whatever conclusions it may lead." - John Stuart Mill.

"Thinking means connecting things." - GK Chesterton.

"What about the dog that didn't bark." - Sherlock Holmes (author Sir Arthur Conan Doyle).

"We are born unarmed. Our mind is our only weapon." - Ayn Rand.

"If you think there is a contradiction, then recheck your premises." - Ayn Rand (from Atlas Shrugged).

This is one of the all time greatest quotes on thinking. When faced with an apparent paradox, the key to resolving it, is often, to reset your assumptions. After reading this quote, I started becoming a lot more perceptive in my relationships, and in office politics.

It is helpful to ask yourself, "What if my assumptions are wrong?" Don't cling to an emotional position with your thoughts. Consider them an abstract thing whose goal is to arrive at the truth. In that context it is much easier to adjust your perspective when new insights or new information are available.

Sometimes it can be helpful to debate a topic with yourself. For example, try to think out ways to support and criticize a given statement.

"Actions speak louder than words." - Unknown.

People show what they really think, by what they do.

"A man who does not think for himself, does not think at all." - Oscar Wilde.

A lot of people just do what is "expected" of them or what they are "told to do" by their bosses. This is a normal, low energy way to go thru life. If a person does this, they will tend to have a decent life, but also a boring life.

"People mistakenly think that ("social") thinking is done by the head. It is done by the heart which determines the conclusion, and then commands the head to come up with a reason for it." - Anthony De Mello.

"Logic makes people think. Emotion makes them act." - Zig Ziglar.

The point of these quotes is that if you want to persuade someone, you had best appeal to their emotion as well as their logic. Young guys tend to over focus on the logic apparently due to a combination of naivete and high testosterone.

Young guys tend to grow up in a world of sports, academics and hanging around with the guys. There are relatively clear cut rules of sportsmanship in this setting. Then they get into the real world and the rules become a lot more "fuzzy," more context driven, and it takes time to figure them out. The best way is to have an older person tell you how things work at the job.

"Ours is an age which is proud of machines that think, but is suspicious of men who try to." - Howard Mumford Jones, 1892-1980, Professor of English at Harvard.

The point of this quote is that it is important to learn to keep your mouth shut in a new environment. If you are asked a question, then answer it, but do not go around spouting off opinions as this will tend to backfire on you. Over the years, I have seen who climbs the promotion ladder and I can assure you that the mature social skill of being quiet and reserved at work is higher yield than being outspoken.

You may think that other people will be impressed by your brilliant ideas. More likely, they'll just be jealous. Better to let them read about your ideas in a published article that promotes your career. That carries a lot more weight than spouting off in a meeting.

"If you are too open minded, your brains fall out." - Lawrence Ferlinghetti

"Don't be so open minded that your brains fall out." - G. K. Chesterton..

"If you bend to far, you show your ass." - Unknown. (my mother used to say this).

"Meek young men grow up in libraries, believing it their duty to accept the views which Cicero, which Locke, which Bacon, have given; forgetful that Cicero, Locke, and Bacon were only young men in libraries when they wrote these books." - Ralph Waldo Emerson from the American Scholar.

"The great thinker is one who can hear what is greatest in the work of other "greats" and who can transform it in an original manner." - Martin Heidegger.

"Man's mind is his basic tool of survival." - Ayn Rand.

One aspect of thinking is to see an issue from multiple perspectives. This helps you to create a more accurate model of the world as it relates to the given topic.

It is good to try to understand competing points of view. It is a sign of a smart person that they can understand an issue from, for example scientific, emotional, psychological, poltical and religious points of view. Even if you totally disagree with a point of view, being able to understand it can help you to refute it.

"People often think that the best way to predict the future is by collecting as much data as possible before making a decision. But this is like driving a car looking only at the rear view mirror-because data is only available about the past.....This is why theory can be so valuable: it can explain what will happen, even before you experience it." - Clayton Christensen from, "How Will You Measure Your Life?"

"The task is not so much to see what no one has yet seen, but to think what nobody has thought, about that which everybody sees." - Erwin Schrodinger.

"That which you mistake for madness is but an overacuteness of the senses." - Edgar Allen Poe.

"I do not suffer from insanity. I enjoy every minute of it." - Edgar Allen Poe.

"Scholars are those who have read in books, but thinkers, men of genius, world enlighteners, and reformers of mankind are those who have read directly in the book of the world." - Arthur Schopenhauer.

"We live in a world of frightful givens. It is given that you will behave like this, given that you will care about that. No one thinks about the givens. Isn't it amazing? In the information society, nobody thinks. We expected to banish paper, but we actually banished thought." - Michael Crichton.

"Curiosity is what separates us from the cabbages. It is accelerative. The more we know, the more we want to know." - David McCullough, historian, author.

"Intuition will tell the thinking mind where to look next....It is always with excitement that I wake up in the morning wondering what my intuition will toss up to me, like gifts from the sea. I work with it and rely on it. It's my partner." - Jonas Salk, inventor of a Polio vaccine.

Occam's Razor is a useful rule of thumb for complex problem solving. Sometimes there will be multiple competing theories to explain something. This concept is that the simplest answer is probably the correct one. The point is that if you have a simple explanation, that is consistent with the available evidence, then it is probably correct.

The reason why people will sometimes try to justify very complicated, false explanations is that those are often more personally convenient.

For example, the simple explanation might mean that the doctor has to do an emergency procedure at night, and the complex one would let the procedure wait until tomorrow.

Here is a familiar quote from on the job, "The patient has a fever and tenderness. There's no other good reason for him to have a fluid collection there. Occam's razor. It's probably an abscess. You gotta drain it, tonight."

Chapter 46.

Neurogenesis.

"Exercise makes you wise." - Peter Rogers MD.

"The brain is a survival machine." - Sam Wang PhD. Author of the Neuroscience of Everyday Life.

"Man's mind is his basic tool of survival." - Ayn Rand

Walking while reading is called a **"Walk and Talk and Read"**. When studying a foreign language, the reading can be done out loud.

Walking increases your attention and helps you to learn and remember. This basic mechanism can be amplified.

Why?

The human brain was designed to **walk down a path in a jungle** and figure out how to survive.
Where is the food? The water? Shelter? Sex partners? Predators? How do I get back home to family and tribe?

All the senses are active when one is in the woods. What was that sound? That smell? That creature over there? Is is a wolf or is it just my dog?

We are going to use these **innate skills** to become better students.

When we walk, our brain secretes increased amounts of **BDNF** (Brain Derived Neurotrophic Growth Factor) which helps stimulate the formation and growth of new neurons in the dentate gyrus of the hippocampus and the subventricular zone. This is called **neurogenesis**. These new neurons are made by neuronal stem cells.

In order for these neurons to survive long term, we have to "put some information into them."

From an evolutionary perspective it is thought that in order to prosper, while walking down a path in a forest, an animal must be able to learn and memorize his environment very quickly. This requires alertness and curiosity, and is primarily visual.

That's why your **attention** level is **improved while walking**, and it's a good time to read, to look at flash cards, to listen to audiotapes and even to "shadow."

Chapter 47.

Shadowing.

"Think grey." - Edward de Bono from "Think! Before it's too late."

By "think grey," he means to think about the **grey matter of your brain.** The grey matter is where the nuclei of your neurons are located, like in the cerebral cortex.

Shadowing is a technique pioneered by **Alexander Arguelles PhD**, perhaps the greatest polyglot in the world. He was working as a professor in Korea, experimenting with methods to speed up the process of learning a new language.

I had done "**Walk and Talk**" in a simplistic way for years, inside my house and on the basketball court. However, Professor Arguelles brought it to a whole new level.

While I was watching his video about shadowing on You Tube, I had an **AO** (Academic Orgasm).

Professor Arguelles said,

"After trying lots of variations on **shadowing**, I have found that **the most effective method** is to walk down a path in a forest, quickly, head up, listening to a foreign language **audiotape**, and speaking out loud, better yet **yelling** the words as I repeat the words of the audiotape, like a shadow, as fast as I can."

"This is the fastest way to teach yourself a new language. **It plants the new language** in your brain. I don't know why this is true, but it is."

"That's it!!!," I exclaimed.

I said to my wife, "Eureka!"

She said, "you don't smell so good yourself." (Joke is from, "PUNdemonium" by Harvey Gordon).

I had heard about an fMRI (**functional MRI** = real time MRI where you can see what is happening in a person's brain while they learn new things) study that showed that more neurons are recruited when more senses are involved, when the person goes faster, and when the person speaks louder.

It matches!

When the person speaks louder, he remembers better because **more neurons are recruited** for the task.

This means that memorization of the information is connected to more neurons in the brain. This suggests that the information will then be more rapidly available for retrieval in the future. Ie. the information will be more widely stored and therefore more quickly remembered. Ie. it will be better learned and better memorized.

When he walks faster, more neurons are recruited.

When he is walking down a path in a forest, his attention is peaked.

When he simultaneously is listening to an audiotape and repeating the words after it, he is carrying out **multisensory processing**. Simultaneously, listening, talking and looking. Auditory, oratory and visual.

It sounds a lot like a **conversation**, doesn't it.

Yes of course!

When you have a conversation with someone about a topic, you remember that better.

When you go to Spain or Mexico or Puerto Rico for the summer in a language **immersion** setting, you learn a lot more Spanish than sitting at a table, doing Spanish grammar homework, by copying the answers off the internet.

The question is, " Why?"

Chapter 48.

Whole brain learning part 1.

The answer consists of 3 great insights converging to produce a profound conclusion that will change your life.

Part one of the answer is "because we are made to walk down a forest."

Part two is that "**we are made to talk to each other**."

These skills are **important for our survival**. Our brain takes this stuff very seriously. It pays attention. It **remembers stuff that is important** for our survival.

Talking to oneself in the process of "walk and talk" or "shadowing" is mimicking the natural process of conversation.

That's an important point.
"**Shadowing**" in this book is defined as a solitary process where you walk by yourself, listening to an audiotape or audio CD and try to say the words immediately after the speaker, like an auditory shadow.

"**Walk and Talk**" is actually what I do more often. Walk and Talk means to walk around, eg. In a circle in your home, or in a park or on a basketball court, etc. And to talk out loud (read out loud, discuss with yourself out loud) while you go thru flash cards or read a foreign language book.

I also often just do, **"Walk and Read"** which is to read while walking. Walking is good exercise. If I just walk without doing anything, I get bored after 15 minutes. Reading a book while walking makes it a lot more interesting, and I can walk for as long as 2.5 hours. Most of the time, I only walk for about 30 to 90 minutes.

Now, some may say, "well I like to walk in the park, and I would feel awkward to talk out loud in public." My reply is, "then self test."

Self test is to subvocalize, to talk to yourself in your head. For example, after studying the anatomy of the brain you could self test yourself by trying to subvocalize the material you learned earlier that day.

For example, you could say to yourself, "the medial surface of the brain is especially important for social intelligence and the lateral, outer, convexity surface of the brain is most important for academic intelligence, for thinking about school stuff." - (as paraphrased from the book, "Social" by Matthew Lieberman).

This chapter is focusing on the benefits of combining the exercise of walking with that of learning with the goal of making new neurons and keeping these new neurons alive by **putting information on them**.

If the new neurons are not given some new information to store, it is thought that they wither away, ie. are pruned off the dendritic "trees and bushes" of the brain.

Now, it is also true that exercise alone, even without simultaneous studying is very good for the brain. There were some landmark studies at **Naperville High School in Illinois** that showed students performed much **better in math class** after exercising.

These students did very well on standardized tests. They also improved in reading. This was pioneered by the Naperville, gym teachers Phil Lawler and Paul Zientarski. Heart rate was used to monitor the intensity of exercise.

At Stanford, I used to spend a lot of time studying and training for wrestling. The exercise of wrestling seemed to increase the stamina of my mind.

Now, in 2014, I am 50 years old, too old to wrestle everyday, and walking is the best exercise for persons in this age range. My dad, an internist-psychiatrist, used to walk his dog every day, and he said that it seemed good for his brain.

The "walking" can be done in whatever way works for you. It can be done on a **treadmill**, an elliptical etc.

There is also an **emotional component** to walking down a path in a forest. At any moment something exciting might happen that starts with the letter "F", fighting, fleeing, feeding, f_____.

So you gotta pay attention.

Part three of the answer is, "**neurons that fire together, wire together**" as described by Donald Hebb in his 1949 book, "The Organization of Behavior."

The short summary is that, **"when we learn in a way that fits with what our brains are designed to do, we learn faster and remember better."**

The longer summary follows from several observations. Answering Spanish grammar questions is a relatively, mundane, unemotional task that your brain accepts reluctantly because it has to to please the teacher, to pass the class. Your brain uses the minimal resources necessary to complete the task.

On the other hand, **a conversation is interesting. There is a lot going on.** You are looking at the other person and analyzing their body language. Is she happy, sad, angry? Is she favorable, neutral, indifferent or hostile to me? Is her body language friendly, suggesting she wants to talk more. Or, is it closed or cold, suggesting she doesn't want to talk. The visual component of a conversation is very important.

The tone of voice is also very important. Is it warm, neutral or cold, etc.?

Real conversation is not about grammar. Grammar is of only minor importance to the brain.

Real conversation is about communication. Communication is very important to the brain.

Conversation is a multisensory social skill. Simultaneously, neurons of vision, hearing, thinking, gesturing and speaking are all active.

I thought to myself, there is a big insight here. What is it?

Neurons that fire together, wire together.

That's it!

The reason you learn the foreign language faster when walking down a path, looking around, listening and talking is because it is using innate skills. It is like exploring, foraging and having a conversation all at the same time.

It is like **using the whole brain.**

It's WHOLE BRAIN LEARNING!

It's neurons firing together and wiring together so that later on they will be able to function together in a useful way, like..........a conversation.

A person that studies Spanish by listening to audiobooks or by listening and speaking in a conversational format will be able to speak better in a real conversation than someone who hangs out with a grammar book.

Ok, so you're probably saying to yourself, I could have saved a lot of time by just saying, **"exercise is good for the brain and conversations about school stuff are helpful for remembering."**

Yes that's true, but, there is so much more to it than that.

A deeper understanding of these processes, encourages a person to be more excited about trying out the methods.

Chapter 49.

Building your brain.

"No subject of study is more important than reading.....all other intellectual powers depend on it." - Jacques Barzun, French writer.

Acquiring the vocabulary to explain the neurologic processes of learning helps us to tweak the system for learning optimization.

Neurogenesis is the most famous of the neurological benefits of exercise, but there are other things going on.

When you exercise, your brain is active and needs more oxygen. In response to this, your brain grows more capillaries, (small blood vessels) on the brain's surface to deliver more oxygen. This is called **ANGIOGENESIS**.

The connection between brain cells, neurons, is called a **synapse**. **Neurotransmitters are chemicals that are released by the presynaptic neurons, that then diffuse across the synaptic cleft to be taken up by receptors on the postsynaptic neuron**.

The most common excitatory neurotransmitter in the brain is **glutamate**. Other neurotransmitters such as GABA, acetylcholine, serotonin and dopamine are less common, but have important effects.

Exercise and learning leads to the production of new synapses. This is called **SYNAPTOGENESIS**.

A synaptic connection that is already made can me modified to fire more or less intensely. This is called **SYNAPTIC MODIFICATION**. The ability of neurons to change their synapses in function and number in order to learn new things can also be called **NEUROPLASTICITY**.

Frank Longo MD, PhD, professor at Stanford, has a lecture on You Tube that is about 1:55 long called, "Learning and Memory: How it works and when it fails."

At 1:53, into the overall lecture, there is a beautiful video of neurons in vivo. You can see the dendrites trying to communicate with adjacent neurons and establish connections. When you see this, you understand what is meant by the brain hungers for knowledge.

Dr. Longo and myself agree that this is the most beautiful and insightful video about the brain that we have ever seen.

"The brain is incredibly dynamic."
- Professor Frank Longo at Stanford, in the You Tube video, "Learning and Memory."

When an athlete exercises, more energy demands are placed on both the skeletal muscles and the brain. It is common knowledge that our muscles respond to this by storing more glycogen.

Well, the less well known, but much more exciting news is that the brain, in response to exercise, also stores more glycogen. **Glycogen** is a storage form of glucose whereby lots of glucose molecules are linked together by chemical bonds.

During exercise, these bonds are cleaved to release glucose into the blood. This provides energy for the muscles and for the brain.

Speaking of bonds, which bond has the most powerful attractive force? James Bond, of course! (Joke from the "Nurses, Day to Day Calendar of Jokes, Quotes and Anecdotes" published by LLC Andrews McMeel Publishing company.)

A landmark science article on brain glycogen storage is "Brain Glycogen Supercompensation following exhaustive exercise" by Ito et al. In the journal of Physiology, February 2012.

This gives the brain more stamina for studying and thinking.

That's Great! Fantastic! Marvelous!

But wait. There's more.

Mitochondria are energy factories. **ATP** in the human body is an essential form of energy. Mitochondria convert glucose into ATP.

Anaerobic (without oxygen), nonmitochondrial metabolism of glucose yields very few ATP.

Mitochondria along with oxygen to facilitate the process, produces LOTS of ATP.   Therefore glucose provides a lot more bang for the buck when mitochondria and oxygen are available.

We already talked about exercise related angiogenesis providing increased oxygen and glucose delivery capacity to the brain.

Well, exercise also causes more mitochondria to be made in brain cells. This is called **MITOCHONDRIAL BIOGENESIS**.

For those of you with time on your hands, there is a scientific paper on the subject called, "Exercise training increases mitochondrial biogenesis in the brain" by Steiner & Murphy et al. Journal of Applied Physiology, October 2011.

Take it from an old guy, this is wonderful news. There are so many things in life that cannot be fixed. For example, my mom is dead from cancer. I can't bring her back.

The fact that you can improve your brain by exercise is a good motivator.

For the young person this can help you to get better grades in school and to function better at work. For the middle aged and older person, it maintains your overall health and cognitive function.

In fact, if you look at these Hollywood celebrities who look so incredibly young for their age, first of all you've gotta concede that plastic surgery and hormonal therapy likely play a big role.

However, there are lots of real life people who look fantastic for their age that are not taking hormones and have never had plastic surgery. In fact, I know women in their late forties and early fifties who look grrrrreat!

The point is that exercise and healthy food are the most important things that keep a person looking young for their age. Sleep is also very important.

Sleep is a key time for the consolidation of memories and for the myelination of neurons.

Consolidation means converting a short term memory into a long term memory.

Myelination is the building of a fatty insulation layer, circumferentially around the axon, (transmission "wire") of a neuron so that it can conduct (transmit) faster. Ie. Myelination helps you to think faster, remember faster, and react faster.

So to summarize, exercise increases **BDNF** secretion, improves brain **NEUROGENESIS, MEMORY, ANGIOGENESIS, MITOCHONDRIAL BIOGENESIS, GLYCOGEN STORAGE**, and **SYNAPTOGENESIS**.

Sleep improves **MEMORY CONSOLIDATION** and **MYELINATION**.

If you are curious to read more about neurogenesis, there is a good article by Fred Gage PhD in the Journal of Neuroscience, February 2002.

The book, "The Brain that Changed Itself" by Doidge is also very good, and talks about neurogenesis in the context of stroke rehabilitation.

Some of the classic books about memory include "In Search of Memory" by Eric Kandel and "Memory and Emotion" by James McGaugh.

Chapter 50.

Whole Brain Learning part 2.

The key point is that when we use more sensory systems together, we remember things better.

Eg. if you read something in a book and then talk about it the next day with a colleague, you will remember it a lot better.

This is one of the reasons that **teaching others is a great way to teach yourself.**

I highly recommended that you tutor others in some fashion in high school, college or med school or whatever school, especially in the relatively difficult subjects.

You learn more because, first of all you need to understand the material better in order to be able to explain it to someone else.

Explaining it to someone else is a social experience, a conversation which has an emotional component and this makes it more memorable.

It is inherently pleasant to teach. People volunteer to teach and to coach. Helping others causes increased release of reward neurotransmitters in our brains.

When a salmon spawns, it dies. It no longer has a purpose. It does not need to teach its baby fish how to read.

Human babies need a lot of nurturing. Adult humans teach a lot to children of all ages including teenagers.

The middle age adults teach the young adults and the tribal elders help everyone.

So those are really the key points. Try to make learning multisensory, and it's good to have someone to talk to about your field of interest.

Chapter 51.

The method is more important than the student.

This observation really clicked for me when I was trying to teach myself Spanish in my late 30's, after my mom had died.

First of all, I screwed up because I should have learned Spanish from her when she was alive. We could have talked on the phone in Spanish instead of English.

That is an important lesson in life. **Learn as much as you can from your parents or other older adults while they are around, because some day, they won't be**.

Even your mom or dad may become less available to you because of a divorce. So when you have a question, go ask them. Don't wait.

Second of all, I started out trying to learn the usual way that languages are taught in the USA, grammar, grammar, grammar. A conventional Spanish teacher told me I was making "great progress".

However, at work when a coworker said one sentence in Spanish to me, it was like a spark plug in my brain misfired.

I said to Jose, "Como estas?"

He said, "Jodido pero contento."

Me, "what does that mean?"

Jose, "it means, I know I'm screwed in life in many ways, but I've accepted it so that now I'm content, and everything is ok."

Me, "Wow. You sure know how to pack a lot of meaning into just a couple of words."

This was an eye opener. How come my teacher says I'm doing well, but I can't understand anything?

How come a smart, hardworking, motivated person like myself can study for a year, and not be able to understand anything?

I was bummed out, and ready to give up studying Spanish.

Being the irresponsible, passive aggressive, lazy dad that I am, I usually try to weasel out of having to drive the kids to their extracurricular activities.

However, on this particular Saturday, I got stuck with babysitting the kids and driving them to a cousin's house. I know what a lot of you are thinking. "It's not babysitting when it's your own kids." Then why does it feel like babysitting?

Anyways, we are about half way to the cousin's house when the usual stuff starts happening. "Are we almost there yet?" "He hit me." "He farted." "He said a bad word." "He took my gameboy."

It dawned on me.

Most of these little kids could not read yet, and none of them had ever seen a grammar book. Yet, they could communicate effectively, could understand a cartoon on TV, and had far more skill in English than I had in Spanish.

I began to realize that **the key to learning Spanish was to focus on communication.**

Two other experiences contributed to this realization. At work I teach residents. I routinely asked them, "did you ever take Spanish classes? Do you know how to speak Spanish?" I asked about 100 of them.

Not one ever learned from school alone. Not one!

The only ones that spoke Spanish were the ones that had communicated in Spanish such as by living in Spanish speaking countries or having relatives that spoke Spanish or a spouse that spoke Spanish.
Very interesting.

Then came another transforming observation. I met several people who had learned English as a second language only by verbal practice. They could not read English. They did not have much education in their original languages.

There it is. The most important secret of language learning.

It is more important to have a good method, than to be "studious." Ie. you could study a Spanish grammar book until the cows come home and you would never get good at conversational Spanish.

Ie. a poor student with a good method can learn ten times as much as a good student with a bad method.

THE METHOD IS MORE IMPORTANT THAN THE STUDENT!

Given that you are reading this book, it is obvious that you are highly inquisitive, and a great student.

Well, combine that with communication based methods and you will learn Spanish superfast.

Communication based second language study can be done with either conversation or techniques like "walk and read out loud," "walk and shadow," listening to audiobooks while reading the text etc.

These study techniques engage multiple senses and lead to a deeper level of sensory processing. For example, the language skills of deciphering text through the **visual process** of reading is combined with the **oratory process** of reading out loud and the **auditory process** of listening to oneself, all of which together engage the whole brain.

Neurons that fire together, wire together.

Whole brain learning. Better learning.

We will come back to language learning techniques near the end of the book.

One set of terms that is good to mention now is L1 for primary-native-original language and L2 for second-foreign language.

Chapter 52.

The future of education.

The most valuable class in American high school for most people is **typing**. It is worth your while to become fast at it. The typing skills developed in high school follow you thru the rest of your life. Hospital charts used to be handwritten. Nowadays, they are typed into a computer.

This current situation in USA of college education, is like my high school wrestling team where the coach was really a football player and only coached wrestling as a way to make a few extra bucks in the winter.

To the individual wrestler, learning how to improve was a big deal. Every weekend, you had to go out and fight some guy from another school. If you didn't improve, you get your butt kicked, thumped.

Once I realized that I was not learning enough in wrestling practice, I bought books about wrestling technique, and I would ride my bike over to the local college to train with the older guys. Nowadays, a frustrated wrestler can learn technique from DVD's or online videos.

The same thing is happening in education. If a student is not getting what they want or need from their school teacher, they can look for information online.

The internet makes it possible for students to seek out better teachers online. The internet, in a sense, increases the efficiency of production. The production of teaching and educational materials.

The internet "giveth and it taketh." As more education is provided online what will happen to conventional schools and conventional teaching jobs?

I don't know. But I do know that change is usually very slow in the academic world. My son is learning the same stuff in college and med school, and in the same way as I did 30 years ago.

Colleges have lots of resources, land, buildings, professors, traditions, alumni, sports teams, ability to grant official degrees. I think that traditional education will continue for a long time in similar fashion. However, there will be an increased variety of approaches for students in the USA and other countries.

One approach is massive enrollment online courses. Some colleges are doing this whereby they can have students from all over the USA and other countries take a course.

Perhaps colleges will adapt to this by recruiting better teachers. Currently the big universities tend to recruit professors for their research prowess rather than teaching ability.

Perhaps an alternative market of "great teachers-tutors" like what has developed in South Korea will expand in the USA.

One likely way that online education will be delayed is in the official recognition of the diplomas. In other words, is a diploma obtained online the same as one from attending a university? I don't know?

 Perhaps the student will have to only go to the school for identification purposes during registration and the taking of tests?

The bottom line is that the educational system, is in transition.   There is more competition in the process of providing education than in the past.

I think it will change the most at the college and grad school level.

The grade school and high school level is currently such a local thing. A lot of companies want to implement computer learning at the grade school level. I think that the schools are going to resist it in a passive aggressive way.

Why shouldn't they? If everything can be taught to a kid on a computer, then who needs teachers? However, I do think that kids need teachers. It is part of human biology for hundreds of thousands of years to be taught by other humans. It is not that easy to replace that with a computer screen.

It is different at the college level. People are already used to the idea of students moving away from home to go attend a college.

Online education provides a "recorded for later" option in education. In other words, you can keep your job and go to school at night watching online lectures.

Online education lowers the cost, of tuition a lot.

The key is how will an "official diploma" be defined.

In the future, perhaps there will be more refined ways to evaluate graduates. For example, are the MCAT for med school and the LSAT for law school etc. adequate?

DVD and online lectures can also potentially tremendously speed up education. For example, if you have a class that requires 36 hours of lecture, that could be 3 hours per week for 12 weeks.

Now, if those same lectures were watched on DVD played at 2x speed, that would be 18 hours of lecture.

Well if you watched 6 hours on Saturday, Sunday and Monday, at 2x speed, then you could complete the lectures during a 3 day weekend

At this rate, you could obtain college degrees very quickly.

There is a new college model called, "Minerva." Minerva may make it possible for it's students to attend classes in a different city each year.

Many teenage boys are addicted to video games. They go online to learn techniques to get to the next level. They will watch You Tube videos for hours in order to improve their video game performance. Perhaps education should be delivered to them thru a video game.

This could be done by solving school like problems. For example, in math the levels could correspond to addition, subtraction, multiplication, division, fractions etc. For biology, each level of the video game could correspond to a chapter. To make could it more interesting for them, instead of clicking on the correct answer they could shoot it.

For **history** class they could fight battles against Greek generals like Alcibiades, then Romans like Caesar, on up to Napoleon, Admiral Nelson etc. They could have a simulated camping trip where they have to use knowledge of **geology**, water, **astronomy** and **botany** to accomplish a mission. Sounds like fun.

Simulators have been used a lot to train pilots. Simulators could be used to train kids how to purify water for drinking, dig a well, prepare soil for growing plant foods. For **geography** the simulators could have them flying to the country they were studying. Then they could have virtual friends from that country. Who knows?

Chapter 53.

<u>Thinking – Edward De Bono.</u>

"Most mistakes in thinking are mistakes in perception, rather than logic." - Edward De Bono.

This quote changed my life.

I could not understand some things in my personal and academic life. I would think about them and the logic seemed perfect, but I could not solve the problem, or predict related events.

Then I saw this quote and I realized that the problem was not the logic, but the perception. This quote is very similar to the one by Ayn Rand of **"If you think there is a paradox, then recheck your premises."**

Quite often when you feel like you just don't get something, even though your thinking seems clear, the trick to solving the problem is to ask yourself, "how can I reframe this, recontextualize this."

Ask yourself, "would it be possible to approach this problem with different assumptions." Ask yourself, "how could this situation be perceived differently?" Run the problem by some other persons.

"If you never change your mind, then why have one?" - Edward De Bono.

"A foolish consistency is the hobgoblin of small minds." - Ralph Waldo Emerson.

"Many highly intelligent persons are poor thinkers. Many persons of average intelligence are good thinkers. The power of the car is a different thing, than how it is driven." - Edward De Bono.

"Unless we have complete information, we need thinking in order to make the best use of the information we have." - Edward De Bono from "How to teach your child to think."

"Many highly intelligent people often take up a view on a subject and then use their intelligence to defend that view. Since they can defend the view very well, they never see any need to explore the subject or listen to alternative views. This is poor thinking......"
- Edward De Bono from "How to teach your child to think."

"Criticism is much easier than creation." - Edward De Bono.

Edward De Bono is a Rhodes scholar, a physician and a pioneer in thinking methods. He is the inventor of the 6 hats method for discussing a topic in a meeting.

"Thinking skills are the software of the mind." - Edward De Bono.

"Critical thinking is just a beginning......Optimal thinking is better......Trying to solve a problem should include optimizing perception, increasing knowledge, constructive thinking and creative thinking." - Edward de Bono (This quote was a paraphrase from memory.)

I am very grateful to Edward de Bono. He helped me to improve my thinking, a lot.

He also developed concepts of vertical versus horizontal thinking. From memory, I think he explained it something like this. If you own a horse drawn carriage, to make it go faster, you can get a faster horse, put bigger wheels on it, lighten the load, etc. That is **vertical thinking.**

Horizontal or lateral thinking would be to do something different such as to invent a car or buy a car. The point is to try to think in a new way about a situation. This is more difficult to do than it sounds, because most people cling to conventional thinking and will mock you when you go outside of it. They might even attack you. That is why it is good to seek out places for your training and future work where your type of thinking is appreciated.

Talking to colleagues is often a good way to resolve a challenging problem. Sometimes they will come up with a solution. Other times, just the discussion will get you to think in new fresh ways. Part of what happens is that this primes your brain with related vocabulary and this makes it easier to think clearly on the subject.

At this point, it's as if your subconscious mind can now more quickly scan your mental library of knowledge and experience, and often the answer just pops into your conscious mind suddenly like light bulb being turned on. It is highly valuable to have smart colleagues so you can bounce ideas off of each other.

Johnny Von Neuman was a famous mathematician in the USA and **he noticed that he did much better work when in environment where he had routine discussions with other scientists.** When he worked in an isolated area, away from other scientists, his creativity and research productivity diminished.

Edward De Bono recommends that schools ought to have a **class called "thinking."** I totally agree with this. In the USA, boys from ages 6th grade to freshman year of high school tend to think they are going to be professional athletes. Then they go to high school and put tons of time into sports. They spend hundreds of hours learning football, basketball and baseball.

Well, I love sports, but why not also learn more about thinking? Why not learn more about how your brain works? About memory systems? About flash cards? Why not learn how to learn faster and better?

"The most difficult thing to think about is that which is right before our faces." - Goethe.

"Creativity involves breaking out of established patterns in order to see things in a different way." - Edward De Bono.

This is part of why enjoying comedy, reading jokes and making up jokes is good for the brain. Most jokes are based on this, thinking in unexpected ways. The "surprise" in thinking is what makes the joke funny.

"It has always amazed me how little attention scientists and philosophers have paid to humor. It is such an important thing." - Edward de Bono.

He's right! Humor is a wonderful, fascinating thing. The older I get the more I love comedians.

This reminds me of somewhere I once read (I think it was in an Edward de Bono book) that the main persons interested in new ways of thinking were business people rather than university people. At first I thought no way! The university guys are smarter, they do research, etc.

Then I read on and the point was made that the business people wanted to think better because their business and money depended on it. Whereas, the university people were often in a fixed pattern of "play it safe, do what is expected, don't make any waves, if we write about this popular topic in the typical way we will get grant money etc."

"The simple process of focusing on things that are normally taken for granted is a powerful source of creativity." - Edward de Bono.

"Creative thinking, in terms of generating ideas, is not a mystery. It is a skill that can be practiced and nurtured." - Edward de Bono.

"Sometimes a situation is only a problem because it is looked at in a certain way. When it is looked at in a different way, sometimes the right course of action is so obvious that not another word needs to be said and the problem ceases to exist." - Edward de Bono.

This quote was also quite helpful to me. For example, I once needed time to write a paper, but there never seemed to be enough time, and I was supposed to go on vacation with my girlfriend. She broke up with me right before the vacation and cancelled the vacation. I was very sad at first.

Initially I just moped around feeling sorry for myself. Then I realized, "Hey! Now, I've got time to write that paper!" The paper was a big success for my career.

"The purpose of science is not just to analyze and to describe, but to make useful models of the world. It is useful if we can make use of it." - Edward de Bono.

Another great quote from our friend Edward de Bono. I love books as a way to "meet" great writers. How else would we be able to "meet" Edward de Bono.

In our attempts to understand life, we construct models of the world. The more accurate the model, the better we can understand what has happened in the past as well as what is happening in the present. Even more important, the more accurate the model, the better we can predict future events.

This reminds me of another quote,

"There's always a good reason, and then there's the real reason."
- J. P. Morgan.

The good reason will make sense, but it will seem under powered. It is important to try to figure out what the real reason is, because it is the key to being able to predict future events.

Again, this quote is encouraging you to try to look for a deeper meaning in some situations. This can also be helpful when taking academic tests. It is definitely helpful in one's social life.

Chapter 54.

<u>Financial intelligence.</u>

"To earn more, you must learn more." - Brian Tracy.

FIQ = Financial IQ.

It is good to learn about money. There is sometimes an attitude in the science departments of universities that focusing on making money is somehow, low class in some way.

For example, when I was an undergraduate at Stanford, the attitude on campus was that the biology professors were these heroic figures expanding the knowledge of the world, and that MD's were a lower echelon, that had to some extent, sold out their research potential to go into clinical medicine, because they wanted to make more money.

This makes sense in a university that prides itself on research and wants to recruit top notch research scientists.

The bottom line is that it seemed a lot more prestigious to be a biology professor than to be a medical doctor.

Anyways, it is helpful to have money. It creates options.

You can increase your wealth by making more money as well as by saving more money.

The key point of this chapter is just to remind you that it is important, and not to neglect learning about it.

Many medical doctors in the USA don't start to really learn about money until they are over 35 years of age and by then it's kind of late.

Be careful about taking on excessive amounts of debt.

Life can be a harsh teacher. Sometimes after you screw up, you feel like Zeus just threw a thunderbolt at you.

For example, Kiyosaki wrote that "your house is not an asset." I figured, what does he know? My dad made a lot of money on his house when he sold it.

Then the housing crisis came in 2008 and lots of persons, including yours truly, saw their homes go belly up.

It is a good idea not to buy a big expensive house, unless you really need it. You start out thinking you own the house. Then after years of working and paying bills, you realize that the bank owns the house.

Then you are stuck in the high paying job, you don't like, because you gotta pay off the expensive house.

You want to take a job that looks like more fun, and has more potential for self development, but you can't, because you can't sell the big house for a reasonable price, that fast.

Avoid the big house, and avoid this trap.

"A man in debt is so far a slave."
- Ralph Waldo Emerson.

Chapter 55.

Thinking by metaphor.

"Boyd thought by analogy, a process that his friend, ever the pragmatist found extremely unsettling…..He found it even more unsettling that Boyd was always right." - Robert Coram from "Boyd."

Earlier, we talked about the limitations of working memory. You can "only hold one thought" in your mind at a time. You can only keep 7 plus or minus 2 items floating around in your head at a time.

Well, **what can you do to improve your working memory?**

The Feynman method! Brilliant! Write it all down on a piece of paper and add to this as you go along. That will certainly improve your "effective" working memory.

However, our ancestors did not have paper. They did not even have a written language until about 5,000 years ago.

How could the human mind have "made itself smarter" in the primitive world?

"A metaphor compares two ...objects or ideas and illuminates the similarities between them. Since the word or phrase used to set up the comparison evokes a mental picture, you might say that metaphor embodies the phrase, "a picture is worth a thousand words." - Elyse Sommer and Dorrie Weiss, authors of "Metaphors Dictionary."

When you make a metaphor for something, that helps you to visualize it in your mind's eye, their is better memory of it because of this deeper level of processing, and the use of "visual" memory.

Thinking in pictures could effectively function as a form of "chunking." Each picture is worth a thousand words.

Let's put this into caveman perspective. By picturing a woolly mammoth, they could let that use up one of those precious 7 working memory units.

Then having seen a rock roll down a hill and hit something, they could perhaps picture throwing a rock at the woolly mammoth.

Having seen one woolly gore another with a tusk, they could conceive of stabbing a woolly mammoth.

Combining the rock throwing concept with the stabbing, they could conceive of throwing a spear at woolly mammoth.

This is creativity. The combination of two ideas to come up with something even more effective.

If only one person thought of this and did not communicate it, progress would be slow. Well, the older persons could draw pictures on the wall of a cave to teach the younger cavemen. More likely they drew pictures in the dirt and danced around holding their hands up to represent woolly's tusk.

This passing down of knowledge to the next generation is a form of cultural evolution. It allowed humans to effectively become smarter and smarter with each generation.

This is a form of **Lamarckian intellectual evolution.** The young ones were able to understand these hunting methods through a **combination of logical thinking, mirror neurons, visual thinking, and motor-procedural memory.**

Getting back to metaphor and analogy, we can see how a **metaphor such as the rolling stones expanded the caveman's working memory and ability to think.**

One can start out with a basic metaphor and extend it or escalate it. One can have double metaphors with ostensible and hidden meanings.

The metaphor enables the caveman to create a model of the world. Then through trial and error, the model is refined and improved.

John Boyd describes this as **a continuous loop of ongoing building of a theoretical model of reality (construction) and discarding of parts of it (destruction) followed by combining with other domains to create something new and better (synthesis, rebuilding and creation).**

For example, use of the spear allowed a stabbing to occur from increased distance, thus protecting the caveman hunter. One could throw a rock at the snake, but those snakes are pretty fast and it might run after you.

Time to look for ideas from another domain.

As John Boyd says, **"whoever can adapt to change faster wins."**

As Darwin says, **"the animal that is best able to adapt survives."**

Chapter 56.

Leitner boxes and intro to Flash Cards

"Flash cards are like legal anabolic steroids for learning with no negative side effects." - Peter Rogers MD

I have seen the resumes of doctors applying for jobs. I have interviewed them. I also did a research project where I interviewed all the top ten percent medical students at the University of Illinois Medical School on how they studied.

Flash cards were an essential method of many of the absolutely best students, students who graduated first in their medical school classes.

The cardboard boxes in my bathroom, are about the size of shoe boxes, and are called **Leitner boxes**, named after Sebastian Leitner who wrote about it in his book, "So Lernt Man Lernen" which we'll just call, "So Learns Man." My translator is on the Fritz.

I keep them in the bathroom because I go thru some flash cards whenever I enter that room.

Leitner in 1972 described a flash card file system consisting of a series of boxes. It is a form of **spaced interval repetition system** (SIRS) that is done **without a computer**.

Spaced interval repetition can also be performed with computer based flash cards such as the **Anki** and **Super Memo** programs. Flash cards can also be viewed on a cell phone.

The David James **"Goldlist Method"** is a brilliant, special type of SIRS, invented by an accountant, that is done with a notebook and primarily used for learning foreign languages.

With Leitner boxes, the student looks at a flash card and if knows it well, then advances it to the next box.

If the student does not know it well, the flash card can be returned to the same pile or even sent backwards one box.

The point is that **although repetition improves memory, in order to be efficient, it needs to be structured, eg. appropriately timed.** Ie. the information that is difficult requires more repetitions than the easy stuff.

This is accomplished by the "easy" flash cards advancing rapidly to the **completion box**. Whereas, the "difficult" flash cards remain in the same pile several times or even go backwards a little bit before they are confidently learned.

Therefore, more time is spent on the difficult flash cards, and all flash cards are learned well before they get to the last box, the "completion box." Thus it is a combination of flashcards, SIRS and of mastery learning.

You can have as many cardboard boxes as you want for a given subject. I find 4 to 5 a reasonable number. The first box is the beginner box and the last box is the completion box. I have the boxes taped to a shelf in my bathroom.

You can have separate sets of Leitner boxes for each subject or you can combine subjects.

Knowing what I know now, **if I could do it over, I would buy a big table and put it into a big study room. If space is limited, then the the Leitner boxes can much more economically placed on shelves.**

I like doing flash cards in the bathroom because, I have to go in there anyways, and might as well learn something.

So, the current set up that I use is to have the boxes on shelves in the bathroom and then the actual flash cards in use, on a table next to the toilet.

I also like to go thru flash cards when doing a "walk and talk" as is discussed later in this book.

There is also a **"handheld stack" variant of Leitner boxes** whereby one puts easy cards to the bottom of the stack and more difficult cards into the middle of the stack with the net effect that difficult cards will be looked at more often.

Chapter 57.

Thinking – Garry Kasparov.

"Enormous self-confidence, intuition, the ability to take a risk at a critical moment and go in for a dangerous play, with counter chances for one's opponent....It is precisely these qualities that distinguish great players." - Garry Kasparov.

Garry Kasparov is one of the best chess players ever, and considered the best ever by lots of experts.

He wrote a very interesting book called, "How Life Imitates Chess." I recommend the book because he talks about how to optimize performance. He talks about the need for constantly analyzing one's performance and trying to improve it. He talks about intuition and other relevant topics.

"Ultimately, what separates a winner from a loser at the grandmaster level is the willingness to do the unthinkable. A brilliant strategy is certainly a matter of intelligence, but intelligence without audaciousness is not enough.

Given the opportunity, I must have the guts to explode the game, to upend my opponent's thinking and, in so doing, unnerve him. So it is in business. One does not succeed by sticking to convention. When your opponent can easily anticipate every move you make, your strategy deteriorates and becomes commoditized." - Garry Kasparov.

His book, "How Life Imitates Chess," motivated me to work harder and to continually try to refine my methods. The audio CD version of "How Life Imitates Chess" is really good.

"The ability to work hard for days on end is a talent. The ability to keep on absorbing new information after many hours of study is a talent." - Garry Kasparov

This is an interesting quote and I think it's true that as one studies more, Eg. in medical school, their study endurance increases. Perhaps it is due to building up a foundation of knowledge, perhaps increased brain glycogen, perhaps enthusiasm for one's progress, perhaps......

"You must enter competitions.........Competition generates hidden reserves of effort." - Garry Kasparov.

Competition is a big motivator. Knowing you have an upcoming competition gives you more energy to work on the task.

"When you take something for granted, is when you are most at risk to lose it." - Garry Kasparov.

Ouch! I have learned this one the hard way several times. When friends and family are trying to warn you about something, it is a good idea to listen! This doesn't always mean that they are right, but it does mean that they might be right, and that they are trying to help you.

"When faced with a problem we search for a relevant past parallel to see what was done and what happened." - Garry Kasparov.

"The one time when you are surely learning is when you are nervously attempting something new." - Garry Kasparov.

Chapter 58.

<u>How to learn any academic subject fast.</u>

"All science is either physics or stamp collecting." - Ernest Rutherford, New Zealand physicist.

Find the best books (see how to select a textbook).

Find the best DVD courses, preferably with a printed **syllabus**.

Put the book on the table in the magic bathroom.

Also read the book during meals when seated.

Check if there is an audio CD course.

Make computer flashcards with Anki and hand held flash cards for Leitner boxes.

Take a school or other educational center course in the subject.

Keep a list of all the stuff you are going to do to learn the subject and check them off as you make progress. For example, you can put a check box next to each item, book number 1, book number 2, DVD number 1, etc.

If the activity is associated with a place, then try to go there.

If there is an accessible expertise place, or person, then go visit and learn.

Try to find an opportunity to practice the activity in a live setting under supervision so that you can get hands on practice, and also receive constructive feedback.

Chapter 59.

Thinking – Thomas Kuhn.

Thomas Kuhn obtained his PhD at Harvard in physics. He was working on a talk about Aristotle's ideas on motion when he observed that many of the old ideas of science were not so much wrong as limited.

He popularized the terms **paradigm and paradigm shift.** The idea is that scientists use a paradigm to guide their work. Most scientists do what he called "normal science" which means doing research projects that demonstrate how the data fits the paradigm.

When scientists doing "normal science" find something that doesn't fit the paradigm, they tend to initially assume that something was done wrong with the experiment.

Eventually if enough exceptions to the current paradigm occur, then someone else comes along and puts forth a new paradigm with this being referred to as "revolutionary science."

The new paradigm is sometimes initially ridiculed and hotly contested.

Then the next generation of teenagers comes along and says, "oh yeah, that's obvious."

So, one might say, "well, why don't more scientists just work on these controversial issues?"

Well, it depends. It depends on the ability to get funding for the research and on how they will be treated.

The benefit of knowing this is to help you recognize that there is sometimes more than one reasonable point of view on a scientific topic.

In the context of medicine, this perspective can be helpful for diagnosing rare diseases or unusual manifestations of common diseases. The key is to keep an open mind to the possibility of an alternative to the prevailing, preliminary diagnosis.

Chapter 60.

Cold showers

I never used this "method" as a student. I tried it once as a 50 year old and it worked.

The idea is to take a cold shower as a way to surprise your body into an increased alertness phase that might be helpful for studying. Apparently the cold water causes a surge in your adrenaline.

Chapter 61.

Peripheral brains and the myth of external memory.

Some persons have said that they don't see the point in reading and studying so much because they can just look stuff up on the internet whenever they need to.

Well, here is the reality. It doesn't work that way.

The following examples are taken from the real world.

Medical residents often carry around small notebooks in their pockets that contain useful clinical information. These pocket notebooks are called **peripheral brains** or scut monkey handbooks. Scut is a medical term for "tedious or dirty work" that is typically done by junior residents rather than the more senior staff.

The residents often write a lot of their own personal notes into these peripheral brains. They can be very possessive of their own customized peripheral brain. For example, when I was rotating thru ENT as a medical student, the chief resident loaned me his peripheral brain so that I could correctly write some chart notes.

Upon handing over the peripheral brain, his phrasing was instructive as to how much he valued this little notebook into which he had painstakingly written so much information.

"Don't lose it or I will kill you!"

Clinical medicine is a fast paced job. Doctors have to work very quickly. It might seem to the uninitiated that doctors are casually strolling around having polite conversations with people.

The reality is that **doctors have productivity objectives for each day.** An office based physician will be expected to see 10 to 30 patients depending on the complexity. A radiologist will read 20-50 CAT scans and MRI's depending on the complexity.

There is almost no time for going on the internet. I spend about 5 minutes a week at the hospital looking stuff up on the internet, if that much. I spend about 30 minutes a week in consultation with colleagues in my own field.

Instead of going to the internet, it is much more efficient to call a colleague and say, "can you take a look at this? Do you think that is a tumor?"

In sports, things happen very fast. Gene Mills, who was known as "mean Gene, the pinning machine", emphasized lots of repetitions in practice of complex technique.

He said, **"it has to be automatic. You just react. If you think, you stink."**

Strong words. "If you think, you stink."

This is true of any sport. You have to practice the maneuver until it becomes faster and faster. This **increase in speed is due to the neural pathway for that action over time becoming hypertrophied with increased neurotransmitter storage at synaptic junctions and with thicker myelination** (fatty, electrical insulation) of nerve fibers (axons).

It is the same thing in conversation. Things happen fast. A good conversationalist and a good comedian need to have a sense of timing and the ability to interject a humorous comment or facial expression.

The internet also suffers from the "pile of crap" or needle in a haystack problem. There are a lot of topics for which there are piles of bad information that make it difficult to find useful information on a subject. For example, this is the case with lots of topics in nutrition and medicine.

Well then, what is the **internet** good for?

It is good for looking stuff up the night before or the night after something happens at school or work. It is good for looking up rare diseases, especially when the are associated with a characteristic image.

The point of this chapter was to remind students that you need to learn a ton of stuff. More than you can imagine. I am constantly learning, and I feel that I don't know enough about a lot of things that are important to me.

Ongoing learning continues throughout life. If you want to work in a high level, technical field, you should plan on being a life long learner.

Here's the good part. Learning is fun. Helping people is fun.

Here's the bad part. Too much work can be tiring. That's why you want to minimize your commute and choose a job where there you will have a reasonable balance to your lifestyle.

Chapter 62.

Thinking and Creativity – John Boyd.

"The goal of the individual in learning is to increase their capacity for independent action."
- John Boyd, American fighter pilot.

There is a great book about John Boyd called, "Boyd: The Fighter Pilot who changed the art of war" by Robert Coram. John Boyd was an American pilot around the time of the Korean war and the Vietnam war. He was an innovator in the design of jet fighters and in military strategy.

Boyd was a fascinating guy. I have seen this pattern before. He was sort of an exile from the rest of the air force. He arranged his life so that he would have lots of time to read. He read everything on flying and on military strategy as well as whatever else seemed relevant.

Then he came up with brilliant, new insights such as the OODA loop.

"If you want to understand something, take it to the extremes or examine its opposites." - John Boyd.

In order to figure out what was going on in a complex situation, he recommended extrapolating the issue out to the extremes as a way to determine what was really going on. This could make the correct answer more obvious.

He also emphasized the usefulness of mentally turning a situation around backwards as a way to understand it. For example ask yourself, if you did to someone else, what they did to you, how would they feel. This can help you figure out a lot of social stuff.

Another way to do this is to ask yourself, "what if the opposite idea could be true?"

This is a useful, hypothetical thought experiment.

Practicing this type of mental flexibility, mental gymnastics, helps you to become a better thinker.

This can also help you figure out medical stuff. For example ask yourself what are the possible scenarios with medical therapy versus surgical therapy. Thinking out the scenarios helps you to choose the best option.

John Boyd was a great thinker.

He also came up with a concept similar to the idea of thinking outside the box with regard to describing how a snowmobile was invented. It incorporates features from multiple different domains such as wheels like a car, treads like a tank, steering wheel like a bicycle that are then combined into something new.

Chapter 63.

Creativity – David Kord Murray.

"If I have seen farther, it is by standing on the shoulders of giants." - Isaac Newton, English scientist.

"It is very important how you define the problem, because that has a big effect on how you come up with the answer." - David Kord Murray.

"If you ask the wrong question, then the answer doesn't really matter." - Thomas Pynchon.

"**The formulation of the problem is often more essential than the solution, which may be mearely a matter of mathematical skill.**" - Albert Einstein.

"**A problem properly stated is half solved.**"- John Dewey, American psychologist, philosopher, educator, writer.

David Kord Murray is the author of the book, "Borrowing Brilliance" which is one of the best books ever written for on the job related problem solving.

He emphasizes that one should, **"look at what other successful places are doing and ask yourself how you can adapt that to your place."**

"Ideas come from other ideas. All good ideas do." - David Kord Murray.

Chapter 64.

<u>Creativity – Gerard Puccio.</u>

"Creative people are constantly reading…They read primarily nonfiction." - Brian Tracy, author of "Change your thinking, change your life."

Gerard Puccio teaches a course on Creativity for thegreatcourses.com. It is a good course. It brings together a lot of information on creativity.

I enjoyed learning about the different types of creative personalities such as an "improver" like the painter Norman Rockwell who refined traditional methods of painting versus an "innovator" like Salvador Dali who went off in more unexpected ways.

Chapter 65.

Creativity – John Molloy.

"Creative persons are highly intelligent. In general, you have to be able to see things in the usual way, before you can see them in a different way." - John Molloy (approximate quote from memory).

This is like the axiom, that you have to know the rules before you know when to break them. This is analogous to how comedians have to understand "normal perspective" in order to help them develop a "funny perspective" on something.

"How to work the competition into the ground and have fun doing it" by John Molloy is a book about creativity. As suggested from the title, this is a very assertive, opinionated book. He was doing research to help companies hire the most creative engineers.

He observed that highly creative persons often had a phase of prolonged loneliness during their childhood or adolescence that was transformative. This is often a time when they read excessive amounts on their own.

"They had a sense of isolation from their peers and sometimes their families as well. They often had few friends. They learned to entertain themselves with their own thoughts and to live in a world of ideas." - John Molloy.

This is a familiar pattern in the lives of Benjamin Franklin, Talleyrand, Napoleon, Faraday and many other great persons.

"Highly creative people are logical, pragmatic nonconformists." - John Molloy.

Like Johnny Von Neuman, John Molloy emphasizes the importance of working in a creative environment. Molloy also talks about the importance of the subconscious mind and how it is good to have pens and papers around the house so that one can write down an idea whenever it pops from the subconscious mind to the conscious mind.

"You have to risk being laughed at. People everywhere laugh at geniuses, and you have to face the fact that, even if you make a breakthrough, it may cost you your credentials, your credibility and your career...........Risk taking is an essential part of creativity." - John Molloy.

"Creative persons have learned from experience that the world does not understand them. They eventually no longer expect to be understood by everyone." - John Molloy.

"To be great is to be misunderstood." - Ralph Waldo Emerson.

John Molloy also writes that young and early middle age adults tend to be more creative than older adults because they tend to be more willing to take risks.

Chapter 66.

<u>**Mastery - Robert Greene.**</u>

"You must value learning above everything else. This will lead to all the right choices. You will opt for the situation that gives you the most opportunity to learn, particularly with hands-on work." - Robert Greene in his book, "Mastery".

Robert Greene is the author of the book Mastery as well as books about Power and Seduction and other books.

"High creativity requires high level knowledge and an open, agile mind." - Robert Greene, author of "Mastery."

The book, "Mastery" is about the process of a student becoming a master expert. It is a very good book and takes a wholistic approach to the topic. Mr. Greene writes about apprenticeship, the intuitive mind and social intelligence.

This is a good book for a young person who wants to plan out their future. A key point is that you need both the academic and the social component to progress most rapidly.

Chapter 67.

<u>The status of brain science.</u>

Most of the things that really do improve the brain were discovered a long time ago, such as exercise, reading, memory systems, flash cards, intellectual conversation, eating vegetables and sleep.

There are several magnificent tools now available for brain research including fMRI, micro-electrodes and computers.

Some great work has been done in the study of memory.

However, brain research is still in its infancy. The more you learn about the brain, the more you realize how little is known about it. Nature and evolution are a lot smarter than doctors and scientists.

In comparison to transportation, brain research is at about the phase of the Wright brothers who worked in a bicycle shop and figured out how to make the first plane powered by pedaling a bicycle.

This is a great time to go into brain research because there is a lot to learn, and the tools are now available to gather information.

Chapter 68.

<u>The three part brain.</u>

The three part brain concept is also called the triune brain theory and was developed by Paul Maclean in the 1960's.

It is a very, oversimplified, but helpful way to conceptualize brain function. The brainstem is the most primitive brain, the reptilian brain. This is for basic, background stuff like breathing and maintaining blood pressure.

The limbic system is the mammalian brain or emotional brain. It is capable of very quick decision making for fight or flight situations. This helps us to survive in the wild. When you see a predator charging at you, you run or climb a tree or get your gun Annie Oakley. You don't try to analyze what type of big cat it is. Big cat, not otherwise specified is enough.

The limbic system is located near the center of the brain, and includes the cingulate gyrus along the medial surface of the cerebral hemispheres, adjacent to the corpus callosum.

Cortex means bark, like the bark of a tree. The outer surface of the brain contains, cerebral cortex. This is referred to as part three of the three part brain, the human part, the neocortex. This is the thinking brain. The frontal lobes are considered the main site of executive function.

The useful aspect of this theory is to remind yourself to try to use your neocortex when you make important decisions. We often have an immediate, emotional reaction to difficult situations and it is helpful to let yourself cool off, when you have the time, and try to make sure that the "thinking" part of your brain has time to contribute to the decision making process.

Chapter 69.

Body language.

What is a chapter about body language doing in a book about study skills?

You need to get along with your teachers and mentors. A basic understanding of body language will help you. It is important to be able to recognize when people don't want to talk to you anymore, so that you will not continue to ramble on and annoy them.

My daughter in 4th grade, "dad, sometimes you sandtrap people."

Me, "what do you mean by that?"

Her, "you go on and on lecturing, and they feel like they are in a sandtrap."

Me, "who says that?"

Her, "everybody says that".

Ok, I admit it. Learning social skills was difficult for me. I think that in general women have much better social skills than men.

In fact, I would wager that **the average dog has better social skills than the average 30 year old, human male.**

At 40 years of age I read a fascinating book about relationships and communication. The next day at work I talked about it with two, lady, ultrasound technologists. I expected that they would be mesmerized by my newfound social insights.

They both had bored looks on their faces. Then one said to me, "Doctor Rogers, we learned all that stuff when we were teenagers."

So ladies can skip this chapter. Men over 50 can skip this chapter. For guys 18 to 30 years old, this information might help you to communicate more effectively.

Open body language (open to conversation) includes arms uncrossed, facing towards you, smiling.

Closed body language (doesn't want to talk) includes arms crossed (can also mean doesn't trust you or uncomfortable with what is being said or the room is cold), facing away from you.

IOI's (indicators of interest) includes big smile (whole face), dilated pupils, leans forward, entire body faces you, moves closer, touches you, plays with her hair, laughs at your stupid jokes, overreacts to you, wiggles her shoe on her foot, asks for another drink, says "my place or yours."

IOD's (indicators of disinterest) includes frown, fake smile (lips only), holds her engagement ring and wedding ring up like a shield, arms crossed, ignores you, faces away from you, looks mad, increases distance between herself and you, slaps you, kicks you, tells you her brother is going to kick your ass, calls security.

It is also important to look for groups or "clusters" of gestures. For example, a person might have closed arms because they are cold.

Here's another piece of advice, if you are a man talking to a woman and she seems to be giving mixed signals, red lights and green lights, trust the red. It's a red light. Do not pass go.

If there is a contradiction between the verbal message and the body language, trust the body language.

From what I've seen, women tend to have more developed social networks than most men.

"Courtship is 99% nonverbal." - David Givens, PhD, author of "Love Signals; A practical field guide to the body language of courtship."

I don't think it's really that high, but it is definitely way up there.

There are lots of books and some videos on body language. The best books on this subject have lots of pictures. It is good to read about communication between men and women.

The book, "Definitive Book of Body Language" by Allan and Barbara Pease, is good.

Once you are aware of it, it becomes obvious that every in person, verbal conversation, also has a significant nonverbal component of communication.

For example, in a school or job conversation, you usually should demonstrate indicators of friendliness, warmth, openness, trustworthiness and thoughtfulness.

When you understand how all this works, it becomes natural to do it even when you are otherwise tired or frustrated about something. You become better at keeping the different aspects of your life separate.

Paul Ekman has written some interesting books on facial expressions.

"The facial expression creates the emotion.....I can generate almost any emotion." - Paul Ekman, American psychologist and pioneer in the study of facial expressions and emotions.

"Where words are restrained, the eyes often talk a great deal." - Samuel Richardson, author of Clarissa.

"When a woman is talking to you, listen to what she says with her eyes." - Victor Hugo.

There are even entire books on eye contact such as "The Power of Eye Contact" by Michael Ellsberg.

Chapter 70.

<u>Maxwell Maltz MD, psychocybernetics and self image.</u>

"The self image is the key to human personality and behavior. Change the self image and you change the personality and behavior." - Maxwell Maltz.

"Our self image, strongly held, essentially determines what we become." - Maxwell Maltz.

"Self improvement is the name of the game, and your primary objective is to strengthen yourself." - Maxwell Maltz.

"Your self image determines the boundaries of what you can achieve." - Maxwell Maltz.

"You will act like the sort of person you believe yourself to be......If you think that you are smart, then you will work to prove that you are smart." - Maxwell Maltz.

Maxwell Maltz was a plastic surgeon back in the mid 1900's. He noticed dramatic difference in patient outcomes that were caused by the patient's self image.

He wrote a pioneering book on the concept of self image called "PsychoCybernetics" which means to drive your mind towards its goals. He also had some very helpful insights on the benefits of "mental visualization practice."

There are some good videos of Dr. Maltz being interviewed on You Tube.

I found his books and videos helpful. They promote a positive mindset, a can do attitude, and you feel happier and energized after learning from them.

"My dear child, you can't be held responsible for someone else's actions." - Maxwell Maltz.

When you view yourself as a good student who is on their way to getting better and better, you will get better and better.

It is also good to set high goals. For example, one can say, "I want to graduate with a degree in chemistry."

You can set even higher goals such as, "I want to graduate with a degree in chemistry and top honors."

When you aim high, you are also likely to achieve high.

Chapter 71.

Development of expertise and Anders Ericsson.

"Two obsessions is one too many...Being really good at anything.....requires a virtually obsessive devotion to one's objectives." - James Watson codiscoverer of the DNA helix.

Anders Ericsson is a psychologist who did research on the development of expertise. He wrote a famous book called, "The Road to Excellence." He found that **to develop expertise it takes an average of approximately 10,000 hours of deliberate practice.**

By **deliberate practice** it is meant, practice that focuses on the development of continued improvement. For example, if a child takes piano lessons and refuses to practice their scales and challenging pieces, but only plays "twinkle, twinkle little star" over and over, to drive their family crazy, this kid is not going to develop too much on the piano.

On the other hand, if the child is a sponge, and cranks thru the scales and the practice songs and the Suzuki or whatever training method is considered optimal, under the supervision of a good teacher, this kid is going to get good fast.

How long does it take to reach 10,000 hours. **At 3hrs practice per day x 365 days you have 1,095 hours which we can round off to 1,000. This corresponds to 10 years of practice.**

Therefore at 6 hours a day of practice, a person will have 10,000 hours within 5 years. What can you practice 6 hours a day? You can study a language or almost any academic field for 6 or more hours per day.

This raises the question, **"how can one accelerate the process?"**

As mentioned, one can increase the number of hours per day.

Better yet, a good teacher, mentor or coach can more quickly focus you on the optimal methods to speed up progress.

Great coaching can make a huge difference. For example, Dan Gable set records as the head coach of the university of Iowa for winning NCAA wrestling championships. Why? Because he was a great coach and he accelerated the development of skill in his wrestlers.

Great athletes sometimes have great physical talent. However, great athletes sometimes have also caught on to a concept that others were less aware of. For example, Dave Schultz (Oklahoma and Foxcatcher) and John Smith (Oklahoma State) are two of the greatest wrestlers that ever lived.

But to look at them, they just look like regular guys. No big muscles. No dazzling speed. I personally ran foot races against Dave Schultz and he was as slow as a turtle. Well then, how could they win so much?

The answer is technique. Here's why. You can only get a little stronger and a little tougher than other top level guys by physical conditioning. The edge for these and other things like flexibility is small.

However, the potential, differential growth curve for improvement by optimization of wrestling technique is unlimited. With increased practice and refinement of technique, one's anticipation speed, recognition speed, and reaction time gets faster and faster. That's the secret. Dave and John were to freestyle wrestling technique what Bruce Lee was to martial arts technique. Their innovative, eclectic styles continually baffled opponents.

The teaching point is to **try to figure out how you can optimize performance in your own field.** The purpose of this book is to help you optimize the academic component as well as to provide you with some pearls in a few other areas. In fact, there are enough pearls here to make a necklace.

High level experts are often, assertive autodidacts. They seek out books and teachers, and they learn whatever they need to learn.

Early success can also lead to a positive feedback cycle of increasing effort and more success.

Also there is controversy about the 10,000 hours number. It is better to think of it as a ballpark number. Some persons learn a skill faster or slower than others. Some are more motivated, have more family support, proximity to training centers, a supportive local culture, adequate financial resources etc.

There are different levels of "expertise", for example, competence, excellence and greatness.

"An expert is someone who has already made all the mistakes in a narrow field." - Niels Bohr.

Chapter 72.

<u>Entertainment and brain idling speed.</u>

This chapter is for people over 30 years old. Younger persons are often so busy that they are less likely to be interested in these ideas.

This chapter is pure speculation based only on some random thoughts with no rigorous data. However, there seems to be some merit to the concept based on personal experience.

We talked about average IQ being 100. Well if you wanted to make money selling something with TV commercials, then it makes sense to try to appeal to the largest audience.

When people come home from work at night, they are often tired and want entertainment rather than intellectual challenge. It is very common that people come home, eat dinner and then watch TV.

For the sake of discussion, let us say that the intellectual challenge level of TV is set at an IQ level of 95. This is a level at which people can comfortably follow the show while eating dinner, washing dishes etc.

Now of course, there are lots of TV channels and some with more intellectually challenging shows.

For the sake of discussion, let's say that a history audiobook is set at an intellectual challenge, IQ level of 115. When played on a CD player, a person can walk around, eat dinner, feed the dog, wash the dishes, floss their teeth etc.

Another nice thing about the audiobooks is that there are no commercials. If you speed up the audio, then it is more intellectually challenging to follow it.

The point is that when listening to audiobooks your brain is "idling" at a brain "IQ speed of 115" and over the years, I think it subconsciously absorbs more vocabulary and more information in this way. The brain is being primed with college and graduate school level vocabulary and concepts.

Teenagers and young adults have a lot of academic, school stuff to keep their brains busy. After 30 to 35 years of age, a person has to make a conscious decision about how much they want to challenge their mind.

Chapter 73.

Interesting speeds.

Average conversational speed of English speakers is in the ballpark of 150 words per minute (wpm) with a range of around 100-200 wpm.

Average speed for books on tape is around 150 wpm.

Average reading speed is about 150 to 250 wpm.

Average reading speed for lower level speed readers is around 400 to 500 wpm.

Average ability to listen to conversation speed is around 450 to 600 wpm.

The interesting things here include;

Being able to listen faster than people speak gives us time to understand them and to prepare our response.

This is also part of why we can become distracted or bored when someone is speaking. You need to make an effort to be a good listener. It is a sign of respect to listen attentively to another person and it makes them feel good.

Being able to read faster saves us a lot of time in life.

Given that our brains have more real estate devoted to visual processing than auditory processing, speed reading seems like a relatively untapped learning frontier for most people.

Chapter 74.

Is there a limit to how much you can know?

Theoretically it is unlimited. The human brain seems able to hold whatever amount of information we are able to put into it. If we could be constantly engaged in high yield learning activities we could learn a tremendous amount. For example, if we were rich and we traveled from one learning seminar or interesting place to another we could go on learning and learning.

But what's the catch.

"Every time I learn the name of a student, I forget the name of a fish." - David Starr Jordan, 1st president of Stanford university.

Theoretically, as you learn more, your brain has more "clutter" which might slow down your ability to recall things.

It seems that memory remains stored in our minds relatively well, but our access to it is variable. In other words, the more recently you have used the information, the more rapidly you can recall it. Use it or lose it.

Probably the main catch to "unlimited" learning is the time issue. The more time you put into thing B, the less time you have for time A.

Chapter 75.

<u>Knowledge Management Systems.</u>

In medical school the overwhelming amount of information that needed to be learned led me to seek out memory systems.

Then in the postresidency world, I noticed that information was piling up and often lost. I saw an article in "Wired" magazine about Piotr Wozniak and I started using computer based SIR (Spaced Interval Repetition) systems.

This was helpful, but stuff was still piling up and getting lost.

I came across the "plate spinner analogy" which apparently was written by Gerald Nanninga per an internet search.

This says that just as a plate spinning, circus acrobat needs to initially put in extra effort to get a plate spinning on the top of a stick, he then has to maintain it. Maintenance is easier and only requires an occasional spin. Life is like that. We have to simultaneously balance our efforts in several different areas and to maintain a variety of skills.

The Leitner boxes, of course, are a helpful part of a knowledge management system.

One can write summaries of a topic on the computer or one can write them in the margins of a book.

The combined use of speed reading, Anki computer flash cards and physical flash cards in Leitner boxes works well as a knowledge management system. One can repeat the item as much as desired in the Leitner boxes, and one can easily use this to remember things for years or decades or even for life.

It is important that any written or typed summary have a categorization method so that stuff can be easily found later. Internal hyperlinks can be helpful.

Chapter 76.

Failure and learning.

"From the ashes of disaster, grow the roses of success." - from Chitty, chitty, bang, bang (the movie).

"If you look at the way humans are designed to learn, we learn by making mistakes. We learn to walk by falling down. If we never fell down, we would never walk.......Failure is part of the process of success. If you avoid failure, you also avoid success." - Robert Kiyosaki.

"When one door closes, another opens; But we often look so long and so regretfully upon the closed door that we do not see the one which has opened to us."
- Alexander Graham Bell, American inventor.

"**Every adversity, failure and heartache carries with it the seeds of an equal or greater benefit**." - Napoleon Hill.

"**Nothing in this world can take the place of persistence. Talent will not; nothing is more common than unsuccessful men with talent. Genius will not; unrewarded genius is almost a cliche. Education will not; the world is full of educated derelicts. Persistence and determination alone are omnipotent.**" - Calvin Coolidge.

"**A basic tenet of my view of education is if you don't fail, you learn nothing. I don't mean by failure you get an "F". I mean if you don't fail while trying to accomplish something, you fail to learn.**" - Roger Schank from "Talks Training".

"**Many of life's failures are people who did not realize how close they were to success when they gave up.**" - Thomas Edison.

Chapter 77.

Flow states.

Mihaly Csikszentmihalyi has written several books on the subject of mental flow states.

When a learner is fully engaged in studying something that is interesting to them, and which is moderately challenging to them, then they are in a pleasant, efficient mode which is called flow.

It is as if the world around them ceases to exist and they lose track of time. It is like being on an intellectual scavenger hunt for clues to the truths they seek.

It reminds me of the language researcher, Stephen Krashen's concept of "comprehensible input" as well as the idea of the "Goldilocks happy medium."

In other words, if the study material is very easy the student tends to become bored.

If the study material seems irrelevant, the student is also bored.

If the material is too difficult, the student tends to be stressed out and overwhelmed.

If you enjoy what you are doing and find it reasonably challenging, the pleasure derived from this can in a sense energize you, and enable you to perform the activity for more time, and this can help you to progress more rapidly.

This is similar to saying, if you enjoy what you do, you are more likely to be good at it, because you will be more willing to work hard, and this will lead to more self improvement.

That is true. I really enjoyed learning and this made it easy to study a lot. **Learning is one of the great, sustained joys of life. You can spend a large amount of time in this flow state.**

There are a lot of enjoyable activities in life, but most are relatively transient in comparison with learning.

For example, exercise is fun, but a workout is typically is less than 2 hours and may last only 15 minutes.

You can study for hours. You can learn new things at any time of the day.

This is a good concept for life, of focusing on sustained, medium intensity pleasures. Peace of mind is a good goal in life.

At Stanford, one day, I was talking to a physics major. I said to him, "Why would you want to go into physics? Do you want spend the rest of your life solving physics problems?"

He said, "Yes! Why not? I like solving physics problems. What do you think I should do? Go around kissing people's asses all my life just to make a little extra money? No! I'm good at physics, I like physics. I can see a good future for myself in physics, and that's what I'm going to do."

Chapter 78.

Overspeed training.

I hesitate to include this chapter. This information seems potentially dangerous when used for athletic training. I do not have any experience with using this for athletic training. **I do not recommend this method for athletic training.** I'm scared of it.

Overspeed training is using artificial methods to increase what an athlete can do. For example an athlete can be be pulled by a motor as they run so that they can go faster. This it seems to me would increase the risk of injury.

Another overspeed method is running downhill. This sounds like it would increase the risk of shin splints.

Well, this book is not about athletic training. This book is about brain training. It seems that something **"like"** overspeed training is kind of built into some "brain training" things.

For example, speed reading books recommend that you practice reading at rates well beyond your comprehension speeds. Video games often speed things up more and more as you get to higher levels. Shadowing in L2 is intensely challenging.

I tried the demos for some of those brain training courses and they reminded me of this.

Now, I realize, that one could say, **"This isn't overspeed. These things are not using artificial methods to increase what the brain can do. These are simply examples of moving the carrot a little faster in front of the horse's face."**

When you are well rested and well focused, you think better and faster.

In the morning, a lot of people think better and faster.

When you are calm or mildly stressed, but not excessively stressed, you think better and faster.

This chapter seems incomplete because it is. There seems to be something more to this "overspeed concept" and it will likely be a productive area of research in the future.

Chapter 79.

Overlearning to improve long term memory.

By overlearning it is meant studying something more than seems necessary initially with the goal of trying to increase long term memory of the item.

Sometimes when I first learn something, I will intentionally study it more, categorize it more, or process it in some way more than perhaps seems necessary.

Another reason to try to "overlearn" something is to try to more quickly push it from the "conscious-effortful-slower mind to the subconscious-automatic-faster mind." Ie. overlearn it so that when I'm at work the information is immediately accessible to me without having to consult a book or a colleague.

There are pros and cons to this. The good thing is that you do learn the item better. The bad thing is that if you do this too much, it can slow you down a lot.

In general, I prefer to try to go fast. Once I've got the information onto a computer flash card and better yet onto a hand held flash card, I know that I am going to see it again.

I know that it is not going to slip thru the cracks. In addition, I have noticed, that the most interesting stuff, and the most common stuff tends to have more emotional significance and be better remembered with even just routine study methods.

Also, if I think that something is especially interesting, I will try to talk about it with someone. Once it has been talked about with someone it takes on a new, increased significance with an emotional component and tends to be remembered well.

Chapter 80.

Biographies.

"The reading of all good books is like conversation with the finest men of past centuries." - Rene Descartes, French scientist and philosopher.

"Imitation of notable models as an effective spring of learning; was the most ancient and effective motivation to learn, to be like someone admirable." - John Taylor Gatto, American teacher and author.

It is a good habit to read biographies of great people. The information in a biography tends to be more interesting, more relevant, more practical and easier to remember than from just reading history in general or from reading fiction like novels.

For example, William Churchill reminds one that public speaking is important when he says, **"There is nothing like oratory. It can make a commoner like a king."**

For example, Frank Lloyd Wright created a magnificent new architectural style by combining old western and Japanese traditions with new American boldness. Notice the similarity of much of his work with shapes one might find in a Japanese garden.

You can also get biographies in person. Highly successful people often have big egos and enjoy talking about themselves. You can learn a lot from them. It is good to ask them, "How did you get to be so successful? Do you have any advice for me?"

Chapter 81.

Waking up early.

"You will find the key to success under the alarm clock." - Ben Franklin.

I didn't know that they even had alarm clocks in those days.

When are you at your best for studying? It seems true that as we get older it becomes easier to wake up earlier in the morning. When I was in college, I remember saying to a friend, "this is ridiculous. Why do they start this class at 8 am? Colleges shouldn't have classes so early. Nobody wants to wake up that early."

When I was older, I would think, "It is good to start classes early, to get them out of the way so that you have the rest of the day for other stuff."

It is good to analyze what is the "sleep-wake" time cycle that works best for you.

I think best in the morning. For example, at 50 years of age, I can function at mental peak level from 5 am until 12 noon. In a crunch, I can function at peak level from 4 am until noon.

The point is that **when you know your optimal time, you can try to maximize that to optimize your results** eg. The last 3 months before a standardized test.

For example, Alexander Arguelles the great polyglot, experimented with wake-sleep cycles and found he could learn the most when he went to bed at 8 pm and woke at 2 am. He claimed that going to bed earlier decreased the number of hours he needed to sleep. This gave him more "morning hours" for studying.

Try it. Experiment with figuring out the optimal times for you.

Chapter 82.

<u>Learning in the car.</u>

The next group of chapters are all about optimizing verbal skills which is helpful for academic life and social life.

Please give the chapters on wit and jokes a chance because they are a useful part of verbal skills.

"Your car should be a classroom."
- Earl Nightingale, Brian Tracy and Robert Kiyosaki

I have learned a ton of stuff in the car. Most of it was just for personal interest and not specifically for school. However, by filling my mind with information about history, biography, psychology and foreign languages, I think it keeps my vocabulary sharp.

For example, there is such a thing as **verbal agility and verbal virtuosity.** After listening to audio CD books in the car, in the kitchen and in the bathroom, I noticed that my verbal agility just kept going up and up.

Believe me, if my love life went up as much as my verbal agility, I would be a happy man. Now some will say, "verbal agility and a dollar-fifty will get you a ride on a bus." I would counter, but what a fun ride it will be.

I have so much fun joking around with my friends and this new found verbal agility also helps me to think more clearly about all kinds of things such as psychology, communication and social interactions.

Boys and men bond by teasing each other and rough housing. This can be very physical. For example, my younger brother was a powerful wrestler, and he would routinely say to me, "do you know what time it is? It's cradle time!" And then put me into a wrestling cradle hold. He would do this to me even when I brought a date to a family holiday event. He thought it was funny. I avoided him for about ten years for just this reason.

As men get older, over 30, the teasing becomes verbal only, for the most part. Here is where verbal agility plays an even bigger role. This is a typical conversation with a male doctor friend who is a big guy who looks like a California surfer dude and was a former college star, soccer player.

Me, "nice Cowboy boots, Tex."

Him, "how would you like a soccer free kick up your ass?"

Me, "we both know what happens when a soccer player runs into a wrestler."

This type of verbal judo between men is a lot of fun and is common between friends. You can't joke this way with someone unless they are a friend, and you become better friends from this type of joking. It sounds silly, but this type of banter helps maintain friendships among men, and it is good to have friends.

Audio CD books and audio CD college courses create a library of information in your mind for the formation of future word associations.

For example, you can buy a 48 lecture, (24 hours total) college class on audio CD for about $30. It takes less than two weeks to listen to this in the car (1 hour commute each way).

In a routine month it is easy to go thru 2 college level audio CD courses in the car. In a year, 24 college level courses.

I've been doing this for 15 years. This is why, I feel that it would be a walk in the park to go back to college. I've already taken many of the classes several times.

In the car, I always have a notepad and a pen. When the lecturer says something interesting, I stop the CD and then wait for a red traffic light so I can write it down. **I only write at red lights. Do not write while driving or you will crash.**

When I get home, I tear out the page from the the car notepad and bring it into the house and place it into a pile by the computer for later processing. This can be entered onto the computer or just placed into a Leitner box.

Another way to learn in the car is to do a **"self test"** or mental rehearsal. For example, I will try to summarize out loud everything I learned the previous day. If I read a journal article or saw an educational DVD, then I will try to describe it in detail. If I can't think of something that I should know, then I will write it down on the notepad and then tear that out when I get home at night and review it at the next opportunity, such as the next day off or a weekend morning.

Chapter 83.

<u>Wit.</u>

Ok, so this chapter seems kind of random. Well, it's helpful in life to have high level verbal skills for school, job and personal life. Wit is one aspect of high level verbal skills. Wit is easily trainable by memorizing a few quotes and jokes and developing a sense of timing, as well as a fun conversational attitude.

"Proverbs are short sentences made from long experience." - Miguel Cervantes.

"There is no conversation more boring than one where everyone agrees." - Michel de Montaigne, French writer.

"Wit consists in seeing the resemblance between things which differ, and the differences between things which are alike."- Madame de Stael (French writer. Friend of Talleyrand).

"Wit is a dangerous weapon, even to the possessor, if he know not how to use it discreetly." - Michel de Montaigne.

"The ability to quote is a serviceable substitute for wit." - W. Somerset Maugham, British writer.

"I quote others only in order to better express myself." - Michel de Montaigne.

"How clever you are my dear! You never mean a single word you say!" - Oscar Wilde, Irish writer.

"I will be so brief that I am already finished. (Then he sat down)." - Salvador Dali from "the world's shortest speech."

Chapter 84.

Wisdom.

Wisdom can be defined in several different ways. The basic idea is that wisdom is the ability to use one's knowledge in a mature way.

Part of wisdom is being able to quickly recognize whether something is likely to turn out good and beneficial, versus bad and harmful.

Wisdom includes knowing how to focus on what matters and not being distracted by trivialities or being bothered by minor annoyances. Social wisdom includes letting a lot of little stuff go to facilitate maintaining good working relationships and a focus on the larger goals.

"Wisdom is knowing what to do next. Skill is knowing how to do it. Virtue is doing it." David Starr Jordan, 1st president of Stanford.

"Knowledge is proud that it knows so much. Wisdom is humble that it doesn't know more." - William Cowper, English Poet 1731-1800.

"There is often not a lot of wisdom in conventional wisdom" - unknown.

"The conventional wisdom is often wrong." - Steven Levitt, from the book, "Freakonomics."

"What makes us human, I think is an ability to ask questions, a consequence of our sophisticated language." - Jane Goodall, primatologist.

"Without freedom of thought, there can be no such thing as wisdom; and without freedom of speech, no such thing as liberty." - Benjamin Franklin.

"To acquire knowledge, one must study; but to acquire wisdom, one must observe." - Marilyn vos Savant.

A lot of wisdom comes from experience. For example, a 45 year old general surgeon is going to have more experience than a 35 year old general surgeon. The 35 year old may have a hot shot pedigree, but the 45 year old has been in the hot seat a lot more.

The 35 year old may have some advantages with a new, high tech method that he just learned in fellowship. However, the 45 year old will have seen a lot more patient's with appendicitis, cholecystitis and hernias.

"It is the province of knowledge to speak, and it is the privilege of wisdom to listen." - Oliver Wendell Holmes.

Chapter 85.

<u>Observations on words.</u>

"When I use a word," Humpty Dumpty said in a rather scornful tone, **"it means just what I choose it to mean – neither more nor less."** - Lewis Carroll.

"I do not agree with the words that you say, but I will defend to death, your right to say them." - Voltaire.

"The difference between the right word and the almost right word, is like the difference between lightning and lightning bug." - Mark Twain.

"Once I was a scuba diver in a sea of words (reading books). Now I zip along the surface like a guy on a Jet Ski (reading on the internet)." - Nicholas Carr, author of "The Shallows: What the internet is doing to our brains."

This quote brought to mind the idea of a book reader being like a diver searching for pearls. Whereas, an internet reader has the pearls floating on the surface.

"A word is a tool to express a thought." - Brian Tracy.

When you know more words, you can express more thoughts. You can express them more precisely. You can also think more thoughts.

"The limits of my language are the limits of my world." - Ludwig Wittgenstein, Austrian philosopher.

"We hear and apprehend only what we already half know." - Henry David Thoreau.

The more words you know, the more types of books you can read, the more complex books you can read, the more you can understand and learn. Words are the foundation of knowledge.

Therefore, the more you read, the more you increase your vocabulary and **the smarter you get.**

"A word is a script." - Greg Dean, author of "Step by Step to Standup Comedy.

Script is meant here in the sense that a word carries with it implied meanings and visual images. It carries with it assumptions and connotations. For example, the word "doctor" conjures up the visual image of someone in a labcoat with a stethoscope who sees patients and works long hours.

Two words can have the same "general meaning" but widely different connotative meanings. Understanding this a key for formulating persuasive statements.

"Words are often chosen as much for their emotive as their cognitive force." - John Harlan, American Supreme Court Justice.

"Reading is the process of deciphering the meaning of symbols called text." - Howard Berg.

A fast reader does this quickly. A knowledgeable reader does it with high accuracy.

It takes a lot of effort to plow thru a book. It is relatively easy to listen to an audiobook. When listening to an unabridged audiobook, you learn different things than upon reading the text of the same book.

Why is that?

I think it is because talking comes first. We converse from early childhood. It is a natural thing that humans have been doing for hundreds of thousands of years.

Writing and reading has only been around for about 5 thousand years or so, and this was limited to a very small group of people up until the invention of the movable type, printing press in China 1041 and Europe 1450.

I noticed that I could **zoom through audiobooks with minimal effort.** I'm walking around in circles eating dinner and the audiobook is as clear as day.

It's like watching a sporting event, a lot of running around, blah, blah, blah, and then something great happens.

Like a Rafael Nadal, beautiful cross court volley, a Pete Sampras serve, a Jim McMahon touchdown pass, or a Michael Jordan, hotly defended, fade away jumper.

The speaker will utter something brilliant, or funny, or just fabulous in how it summarizes so much in a memorable phrase.

I will put the food down and run to the associated, course guidebook or a notepad and write down the phrase in the margins. This is short term memory capture. Later on, I will look at these notes and decide if I want to add that to my long term repertoire of knowledge and conversational pearls.

The speaker has several advantages over the writer. The speaker can convey meaning by intonation, cadence, pauses for effect and other oratory tricks.

The same, long book which might be boring to read from cover to cover, can be fun to listen to en toto.

On the other hand the book has advantages such as you can go straight to the desired chapter, can write in it, can easily review it, etc.

Although it takes a lot of concentration and effort, the reader can go usually go thru a book a lot faster by reading it than by listening to it.

Chapter 86.

Jokes and joke books.

Telling jokes and laughing at jokes are highly enjoyable, high level verbal skills.

For example, only very advanced students of a second language can tell or understand jokes in L2.

"A serious and good philosophical work could be written consisting entirely of jokes." - Ludwig Wittgenstein.

"Laughter is sunshine. It chases winter from the human face." - Victor Hugo, French writer.

"The highest forms of understanding we can achieve are laughter and human compassion." - Richard Feynman, American physicist, Nobel prize winner in physics.

Humor is the by far the most significant activity of the human mind." - Edward de Bono MD, PhD, Harvard and Oxford professor, expert on thinking and creativity.

"The basic anatomy of a joke is first a setup line that contains a connector word which has at least two meanings. The setup line carries with it an implied assumption. The second line is the punch line which then uses the unexpected meaning of the connector word which creates a humorous surprise." - Greg Dean. (based on the "script based semantic theory of humor" by Victor Raskin)

"I never knew what real happiness was until I got married. And then it was too late." - Max Kauffmann.

"The best thing about being married is that it prevents you from getting married again." - Sam Kinison.

Isn't that magnificent! It is because that moment of figuring out the surprise of the joke gives us a dopamine rush in our brains.

Laughter reverses the acute stress response and is very healthy for us. Laughter lowers cortisol and optimizes blood pressure.

Greg Dean writes books about how to write jokes, and he teaches classes on how to become a stand up comedian. I enjoyed his book, "Step by Step to Standup Comedy."

Understanding the anatomy of a joke is helpful for being able to write jokes.

Telling a joke is similar to telling a short story. Bill McGowan in his book, "Pitch Perfect," describes the sequence. **"There is the buildup, the reveal and the exit."**

It is good to exit on a high note. This leads the listener with a positive feeling about talking to you, so they are more likely to be happy to see you in the future.

When I'm walking or eating I sometimes read joke books, because they relax me. In the typical joke book you have to read about 100 jokes to find a good one, but it's still worth it. When you find that great joke it is such a pleasant experience.

Joke books are good for the brain. In each joke you are searching for the surprise, for the clever insight. This keeps you thinking. This challenges your brain. The laughter moments make you feel good.

Reading joke books is also helpful for improving verbal agility. I have found that almost no one at work wants to talk about the recent book that I read. However, they enjoy it when I make a joke.

Usually it's just a little spoof on some everyday topic, but it creates a surprise and some fun.

Bill Murray, the famous comedian actor, once said, "most conversation is predictable. You know what the other person is going to say before they say it. You know what you are expected to say. All you have to do is throw in a little surprise and things become fun."

How true that is!

Oscar Wilde wrote, **"Some people bring happiness and laughter into whatever room they enter. Others remove it."**

My mom was like that. She brought a lot of happiness into the world.

When I was young, I mostly imitated my father who was a physician and a big reader, but kind of serious and didn't talk much.

As I got older I tried to take after my Mom more because everywhere she went, people where smiling and happy. She was always saying nice things, funny things and doing nice things for people. That is a good way to go thru life.

"The intelligent man finds laughter in most things. The sensible man in hardly anything."
- Goethe.

Ever since I was about 26 years old, I have kept a **joke file** and added to it each time I make up, hear or read a good joke. The jokes are categorized by topic and the joke file now includes thousands of jokes. Just keeping the file organized helps me to remember the jokes. A lot of fun has come from this.

Geoffrey Miller, the psychologist, who is a professor at the university of New Mexico, wrote a book called, "The Mating Mind." He writes that women like men who are funny because this is an indicator of intelligence that is hard to fake.

I showed this to my wife and told her, "if you ever divorce me, I will be able to attract a another woman with my funniness."

She said, "You don't understand. Women like a man who is confident with a sense of humor. That's different. You are funny like a clown. Women don't like clowns."

Ouch!

Chapter 87.

How to write better.

"There is no such thing as a moral or immoral book. Books are either written well or badly. That is all." - Oscar Wilde.

Writing is an important skill for school, work and life. Everybody is taught the utilitarian style of "use active voice and remove the fluff."

However, there is a lot more to good writing than that. It becomes fun when you learn about cumulative sentences and rhetorical devices.

"I was working on the proof of one of my poems all the morning, and took out a comma. In the afternoon, I put it back again." - Oscar Wilde.

"I'm writing a book. I've got the page numbers done." - Steve Wright, comedian from the United Kingdom.

"If you write fiction you are in a sense, corrupted. There's a tremendous corruptibility for the fiction writer because your're dealing mainly with sex and violence. These remain the basic themes. They're the basic themes of Shakespeare whether you like it or not." - Anthony Burgess, English writer.

"Capitalization is important. There is a difference between, 'helping your uncle Jack off a horse,' and 'helping your uncle jack off a horse.'" - old joke, unable to find a source on internet.

"Substitute "damn" every time you're inclined to write "very." Your editor will delete it and the writing will be just as it should be." - Mark Twain.

"Short words are best, and the old words, when short, are the best of all." - Winston Churchill.

"People complain about my exclamation points, but I honestly think that's the way people think." - Tom Wolfe, famous writer.

"A library outranks any other one thing a community can do to benefit its people." - Andrew Carnegie.

"All I need is a sheet of paper and something to write with, and then I can turn the world upside down." - Friedrich Nietzsche.

"I don't want to be a prose prude." - Willam H. Gass the famous writer (this is an approximate quote from memory. I couldn't find the original quote. Of course this calls up the quote, **"I'd rather be a prose peacock than a prose prude"** of which I also can't find the source).

"There were several experienced verbal stunt pilots in the Glass family." - J.D. Salinger from "Franny and Zooey."

Earlier we talked about how the key to getting better grades in high school and college writing classes is to write the way the teacher wants you to, to think your way into their head.

"Schools teach you to imitate. If you don't imitate what the teacher wants, you get a bad grade.......Taking the essence of the instruction and going ahead with it on your own. That got you A's. Originality.....could get you anything from an A to an F." - Robert Pirsig, author of "Zen and the art of motorcycle maintenance."

The next general piece of advice is to just read a lot. When people read a lot, they get better with words. Listening to audiobooks is also helpful in a similar way.

"You want to know how to paint a perfect painting? It's easy. Make yourself perfect and then just paint naturally. That's the way all the experts do it." - Robert Pirsig.

"He then learns that in going down into the secrets of his own mind he has descended into the secrets of all minds." - Ralph Waldo Emerson from "The American Scholar."

It has been shown, as described in books by Stephen Krashen, that as students improve at reading, they improve at writing and that their writing ability largely comes from their reading ability.

The book, "Revising Prose" by Richard Lanham is great.

The book, "Power Language" by Jeffrey McQuain and William Safire is chockful of fun quotes like, **"Power language is better than meek speak"** and **"Sins of syntax."**

I liked the book, "Classical English Rhetoric" by Ward Farnsworth because one can listen to the audio CD version while following in the printed book.

I found the audio CD course with guidebook, "Building Great Sentences" by Brooks Landon to be very helpful when I was in my forties.

It just seems to go beyond the usual, conventional advice.

The best part was the discussion of how to build powerful sentences using cumulative syntax. The discussions on metaphor, prose rhythm and generating suspenseful sentences were also helpful.

Chapter 88.

How to learn grammar.

If you learn Spanish or any other foreign language, you will see L2 grammar compared to English. In so doing, you will learn English grammar.

Sentence diagramming is also a good way to learn English grammar. I like the book, "Drawing Sentences" by Eugene Montoux.

Chapter 89.

Public Speaking- Oratory.

"There is nothing like oratory. It can make a commoner a king." - Winston Churchill.

In the academic world, you will eventually need to do some public speaking. As usual, a good place to start is to ask the locals what is expected of you.

"People may forget what you said, but they will never forget how you made them feel." - Maya Angelou and Carl W. Buechner.

Brief is better.

"A good speech should be like a woman's skirt. Long enough to cover the subject, and short enough to create interest." - Winston Churchill.

Rhetorical devices such as repetition can improve the emotional impact of oratory.

"We shall fight on the beaches, we shall fight on the landing grounds, we shall fight on the fields and in the streets, we shall fight in the hills, we shall never surrender." - William Churchill.

The public speaking course by John Hale of the great courses.com site is quite good.

The book, "How to win friends and influence people" by Dale Carnegie is also good.

Brian Tracy also wrote a good book about public speaking, including at an advanced level before big audiences.

"Everyone plays a musical instrument. It's called the vocal chords." - Gerry Spence, famous lawyer and author of "How to argue and win every time."

"Always hydrate before you orate." - Bill McGowan from the book, "Pitch Perfect." Hydrate with water because improves speech. Do not drink milk because can increase mucus secretion.

Some of the things that make a speaker more interesting include variability of voice tone, telling stories, jokes, information that benefits the audience, rather than the speaker just spouting off about tables of data that no one cares about.

I always liked public speaking. That is an environment that brings out the best in me. **If you are well prepared, and enjoy speaking, then it's fun. It's an opportunity to share some insights, tell a few jokes and makes some new friends. Maybe even get to travel a little bit.** In fact one of the biggest regrets of my life is that I ended up working at a place where I seldom do any public speaking.

Now young people will say, "well then why don't you just change where you work?" The answer is that it is sometimes not that easy to change jobs once you are married with a bunch of kids, a devalued house and a specialized career niche. Much better to choose your first job wisely and to keep your options open, early on.

"Herbert Humphrey talks so fast that listening to him is like trying to read Playboy magazine with your wife turning the pages." - Barry Goldwater.

Chapter 90.

Cramming.

Cramming refers to studying a lot just before the test.

Let us look at how this fits into an overall strategy. It is best to study a lot right from the first day of a class. The goal of this is to really learn the material.

Short term memory lasts approximately 2 weeks. So the purpose of cramming should be to crank up short term memory the last 2 weeks before a test.

This can involve detailed summary sheets. For example before a physics exam it is good to have a "plug and chug" sheet summarizing the common equations and formulas.

It is normal to do some cramming, but you should be smart about it. Make sure you are getting adequate amounts of sleep.

It is during sleep that you consolidate your memories. Your brain "recharges its battery" during sleep. Your thinking will be a lot sharper when you are well rested.

Some students will say stuff like, "oh man, I pulled an all nighter before that test."

I do not recommend that. I never did that.

Walking into a test, I want my brain well rested and ready to think well.

Chapter 91.

Rip and read technique.

This involves ripping pages out of magazines or journals and then reading them later at your convenience.

I have been doing this for 20 years, but I didn't learn to call it "rip and read" until I heard Brian Tracy call it that. I have learned a lot from Brian Tracy.

In the old days, before the internet, doctors and nutritionists used to do this to make their own file system of topic on given subjects.

For example, all the papers on protein go here and all the papers on fat go there.

Chapter 92.

Tape it to the fridge.

It is good to have habits that save time. For example, if you always put your keys in the same place, you will never lose them.

When you need to remember something for tomorrow morning, it is helpful to make a note to yourself and tape it to the fridge or put it on the countertop near the bathroom sink.

This is usually done for one's daily "to do list", but the same thing can be done with a written summary of an academic topic to get yourself to review it the next morning.

Chapter 93.

<u>Learning history.</u>

"If you don't know history, then you don't know anything. You are like a leaf that doesn't know it is part of a tree." - Michael Crichton, American writer, author of "Jurassic Park."

"The purpose of history is to explain the present – to say why the world around us is the way it is. History tells us what is important in our world, and how it came to be. It tells us what is to be ignored or discarded. That is true power – profound power. The power to define a whole society." - Michael Crichton.

"Study history, study history. In history lies all the secrets of statecraft." - Winston Churchill.

Some people question the value of studying history. I did, but no longer.

Reading history is very useful because even though some things change due to modern technology, **human nature remains the same.**

Amy Chua, the Tiger Mom, had a great line in her recent book, "Triple Package," where a Chinese-American parent said to a complaining kid, **"what are you complaining about? You only have to learn around 200 years of American history. I had to learn 5,000 years of Chinese history."**

Chapter 94.

Bloom's taxonomy.

Benjamin Bloom was a pioneering, American educational psychologist. He is the editor of the book, "Developing Talent in Young People." He led a committee that designed the diagram called Bloom's taxonomy..

There is a revised version of Bloom's taxonomy.

I have made up an even more modified version because I think that it is good to understand something before you memorize it. Then I made up the mnemonic URAC which makes it easy to use.

U – Understand = learn it
R – Remember = memorize it
A – Apply it = to a situation or by analogy
A – Analyze how well the application worked
C – Create something new.

Each step gets you to process the information more, and learn it better.

Benjamin Bloom's research and experience showed that students can benefit tremendously from good teaching.

Chapter 95.

Mastery learning.

Benjamin Bloom also developed the concept of mastery learning. Mastery learning refers to mastering level one of a subject before moving on to level two.

The application of it is to help all students in a class complete a given level before moving on to the next. Some students will progress slower or faster than others.

It is thought by some that making sure a student has mastered the previous level before they move on to the higher level is beneficial to help increase the likelihood that they will be successful at the higher level.

Salman Khan, the creator of KhanAcademy.org has shown that mastery learning can help math students a lot. He wrote about this in his book, "The One World Schoolhouse."

Both Khan and Bloom emphasized goal attainment by mastering one level at a time was more important than student comparison by grades on a curve. In other words, the important thing was that all the students learn, not that some get better grades.

Chapter 96.

Obsessive Compulsive Disorder.

If you start washing your hands too much, there's a problem.

In med school I went thru a phase like this and my mother used to tease me, "oh look, it's the boy who couldn't stop washing."

Sometimes students go thru an OCD phase. For example, when medical students start learning about infectious diseases, they sometimes go through a excessive hand washing phase.

In the book, "The Brain that changed itself", Dr. Norman Doidge writes about the work of the UCLA psychiatrist Jeffery Schwartz for treatment of OCD which includes volitional inducement of beneficial changes.

Chapter 97.

Self discipline, habit and routine

"If I miss one practice, I notice, two the critics notice, three, the audience notices." - attributed to Franz Liszt, Anton Rubinstein, and Ignacy Paderewski.

It is good to develop a daily routine that centers on your priorities. This involves minimizing distractions so that you can study more.

Once you have developed the habit of studying at certain times during the day, it becomes easier to maintain that habit.

Chapter 98.

The purpose of an exam.

Tests can be given for the following reasons;

1. To determine grades, like a dog race.
2. To sort candidates for determining who is allowed to go to the higher level, like the MCAT.
3. To determine a standard level of competence like a boards examination.
4. To motivate students to study.
5. To compare students from different schools.
6. To find someone to do something.
7. To keep the students busy while the teacher checks their email.
8. To sort new employees for different types of additional training

Chapter 99.

Stigler's law and the Matthew effect.

Stigler's law is based on the work of Stephen Stigler and Robert Merton. It is along the lines of "the rich get richer" with regard to academics.

People who read more, learn more, and are then, over time, able to learn more.

Over time the curve between readers and nonreaders continues to diverge, to get farther apart.

It is very important that kids read as a hobby in order to develop their vocabularies.

Chapter 100.

The Zeigarnik effect.

The Zeigarnik effect is based on the work of Bluma Zeigarnik.

In general, humans tend to want to finish what they start.

By intentionally leaving something unfinished, we can get ourselves to dwell on it and to thus remember it better, and this is called the "Zeigarnik effect."

Chapter 101.

Checklists.

Checklists have been shown helpful for complex tasks, and are now a routine part of medical invasive procedures.

They help to make sure that the medical team has checked that the patient is not taking blood thinners (anticoagulant and antiplatelet medications) etc.

The checklists are helpful to prevent oversights and they also free up mental bandwidth so that members of the procedure team can focus more effectively on additional items if necessary.

Having a daily "to do" list can work in a similar way for you.

By writing stuff down, you free up your brain to focus on other things.

Sometimes a thought can become obsessive or distracting.

For example, you are getting ready to go to bed and you start thinking about something important that you need to do tomorrow.

You can write it on a piece of paper and put that by the bathroom sink or tape it to the fridge so that you will see it first thing tomorrow morning.

Chapter 102.

<u>Summer time and vacations.</u>

If you need a rest, you need a rest.

However, summer time and vacations can also be great learning opportunities.

For example, you can finish college in 3 years instead of 4 by going to summer school.

You can learn a new skill by focusing on something new in the summer.

You can do a lot with a 2 week vacation.

It can be helpful to free up time in the weeks or months before a standardized exam so that you will have more time to study.

In the summer between the first and second years of medical school, I volunteered to help out in the emergency room to "make my resume look better."

The ER doctor said, "What are you doing here? You should be studying for boards part 1. That will help you a lot more for getting into a good residency program." This was good advice.

Chapter 103.

<u>Focus on your strengths.</u>

Everybody has their strengths and weaknesses.

It is better to focus on your strengths, to develop these. Try to figure out a way that your strengths could be used for a job that you enjoy and will be paid for.

You might need to improve some of your weak areas as part of that job.

However, it is easier to develop a strength than to develop a weakness.

Also a person tends to enjoy the things that they are good at.

Chapter 104.

<u>Research.</u>

"If we encounter a man of rare intellect, we should ask him what books he reads." - Ralph Waldo Emerson.

Why do academic and artistic geniuses seem to be clustered around certain times and locations in history?

The city needs enough food production and wealth, that some persons are free to devote themselves to academics or art.

The local culture also needs to be supportive of science and the arts..

For example lots of art was produced in Florence between 1460 and 1520 during the Italian renaissance because art was highly valued.

For example, there is a reason that so much research comes out of big famous places like Stanford and Harvard. These places have a lot more persons who are entirely devoted to research. They have grad students and research assistants to do a lot of the "grunt" work, including cranking out the numbers and collecting the data.

Every hospital and university will "say" that they promote research. However, very few actually have a true interest in research. Here's what happens in the real world.

At Harvard, I said I had a research idea and I was sent to meet with the statistician who was a beautiful girl, and then with a research fellow who was a fully trained doctor from Japan to help fill out the forms and write out the project plan.

At Harvard, I'm out at a fancy, steak dinner restaurant, paid for by a company that makes surgical equipment, 9:00 on a Saturday night with some doctors including a famous research guy.

This research guy gets a cell phone call. It's the Japanese research fellow with a question about how to feed the lab animals in an atherosclerosis research project.

A flash of insight.

We are sitting around eating steak, giving ourselves atherosclerosis and the research fellow is busting his butt trying to figure out how to prevent atherosclerosis. The famous research guy was smart, but his productivity benefited by the incredible resources available at Harvard.

I spoke with the research, fellow. He said, that the papers he published here were good for his career, and helped him to get promoted at his job in Japan.

At a local hospital, I said I had a research idea. The boss told me, "Look. We are very busy here. You do this on your own time."

The "research committee" gave me stacks of forms and off the record told me that my project was not going to be approved even though it was a simple project about topical, local anesthetics. Research was basically considered goofing off. The attitude was that a doctor is paid to take care of patients and that research should be the province of PhD's.

The reality is that the best medical research gets done when there is collaboration of persons from multiple different fields such as MD's, DVM's, PhD's etc. If you want to do research, make sure that you go to a place that really promotes it.

"It is necessary to be a little bit underemployed if you want to do something significant (in research)." - James Watson, codiscoverer of DNA structure.

Chapter 105.

<u>Choosing your classes & taking class notes.</u>

When deciding whether or not to take a class, the following questions can be helpful;

Can I learn this on my own with a library card?

Will this help me in my major? Grad school? Career? Or outside life?

For example, in college I took an electives in Russian literature. I should have studied the Russian language instead. I could have read Tolstoy and Dostoyevsky on my own time.

If I could do it over, I would have taken a more useful class like **accounting**.

Sometimes you can audit a class and check it out before deciding if you want to take it the following semester.

In college your grade point average (GPA) is more important than your course load if you want to get into medical school. For other majors, you need to ask the older students at your school or the professors.

Especially when you are starting out, it is better to take fewer courses until you figure out how to make the adjustment from high school to college.

In general, the biggest difference is that there is a lot more homework in college compared with high school. It is the same thing with med school. The classes in med school were actually intellectually easier than college.

It's like the old joke. "What do you call someone who graduates last in their medical school class? You call them "Doctor." The point is that everyone is expected to graduate from med school, unlike college where only a small percentage of premeds make it into med school.

In med school, there is a ton more work than in college. In college it is mostly the red hot premeds that are hardcore study nerds. But in med school, everyone is a study-a-holic, even the ones who pretend that they are not.

This is a good time to dispel the genius myth.

There is often some person that other kids say, "that guy or gal is a genius. They don't even study. They just remember everything after only hearing it once." Well let me put this one to rest.

I have never met one of these "geniuses" in my life, and I have been around a lot of very smart people at Stanford, U. of Illinois, Northwestern, Harvard and other places. Everyone of these so called geniuses, just had nonchalant personalities and studied privately, but they studied a lot.

In addition to taking fewer classes, it is also easier to take a class in summer school. The students tend to be less competitive and you have more time to focus on a difficult subject. You can take a difficult class at the local junior college.

It can be helpful to get "off track" from the "red hot premeds." This means to take the college classes out of synch with the other premeds. Ie. Orgasmic (I mean organic) chemistry is less competitive when the philosophy majors are taking it out of curiosity than when the red hots are scribbling their notes furiously.

Taking notes.

How old fashioned of me to say, "scribbling notes." As I am informed by my son, "Everyone types their notes. No one writes their notes anymore."

To each his own. I like writing notes. The brain is connected to the hand. This permits all kind of shorthand symbols, abbreviations and sketches etc.

The abbreviations increase your speed so you can keep up with the teacher.

You can put numbers on the left hand side of the page as you go along. This can be helpful for later when you go over the notes.

Try to write legibly so that you will be able to read the notes later. When you go over the notes later, you can touch them up.

If given a handout, it can be helpful to write on it. For example, **when given power point slide printouts, I like to write sage comments by the teacher onto the actual printed version of the slide and then later cut this out and use it as a flash card.**

Alternatively, typing can be more legible and permits synching the info with one's other electronic devices. That choice is for you.

Me personally, I'll stay with handwritten notes. It's easier and more portable.

It is also helpful to figure out the psychology of the professor. Eg. My first quarter at Stanford, for the English writing requirement, I was randomly assigned to a class called "the literature of alienation." It was a strange class. The teacher and I were alienated from each other.

No matter what I wrote he always gave me a "B". I felt like saying, "why don't we both just save time. Just give me a "B", and I'll save time by not writing the paper and you'll save time by not reading it."

Luckily one of my dorm mates told me that the dorm supervisor was also teaching freshman English and that he was a good teacher and a fair grader. My dorm teacher was a tall skinny guy with a ponytail and glasses which is kind of a stereotype at Stanford.

You show me a tall, skinny guy with a ponytail, who rides a unicycle and juggles and I'll show you a math or physics graduate student or professor.

The math genius gene seems to go with the unicycle and juggling. The ponytail seems to go with the desire for the freedom of being at a university, perhaps with the desire to be able to pursue one's research interests rather than be a corporate slave or a "babykiller."

The "babykiller" comment refers to math and physics majors getting teased if they went into jobs with the department of defense. It was only a decade after Nam and let's just say ROTC was not the most popular extracurricular activity on campus.

Lots of other types go into math and physics but for some reason this stereotype persisted at that time. Anyways, Dennis was a great guy and I learned a lot from him. We had a sort of "limbic resonance". When he said something, I understood what he meant. Also, I could sense what he expected of me on a writing assignment.

As Herbert Kretzmer, author of the English version of the lyrics for the Les Miserables said, "now that the code was broken, the words came fast."

It just goes to show you, how important the professor is in a subjectively graded class like English composition. Make every effort you can to find a teacher that you like for English class and other classes that require handing in written papers.

I always liked standardized tests because they seemed more objective. You just had to answer the questions.

Chapter 106.

Super Memo and Piotr Wozniak.

"If you want to be a genius, you need a healthy brain (good hardware), a good learning system (good software), lots of study to acquire knowledge (good data) and minimal negative interference (time wasted)." - Piotr Wozniak.

Piotr Wozniak is the Polish inventor of the Super Memo computer based spaced interval repetition program. Piotr Wozniak is a genius and his website **"supermemo.com" is a masterpiece.**

There is so much great information on his website, I had several AO's (Academic Orgasms) reading through it.

There was also a very nice feature article about Piotr Wozniak in "Wired" magazine.

Thomas Szysnalski the polyglot used super memo to learn English to a very high level.

The Super Memo program can simplistically be characterized as computer flash cards.

However, it has a lot of features that go beyond that.

Piotr Wozniak emphasizes the importance of sleep for learning. He recommends to try to minimize stress in your life. He recommends to avoid using an alarm clock when possible.

"Rage to master is characteristic of a true prodigy." - Piotr Wozniak.

Chapter 107.

Ebbinghaus.

The research of **Ebbinghaus** is a good place to start for a discussion of spaced interval repetition systems (SIRS). Ebbinghaus was a scientist who in 1885 did experiments on himself to study memory.

He practiced memorizing nonsense syllables under several different circumstances and this led to foundational insights about memory.

He would look at a list of nonsense syllables and then test himself to see how many he could remember. He repeated this test of himself at timed intervals and plotted it on a curve. This curve is called the **forgetting curve**.

Basically, the more time that goes by, the more you forget.

Ebbinghaus found that if he restudied the same material he could then remember it better and for a longer amount of time. He also observed that **"restudied material" was easier to learn the second time around.**

This is a typical situation for medical students. They learn tons of diseases that they might not see until 5 or more years later. By that time, they only have a vague recollection. However, when they go to look it up, it often quickly seems obvious, because they had learned it before.

It is almost as if, their mind had the information filed away in its own mental library and one simply needed to relocate it and bring it to the forefront.

The Ebbinghaus research is limited by the subject material.

No one cares about nonsense syllables. There is no emotional component to this. Emotion is a key aspect of memory.

While a scientist can intentionally simplify a research method to reduce the number of variables, to help keep their data objective, and to ferret out the detailed functioning of a tiny part of the overall system, this can also detach it from the real world.

It's like the difference between studying an animal in the wild versus looking at it's skeleton in a museum. Yes of course, one can learn a lot about a tiger from looking at its skeleton in a museum. However, if you have to deal with tigers in the real world, you'd better also study them in the real world.

Spaced interval repetition is a way to overcome the forgetting curve of Ebbinghaus. Let's say you learn something to a 100% comprehension level and you don't review it again. By that night your comprehension level might be down to 60%, by the next night 40%, the next 30% and then 20%, etc.

Use it or lose it.

Forgetting is rapid early on after first learning something. After having put all that effort into learning something, you will want to know it better than 60% that night. To prevent this, one should review the material soon after learning it, for example, right before going to bed that night. This can bring your comprehension level up to 90%.

Then the next interval to reviewing the material can be a little longer, for example, tomorrow afternoon. This can bring you up to 100% again. **With each repetition, the duration of memory increases.**

After a sufficient number of repetitions, the information item gets put into long term memory. Now it is available to you for as long as you need it.
There is something bigger than SIRS which is called **"knowledge management systems."**

This integrates SIRS with other methods for maintaining your expertise level in a given topic.

Learning the vocabulary of learning, memory and expertise maintenance helps you to optimize your own methods.

"Learning the proper definition of terms is the beginning of wisdom." - Socrates.

"Fear of God is the beginning of wisdom." - Old testament.

"**Fear of women is the beginning of wisdom.**" - Peter Rogers MD

Chapter 108.

Formatting and how to make a flash card.

There are several things to consider when making flash cards.

First of all is the **size**. You can buy small, blank flashcards 1.5 x 4 inches is a good size for short, simple phrases.

For longer phrases, 2 x 4 inches is better.

For on the job flashcards, eg. when on a "field trip" or during clinical work as a health care professional, you want something bigger to write on such as 5 x 7 inch notecard for your pocket.

Next question is **color**. Eg. when studying languages I used yellow for Spanish, blue for French, light green for Italian and pink for Polish.
When studying medical subjects one could use yellow for neuroanatomy (yellow like the myelin covering of neurons), blue for pulmonary, pink for cardiac, light orange for renal etc.

The point of having multiple colors is to keep the subjects separate if you mix them into the same set of Leitner boxes.

Of course, you could have separate sets of **Leitner boxes** for each subject.

Students sometimes ask me if it is good enough to just have computer flash cards. I tell them that computer flash cards are great, but it is better to use multiple methods.

The brain remembers stuff better when you write it out by hand, than when you type it. This is one of the benefits of making your own, handwritten flash cards.

The computer may crash, your internet service may be down, the flash card website you use may go out of business etc. These are all ways that the computer based flash cards might become unavailable to you.

It is a good idea for many subjects to have a **backup, handwritten version of the flash cards.**

There are many ways to make flash cards.

"Every picture tells a story." - Rod Stewart.

I like **picture flash cards.** You can draw your own diagrams or illustrations.

I often buy 3 copies of a book that has lots of good illustrations. For example, for a biology textbook.

The first copy is for reading, and studying and making margin notes.

The second is for cutting out the picture on page A to make a flash card. Cutting out the picture on page A, often ruins the picture on page B, on the other side of the same piece of paper page.

That's the reason for buying the 3rd copy, to be able to cut out the pictures from side B of the page. Of course, this can be an expensive habit. Therefore, one can buy cheap used versions of book and even older versions of the same book. Or, one can just draw onto a 5 x 7 inch blank notecard the key points from the book illustration and use that as a flash card.

When reviewing these flash cards, I just look at the picture and try to describe the key aspects of it. Better yet to describe them out loud. While the picture flash card itself can only be looked at from the Leitner boxes, the key aspects of it can be put onto computer flash cards.

I really like **DVD courses that come with a printed syllabus.** The ideal syllabus is one that has actual copies of the power point slides used in the lecture, printed typically 6 on an 8 x 11 inch page.

While watching the DVD course, one just follows along with the lecturer and then writes notes in pen on the syllabus on the corresponding printed power point slide. Then after the lecture, I cut the useful slides out of the syllabus. This will be about one out of three with a lecture that covers relatively new material and one out of 10 with a lecture that is mostly review.

This process of picking the slides to be cut out and sometimes writing additional information on them is review number one of the material in the DVD lecture.

The **cutouts are then put into a pile in front of the computer.** Then, perhaps a day or two or three later, the information from the cutouts is entered into a computer based flash card system such as Super Memo or Anki. This is review number 2 of material in the DVD lecture.

After the cutout has been entered into the computer, the cutout is then put into **Leitner box number one.** The flash cards on the computer and the flash cards in the Leitner boxes are then reviewed periodically.

Next review of the computer flash card is review number 3 of the material. Then the Leitner box cutout flash card is looked at to serve as review number 4 of the material.

This is 4 repetitions of the material and it has only moved (most likely) so far to Leitner box number two.

The **computer based flash cards** have a SIRS timing system whereby after answering the card you indicate whether it was easy to answer or difficult.

If easy, then the duration is lengthened before subsequent rehearsal. If the card was difficult, then the duration is kept brief before subsequent rehearsal.

The timing is set up so that the more difficult cards are looked at more frequently and more often.

This is great because it efficiently focuses your time. You study what you need to study, rather than wasting time going over stuff that you already know well. The intervals are spaced out to keep your memory and comprehension of it at high level, to enable you to have risen above the forgetting curve of Ebbinghaus.

Piotr Wozniak on his supermemo.com website has written a lot about how to format information and it is well worth your time to read his detailed perspective on the subject.

A couple of key points are as follows; **keep it brief. The brain remembers better if you give it small pieces at a time.** For example, a simple question like "who was the most important French diplomat to work for Napoleon? Talleyrand."

That is a good, straight forward question. The brain seems to prefer to store information in simple packets like this. In general it is less effective to try to put too much information into one flash card.

For example, "Which important French diplomat had a club foot, was forced by his family into the church, read a lot, was fascinated by finance, left the church, felt that France was better off making peace with England and helped represent his country at the Congress of Vienna? Talleyrand"

Now that was a mouthful to type or to remember all at once and the brain would prefer that it be separated into shorter parts at a time.

So you may ask, "**do I always make my flashcard questions brief?**"

Well the answer is, "no."

Why?

Because, sometimes, time is of the essence. There are often lots of flash cards to be written out and/or entered into Anki.

By the way, I started out learning about computer based flash cards with Super Memo, but my computer was then switched over to Linux by my computer expert friend and this led to the Anki online flash cards being the most convenient method for me. We'll come back to the Anki website later.

In order to get lots of flash cards, let's say, 200, written out/and or typed into the computer, I just do it as fast as possible. This works for me now, because most of the stuff I study nowadays is just icing on the cake. Ie. it is just a refinement of stuff I already know.

For example, there is a disease called PRES (**posterior** reversible encephalopathy syndrome) which is typically located in the posterior part of the brain. Rarely it can extend, in continuity, all the way forward to the anterior part of the brain, the frontal lobes. I made up a "memory trick-word association" name for this, "Full Court" PRES. In the sport of basketball, this is a special type of defense.

This idea just popped into my head. I quickly wrote it down. Then I made a written flash card and typed it into Anki. That way I would be sure to remember it.

Then someday I will likely see it in clinical practice, perhaps one, two or three years from now. Then I will call up my neurology colleague and tell them the diagnosis as well as the memory trick-word association name of "full court" PRES.

Typically this will please them as it helps them to teach their neurology residents. The whole process helped me to remember the disease, to diagnose it correctly, to help the patient and to help the neurologist.

And then secretly I hope that they will forgive me for any screw ups I might have made in the past, like possibly missing the same diagnosis 10 years ago when I (and almost everybody else) had never heard of this variant of PRES.

What do I recommend?

If you have the time, then try to optimally format your flash cards with short questions and concise answers. You can write the question on one side and the answer on the other.

In actual practice, I usually just write on one side and then look at the card and think about it. I try to see the concept in my mind's eye. I try to form a mental picture of the topic, what it means, what it looks like, what it relates to. This should happen instantaneously.

I consider it a success if I can look at the card and immediately know the answer and picture it in my head. That means I know it, that I own that information. **This card is then advanced forward to the next Leitner box or the "that was easy" box is clicked on Anki.**

If you know it quickly like this, then you are likely to also recall it quickly when you take a test. In a sense, you are overlearning the material so that it copies of it are put into the "automatic, fast" part of your brain as well as the "conscious, logical, effortful, slower" part of your brain.

If there is a delay in mentally picturing or explaining the picture, it goes backward, into the earlier Leitner box or online, the "that was difficult" box gets clicked on Anki.

Piotr Wozniak calls this process of keeping flash card questions simple and brief, **the "principle of minimal information."**

"Less is more." - Robert Browning and Ludwig Mies van der Rohe

Piotr Wozniak also emphasizes the importance of formatting your flash cards to promote **"active recall."** I think that he is totally right. However, I didn't use flash cards until I was done with medical school. I learned college and medical school with other methods, especially "condensed notes." In residency I had a simplistic flash card system.

In residency, I would carry a couple of 5 x 7 inch notecards in my pocket. Anytime something interesting happened in clinical work or was mentioned in conferences or lectures, I would write it down. Someone once said, "the best form of memory is writing with a pen."

Then when I got home to my apartment, I would put the 5 x 7 inch flash card into an "inbox." Then I would review the material and perhaps look it up in a reference book. **Then, I would add any relevant information into my condensed notes system which consisted of adding margin notes to an outline format book called "Radiology Review Manual" by Dahnert.**

Then the 5 x 7 inch flash card would go to an **intermediate box and then to a completion box.** This was basically a 3 box "Leitner" system. The condensed notes book of Radiology Review Manual by Dahnert was kind of the equivalent of what I might use the Anki flash cards for nowadays.

This system worked very well for me, and I got a 99% on the diagnostic radiology written boards test.

The key was that by taking notes of stuff that actually happened that day, an emotional component was added to the information. This in a sense told my brain that the information was especially important to memorize.

I can tell you that none of the other residents in my cohort took notes during conference or lecture. This seemed odd to me. It seemed due to **peer pressure**.

For some reason unbeknownst to me it is considered more "cool" to try to just "be smart," than to act like you are "trying to be smart." I was actually teased a little bit about taking notes.

My attitude was, "I just want to be the best student that I can be. I will use whatever method helps me to accomplish this goal. I am the best student in the class. I don't care what people say about my methods or if they tease me, because I know that what I am doing works for me. If they want academic success, they should be copying me, instead of making fun of me."

Peer pressure is not just a high school thing. It is a life long thing. For example, I lived in a subdivision and had a well. Every other house in the subdivision sprayed their lawn with herbicides to prevent dandelions.

I did not want to spray herbicides on my grass because I thought it might be bad for my dogs or my kids or the well water or the soil. A couple of dandelions on the front lawn. No big deal, right? Wrong!

My kids got teased about it, even scolded by the neighbors. My kids were embarrassed to bring their friends to the house. My wife threatened to divorce me. Now that's peer pressure. My kingdom for a horse.

If I had the opportunity to do it over again, I would try to go by the recommendations of Piotr Wozniak as much as possible.

He also talks about other formatting processes such as **"cloze deletion"** etc.

Another thing that helps with making flash cards is to **try to phrase things in a memorable way** when possible. For example, the same thing can be said in a clear simple way or a complex, confusing way.

Chapter 109.

<u>More about flash cards.</u>

You can buy a **metal "flip ring"** and put the flash cards onto that. This helps keep them together and can be a way to organize the flash cards by subject.

Eg. I used this method to study foreign languages. Green is a "go" color, an "action" color, so I used it for verbs.

Blue, being related to moods for some reason seemed like a good choice for adjectives. Yellow for nouns. Red for conjunctions and prepositions etc.

Other points about flash cards include, only make something into a flash card if it is worthwhile to review, if you are satisfied with the way the information is written.

For example, don't just cut every picture out of the DVD course syllabus and make them all into flash cards. That defeats the purpose. The actual process of choosing the select few slides to make into flash cards and writing notes onto the margins of these involves you with the material. You are classifying or categorizing this particular information as useful, as worth memorizing.

When you process information at a deeper level, you are telling your brain that it is important to you, and should be memorized.

You can use a **four color pen** to color code parts of the flash card. Eg. You could use a blank, white flash card and write the question in blue ink and then the answer on the other side in black ink or some other color.

This is another reason that I don't usually use the question and answer format on my flash cards. It takes a lot of extra work to make them like this. You you have to have a method so that you know which side is which.

The process of figuring out how you want to do it can be part of how you classify the information.

It is a lot easier to use the question and answer format with the online flash cards, because they are designed for that. You just type in the question in the space for questions and the answer in the space for answers and then you can review them that way.

When a teacher at school lectures from power point slides, you can ask them for a print out or to make the slides available at a website for the class.

After a written flash card has made it to the completion box, I file it away into a more remote box, on a shelf, in a closet. This is a "just in case" box. Eg. if for some reason I am away for a subject for a couple of years and then find out I am going to need to relearn it, then these old flash cards come in handy.

For a college age student, this would be applicable to a class you took during the first or second year of college and then you wanted to review that material a during your 3rd or 4th year for a standardized test such as the MCAT or LSAT.

A good time to look at some flash cards is right before going to bed. This can help the information to get put into long term memory while you sleep that night.

Chapter 110.

<u>Anki computer based flash cards.</u>

This is the system I currently use.

It is free. It is easy to use.

You can make the flash cards online regardless of what type of computer or operating system you have. The online Anki flash cards are fast to make and fast to review. You can classify them into separate "decks (of cards)" for each subject.

Eg. for the brain, I have about 30 subdecks for subjects such as arterial anatomy, venous anatomy, neurotransmitters, cystic lesions, tumors, epilepsy, pituitary etc.

Then for spine, I have about 15 separate decks eg. DJD, tumors, craniocervical junction, cervical, thoracic, lumbar, sacral, trauma, vascular etc.

This ability to subcategorize the subjects is very helpful. If facilitates focused review.

When I used to use a Windows based computer, I used the **downloaded version of Anki. This allowed much fancier formatting.** If you have a computer that allows this, and you want to use Anki, then go ahead and do it this way.

With this version you could color code the text in a way that was helpful.

For second language (L2) learning, you could take L2 text and paste a sentence or paragraph at a time into Anki and then just put a key point into the answer section.

With each review of L2 text, you could color code it eg. Green for verbs etc.

Chapter 111.

How to make a study room.

The main things you need are adequate room space, adequate desk-table space, quiet and minimal distractions.

This room should be dedicated to study. Try to minimize other sorts of activity in this room if possible.

The light should be good. This improves vision because it allows the fovea to use more cones.

It is good to have a big desk. A serious student will often have several books open simultaneously, and this requires a lot of desk space.

Nowadays, a computer is typically a key part of the study room and the monitor will take up desk space. Other things being equal, I prefer books because I can write in the margins, cut out pictures and bring them anywhere.

The internet is great for looking stuff up, but it can also be a big time waster as there are so many distractions like email.

The room should be quiet. I also keep ear protectors that look like headphones in my study room. These are very helpful when the house is noisy.

It is good to have **bookshelves that are arranged by study topic.** All the books for a given topic should be located together. This just makes it easier to keep track of stuff. This is also helpful for the long term perspective.

For example, you may take a class your first semester of college, that you will need to review at the end of your third year of college for a standardized exam.

If all the textbooks, question books and class notes for that subject are together on a specified bookshelf, then it will be easy to review.

If the books and notes are all over the place because "you moved," "forgot them at your parent's house," "friend borrowed them and never brought them back.". Then it will take longer to review the material.

It is good to study somewhere with minimal distractions. Keep this in mind when choosing where to live.

For example, my first year of medical school, I lived at my parent's house. This wasted a lot of time, because I had to drive to school. I would sometimes sleep in or rationalize, "that class is easy, I don't need to drive over there early just for that class."

I would miss out on important things like an informal list of study questions being handed out. I had less time to talk with other medical students.

My second year of medical school, I lived on campus and that was much better. I just rolled out of bed and walked to class, across the street.

It was easy to go home for lunch when I wanted to. I did not waste time commuting. I never missed a class. My punctuality was much better. I had a lot more time to talk to other students in person. I still went home on weekends, and my mom did my laundry.

The relationship between a parent and a child is unequal, because the parent usually loves the child more than the child loves the parent. Moms do a lot for their sons. My mom was happy to do my laundry. She would say, "don't forget to bring your laundry home."

Lots of guys, myself included, wish our wives loved us like a mother loves a son. Yeah right. Good luck.

I had an Asian medical student friend who had also lived at home his first year of medical school. I think that he was of Chinese descent. We talked about it one day. I said, "I love my mom but she drives me crazy."

He said, "I know what you mean. My mom is always telling me what to do. She says stuff like, "you shouldn't talk on the phone so much. You are in medical school now. You should not go out with your friends so much. You don't need to be dating so much at your age. You don't have time for that. You are in medical school now. You need to study more."

I started laughing. He said, "what is so funny?"

I said, "my mom is the opposite. She says to me, "Peter, you study too much. You are not normal. You are a nerd. Why don't you go out more often. Are you going to get back together with Carol? You know that girl Lisa at the tennis club. She is very nice."

Thank God for my mother's love. But I do wish my parents had coached me more, especially my dad.

Although my Asian friend's mom might seem a little pushy, he was a very successful student. Family attitudes can have a big effect on students.

The book, "Tiger Mom," by Amy Chua is interesting. She writes about her own life as well as raising her children, and she explains how many Asian families place a high emphasis on education. She said that children are often told that they should try to do well in school for the sake of family honor. This parental encouragement helps kids do better in school, but it can be overbearing.

Chapter 112.

When to study.

"Conversation enriches understanding, but solitude is the school of genius." - Edward Gibbon, author of "The History of the Decline and Fall of the Roman Empire."

The best time to study something is right before you need it. For example, read about the topic just before going to a lecture on it.

This will increase your attention, learning and memory of the information.

When I was less than 30 years old, my brain seemed equally sharp all day. Now at 50 years old, I am a lot smarter between 4 am and 2 pm. Especially after 6 pm, my brain seems to slow down.

Therefore, **I do my challenging reading and studying in the morning.**

"Think in the morning. Act in the noon. Eat in the evening. Sleep in the night." - Willam Blake, English writer and painter.

It is good to evaluate yourself. **If you have a time of the day when you study best, then use that time for your most challenging subjects.**

Use your "mentally slower time" for studying easy subjects or for other stuff, like eating dinner and talking on the phone, etc.

Alex Arguelles used to wake up at 2 am to study. Now that's a bit radical, but it is interesting to hear him talk about it on his internet videos.

For some people, it might be helpful to get into the habit of waking up a earlier.

"Early to bed and early to rise, makes a man, healthy, wealthy and wise." - Benjamin Franklin.

Now, we all read about what a great man Ben Franklin was in the 1700's.

But did you know that children of the late 1700's and in the 1800's hated him.

Why?

Because their parents were always bugging them with all those "annoying" sayings.

Evaluate where you get more work done, eg. at home or the library or a friend's house.

Does exercise perk you up? Then study the difficult subject after exercising.

It is good to develop a routine to make sure you are getting enough study time.

In general, medical students study a lot more than college students, and they often notice that over the course of the year their study "endurance" actually increases.

You can write out your study schedule on a calendar to help you get organized an to keep track of when homework assignments and papers are due as well as the date of quizzes and tests.

It is also good to learn how to make the most out of **"hidden moments"** (so named by Barry Farber, author of "How to Learn Any Language" which is a great book).

This means for example to listen to audiotapes in the car, or look at flashcards when walking etc.

Chapter 113.

What to study.

For most classes, teachers try to be fair, and they usually make a big effort to emphasize the material in class, that will be on the test.

This is another reason why you should go to every class. Also, hearing a human voice adds interest and emotion to the material and helps us to remember. One can often hear the echo of the teacher's voice in their heads emphasizing a key point.

For a lot of subjects, there is way too much material to potentially teach in a given semester. For example, English literature, biochemistry, anatomy. The teacher chooses the material to emphasize and picks a book to fit with that.

That's why you need to know what the teacher wants to emphasize.

The second most important thing to study is whatever handouts or study questions are provided by the teacher. If the teacher has a website or online videos, then one should watch them. Diligent students will be rewarded for this extra effort.

If you will have to take a **standardized exam** like the MCAT or USMLE etc., then it is good to begin studying for it as part of your regular classes. This can be done by going thru "review books" or specialty question books.

Chapter 114.

<u>Winning mindsets for school.</u>

"There is one quality which one must have to win, and that is definiteness of purpose. One must decide what one wants, and have a burning desire to achieve it." - Napoleon Hill.

It is helpful to have a positive mental attitude. It is good to have an "attitude of gratitude."
When one says things to oneself like, "I am lucky to have this opportunity to get an education." they feel more appreciative and happier.

It is better to focus on LEARNING THE MATERIAL, than just getting the grades. In college, med school and residency, I primarily focused on learning the material rather than the grade.

Of course the grades are important and you should try to optimize them. However, the mindset of focusing on learning the material is more enjoyable. When this was my mindset, and it usually was, I felt good about school in a serene sort of way.

I knew that I was doing my job of learning the material and that everything was as it should be. When studying pharmacology, I imagined that I might become an anesthesiologist and manage complex situations. Dreaming about trying to become a better doctor was a big motivator. I would say to myself, "learning this will help me to help other people and maybe save someone's life."

When you enjoy what you are doing, and are positive about your goals, you have increased energy for studying because it's fun.

Medical students study a lot. I have a friend who was in college when I was in med school, who said to me," man, school has been kind of intense lately, I studied 5 hours on Saturday!"

Do you know why a medical student would smile upon hearing this?

Medical students often study 5 hours on a Monday thru Friday. Five hours on a Saturday would be taking it easy. For example, wake up at six am. Study from 7 am to 1 pm (with some break time in there). Take a nap, do laundry, workout, and then go on a date. Easy day.

Chapter 115.

Approach to class.

Live as close to the lecture hall as possible. Walking is best, followed by bicycle distance, moped distance and then car distance.

Preread the material the night before.

Go to every class because it motivates you, organizes you, gives you the teacher's emphasis and gets you out of bed.

You will get all the handouts. You will know when all the quizzes are.

While doing the homework and during the test, you will run into situations where you will hear the teachers voice in your head, and it will tell you the correct answer. You will only have this if you went to the class.

Sit in the front row. This enables you to hear better as there are better acoustics up front. Sometimes the acoustics are not so good in the middle and back of the room.

You can usually see the slides better from the front row.

You can see teacher demonstrations better when you are up front.

A front row seat minimizes distractions. In the back rows there is a lot more talking and other sorts of goofing off.

A front row seat shows the teacher that you care about the class.

You associate yourself with other students who are serious about the class.

Take notes either handwritten or typed. Try to look at them soon.

Yes it is true that sometimes you might be teased about sitting up at the front or near the front. So what? This is really just jealousy of your self discipline. Better to take it as an indirect compliment.

Doing well in school is your ticket to better opportunities in life. No matter what you do in life, you are sometimes going to be teased, and you will have obstacles. That is part of life.

Might as well optimize your chances for academic success and the opportunities that follow from it.

Chapter 116.

<u>Teaching assistant jobs.</u>

It is good to work as a teaching assistant or tutor. You learn the material better by teaching it. It is fun to teach. A good thing to do is to tutor 1st year classes when you are a 2nd year student. This gets you to review the 1st year material so that it will be fresher in your minds for a future standardized test.

The one pitfall, is that you need to remember, to focus on your own exams first.

For example, in the winter of second year of med school, I was asked to give a lecture to the first year students, one week before my final exams.

I should have said no. Foolishly, I went ahead and gave the lecture.

The time spent preparing for the lecture detracted from my studying for finals. Those last 2 weeks before finals are precious. You should be selfish with them.

I did ok on my finals, but not as good as I would have otherwise expected to do.

Lesson learned.

This is a typical way that things are learned in the real world. You make a mistake. You are bummed out for a little while. You think about it or discuss it with someone. You realize what happened. You vow not to do it again. You are now a little older and wiser.

I worked as a teaching assistant and tutor during my first thru third years of medical school.

Chapter 117.

Learning things in multiple ways.

"Satisfaction of one's curiosity is one of the greatest sources of happiness in life." - Linus Pauling, American scientist.

"You don't understand anything until you learn it in more than one way." - Marvin Minsky, MIT scientist, AI expert.

When I was in medical school, I would often have several picture books or diagram books for a given subject.

I would open all the pictures and diagrams on a big desk and then ask myself questions like;

How could these all be combined into one diagram?

What is the most concise way that all the important key points could be summarized with a drawing or a mnemonic?

Then I would try to draw that diagram or write that mnemonic.

Often the first book would summarize one part well, the second a second and the third a third.

The net result was by consulting multiple sources of information early on, a deeper level of understanding was achieved with good visual imagery.

This led to improved memory of a topic. This also gave me a lot of confidence as a teaching assistant and later as a physician. I was confident that when I discussed a medical topic that my summary was the best available, because I knew what was in all the books.

This begs the question. "Doesn't that take too much time to study that way?"

I don't think so.

The reason is that when I memorized something like a biochemistry cycle, for example glycolysis, I knew it. I didn't have to review it that much. So, even though more time was spent up front in the "memory encoding phase," time was saved in the long run by better long term retention.

Chapter 118.

<u>Harry Lorayne and the letter number alphabet.</u>

"There are only two types of memory, trained and untrained." - Harry Lorayne.

"The best memory-enhancing over-the-counter preparation is me!" - Harry Lorayne from his book, "Ageless Memory."

"To me, the words, "learn" and "remember" are synonymous. To learn is to remember." - Harry Lorayne.

"Decide what you need to know. Understand it, and then memorize it." - Piotr Wozniak, inventor of "Super Memo program" (paraphrased quote).

It is a lot easier to memorize something that you understand, than something that you don't.

Harry Lorayne is a great pioneer of memory techniques and he is one of the most famous memory experts in the world. He has written multiple books about memory. I recommend his book, "Super Memory, Super Student."

The actual techniques of memory have been around for thousands of years. In the ancient days of Greece for example, most people were illiterate and paper was expensive. Information was passed along verbally from generation to generation.

In order to remember something complex you had to have a good memory, and better yet a memory system.

The following are the general principles of memory systems;

1. They have a foundation that consists of a **filing system that maintains sequential order** from first to last.
2. This filing system can be spatial or numerical.
3. **Spatial systems** are based on places familiar to you such as the rooms in your home or places on the your path from home to work.
4. **Numerical systems** are based on converting numbers from 1 to 100, into "picture words" (sometimes called "peg words") or into "people" to make them more memorable.
5. The things to memorize are often intangible.

6. These things are converted to tangible, by using word association tricks.
7. The **things to remember are** then **associated in order to** the corresponding spatial or numerical part of **the filing system by using word association trick**s such as exaggeration, motion, violence, word substitution, sex, taboo, rhymes, puns, stories etc.
8. This use of a filing system with sequential order enables the list of items to be memorized in numerical order and this can appear quite impressive to other people.

The letter number alphabet is a good system for memory. Here's how it works.

The number one is represented by the letters "t" or "d" because they have one downstroke.

Number two by "n" because two downstrokes.

Number 3 by "m", three downstrokes.

Four by "R" because you yell "four" at the golf course and the capital letter "R" looks like a person bent over as they hit a golf ball.

The letter number alphabet goes from 0 to 9. Then it is used to make "words" that correspond to the numbers. Vowel sounds and silent letters do not count towards making up the "number words".

For example, number one is represented by the word, "Tie" because the "T" has one downstroke and the long "i" sound is a vowel sound and the "e" is silent. Number three is represented by "Ma,"

Harry Lorayne calls them, **"peg words"** because it is like hanging your keys on a "peg" so that you will remember where they are.

In his books, Harry Lorayne often lists these letter number "peg words" going up to 100. On the internet you can find lists of these going up to 1,000.

With this method, it is easy to remember up to 100 things in order and to remember each one's exact place in that order.

What do I actually do? I like the concept of the letter number alphabet and it was helpful for remembering the dosage of "amiodarone" in the first chapter.

However, **I seldom use the letter alphabet for memorizing school stuff. Instead, the main thing that I use all the time, everyday, is word associations.**

The reason is that, I seldom have to memorize long lists of stuff. The letter number words and other memory tricks like the loci memory palace method are great for participating in memory contests and memorizing long lists of things.

For example, if you have memorize all the USA state capitols, then the letter number words would be very helpful.

In real life, I usually need to memorize things like anatomical regions, disease manifestations, foreign language vocabulary words etc.

The point is that, these are mostly ISOLATED items.

The best way to memorize these is usually by WORD ASSOCIATION to lock it in initially, and then to enter it into some form of spaced interval repetition system (SIRS) so that it will be placed into long term memory.

There are lots of other books on improving your memory and they tend to emphasize pretty much the same sort of stuff.

Each one will add a few interesting things. For example, the book, "Memory Power" by Scott Hagwood was inspirational as he overcame a lot of obstacles to become a memory champion.

Dominic O'Brien caught my interest with his approach to numbers.

Chapter 119.

The Dominic O'Brien number memory system.

Dominic O'Brien is a former world champion memory expert who pioneered a brilliant method of memorizing numbers.

He is a very good looking guy with long, flowing black hair parted in the middle and a muy macho moustache. Women love guys that look like that. I wish I looked like that.

He converts the numbers into people. I recommend that you buy one of his books to learn the details about it.

The general idea is that numbers by themselves are quite intangible. The letter alphabet and corresponding letter-number words together are a good system, but at times a little bit cumbersome.

Mr. O'Brien noticed that he could remember numbers better and faster if he associated them to people, and he developed a systematic way to do this.

It is relatively easy to think of a famous person who represents the numbers from 1 to 100 in order and to imagine them interacting with the memory item of interest.

For example, Walter Payton was a running back for the American football team, the Chicago Bears in the 1980's when they won the superbowl in 1985. Walter was a beautiful athlete, fast, powerful, brave. At the touchdown line, Walter would dive over the opposing defense like a dolphin jumping thru a hoop. He would run over opposing defenders like a freight train.

Walter's number was number 34. Whenever I see the number 34, I just think of Walter interacting with the item to be remembered.

This can be done for all the numbers 1 to 100.

Chapter 120.

<u>Autobiographical perspective on study methods.</u>

"Life can only be understood backwards; but it must be lived forwards." - Soren Kierkegaard.

"I had an analog childhood and a digital adulthood." - Nicholas Carr, from "The Shallows: What the internet is doing to our brains."

In a perfect academic world, kids would start learning about this stuff in junior high. In the real academic world, kids are taught lots of information, but few skills.

What I'm saying, is that, instead of spending all of junior high and high school teaching information, kids should be taught the skill of learning.

They should be taught how to learn faster and memorize better. They should be taught about flash cards, memory systems, spaced interval repetition, and neurogenesis.

Just like Wade Schalles, Gene Mills, Randy Lewis, Dave Schultz and John Smith dominated the wrestling world by recognizing the potential for improvement by optimizing technique was unlimited, the persons who develop these methods will have a huge advantage in academic performance over untrained persons.

From an autobiographical point of view, I didn't have any tricks in high school except that I read a lot on my own for curiosity, and I exercised a lot.

In college, I became a lot more organized, studied a lot, talked with Jay Rehm about school stuff and used condensed notes, analyzed my teachers to think my way into their minds, did lots of practice problems, and used old tests for two chemistry classes.

Even though Stanford is in California, my first year there I studied so much that I became vitamin D deficient. Condensed notes was the game changer in college to propel me to the to being a top level student. I was also exercising all the time as captain of the wrestling team.

In med school, the game changer was prereading the night before class. When I started doing that, I surged to the top of the class. I continued to use condensed notes extensively. Use of picture books, mnemonics, word associations, and margin notes were also very helpful.

These were my power methods in med school for optimizing academic performance;

1. prereading
2. condensed notes
3. mnemonics (extensive, sophisticated, written by me)
4. word associations (lots and lots of these)
5. picture books (I went thru all the Netter books and many other illustrated atlases)
6. learning things in multiple ways, an eclectic approach
7. deep level understanding. Having studied an item from several different sources, I understood the underlying significance, how and why it was significant for the test and clinically.
8. lots of exercise (I coached high school and college wrestling teams)
9. little wasted time or distractions (my Mom did my laundry, lived across the street from school, had no wife or kids at that time)
10. Go to every class

I started reading about memory systems in med school, but mostly only used the word association tricks.

In residency, I started using flash cards. These just consisted of writing notes on 5 x 7 inch note cards about whatever I learned during the day.

Then I would go home to my apartment which was just 3 blocks away from Northwestern hospital. I would throw the notecard into a cardboard box and try to look at it soon, that night or by that weekend.

Then I would enter the notecard information into a big, outline format book called "Radiology Review Manual" by Dahnert. This served as my condensed notes.

I wrote my own mnemonics, hundreds of them, for anything that seemed to require a short list of items to be connected to each other.

There are several key points to this chapter. The first is that, the farther you go in the academic world the more competitive it gets. The second is that you should keep trying to improve your methods as you go along. The third is that I wish I had this book back in high school. It would have made everything a lot easier.

The average SAT score at Stanford is middle of the number one percentile and it's higher in the premed classes. Medical school admissions are very competitive. Only 4 out of 12 persons from my freshman dorm who started out as premeds made it into medical school.

Only, approximately the top 20% of medical students were able to get into diagnostic radiology in the early 1990's. My study methods progressively improved over time as I learned more techniques and experimented with more methods. I got a 99% on the written boards exam in diagnostic radiology.

In applying for a fellowship at Harvard (based at Brigham and Womens hospital with rotations at Massachussetts General Hospital) in imaging guided surgery (interventional radiology) there were 180 applicants for 2 spots. I think they took me because I told the head doctor that I would accept an offer on the spot and that I would help him to write his book.

Then I did a neuroradiology fellowship at Rush hospital in Chicago. Rush was a very good hospital. My study methods were better at that time than they had been in residency. Only, approximately the top 25% of radiology residents were able to obtain neuroradiology fellowships at that time. It was one of the more "egghead" type fellowships for radiologists.

Then there was neuroradiology boards. After the test one of the examiners called me aside. He asked me where I trained. He said that my performance had been extraordinary. He asked me where I went to med school and residency. He asked me how I had prepared for the exam. This examiner notified my fellowship attending and told him that I had achieved a perfect score. He was not allowed to tell me that in person.

In clinical practice, I use some of these number memory systems, to memorize patient medical record numbers, and dictation codes so that I can read out my procedure cases without having to refer to the paper.

I also use the number systems to memorize phone numbers.

Chapter 121.

The loci and memory palace systems of memory.

These are spatial filing systems for memory. Several of the great world champions of memory highly recommend these systems. This is a normal way to remember things.

The human brain is designed to help you survive when you walk down a path in a forest. It is very good at memorizing the locations of food, water, shelter, potential predators, landmarks to find one's way home etc.

You can think of the **loci system as the location system.** For example, you can write down in sequential order, the landmarks that you pass on your way to school.

For example, your front yard, your neighbor's house, the big building, the lake etc. Then when you want to memorize a list of items, you just mentally associate them to these landmarks in order.

The **memory palace system** is the same sort of concept as the Roman room method. You just memorize key features of rooms in your home in some sort of a sequential order and then use these as a sequential filing system to which you can associate a list of informational items from an academic topic.

Chapter 122.

Counting cards and becoming a gambler.

"Sex is like bridge, you need a good partner or a good hand." - Charles Pierce (also attributed to Mae West).

Memory systems can also be used to memorize one, two or even more decks of cards. This could help you to become good at playing cards.

There is a movie called, "21", based on a book called, "Bringing Down the House," that is about MIT students that used their card counting skills to win lots of money playing blackjack.

Chapter 123.

Mnemonics.

Mnemonics are great for memory. In med school, I never used any of those number list systems. I used mnemonics.

I wrote my own mnemonics almost all the time. I rarely used traditional mnemonics unless they were really good, like "DR CUMA" for the brachial plexus.

A typical mnemonic method is to take the first letter of a group of items and make these into a word. A classic example is "HOMES" for the great lakes;

H – Huron
O – Ontario
M – Michigan
E – Erie
S – Superior

This mnemonic enables you to remember one word to serve as a "placesetter" for 5 words. It is easier to remember one word than five words.

The process of looking at the mnemonic or better yet writing it yourself involves you with the material at a deeper level and improves your memory of it.

The shorter the mnemonic the better. It is good for it to be as short as possible, from which all the necessary info can be recalled or "derived."

The mnemonic also serves as a convenient method to rehearse and self test the material. For example, just say to yourself, "HOMES" and then say the names of the great lakes.

The mnemonic also then serves as a scaffold to attach other information. For example, after saying the names of the great lakes, you could start to verbally rattle off information about the individual lakes.

Eventually, you won't even need the mnemonic. You will just know the information.

Chapter 124.

Mind Maps.

Tony Buzan has written several books about mind maps.

You write the main topic in the center of the page and draw a circle around it. Then you draw curvy lines from the center circle to the subtopics and so on outward to sub-subtopics.

Drawings can be added and colors can be used.

Part of the idea is that this kind of neural, network like system is thought to be more analogous to how the brain thinks than just making a list of items or making a conventional outline format.

I never used this method for school. I tried it a few times for fun around the time that I read about it, and it does seem to work well.

For high school and college students, I recommend that you give this method a try. It seems like a good way to self test. For example, after reading a chapter you could try to make a mind map of it. This will show you what you have retained well versus the stuff that slipped thru the cracks.

Chapter 125.

<u>Standing table.</u>

It is good to have a table for reading while standing.

Too much sitting is not healthy. Once in a while I will read at a high table so I can stand and read.

I especially like to do this after having eaten a big meal.

Modern humans tend to spend excessive amounts of time in the sitting position. When I am studying or working in a seated position, I like to stand up to talk on the phone.

When you stand up, your muscles get more exercise. This is another reason to take periodic study breaks, and it is good to walk around a during these breaks.

Chapter 126.

<u>Posters and study walls.</u>

The poster technique is something I used to do before I started using flash cards more.
It is still a good technique.

This involves cutting out pictures from course syllabi or books or journals and taping them onto a large poster board.

You can get one of those folding, poster boards that are used for high school science fairs.

For example, I made a poster board of cerebral aneurysms to help me memorize subtle distinctions on this topic.

The benefit of a poster board is that all of the relevant material for a given subject is there, together on that poster board to facilitate easy review. You learn a lot from making the poster.

The down sides are that posters become cumbersome to store. They are not that portable. It can be awkward to look at the stuff at the bottom of the page.

A study wall is defined here as functioning like a "poster." For example, on the door to my office bathroom, I taped lots of pictures of the temporal bone. The temporal bone is the home of our hearing apparatus. It has complex anatomy and is associated with a bunch of rare diseases that I have to know about for my job.

When studying for a neuroradiology test, I would just look at that wall and talk out loud as I went thru the anatomy and diseases of the temporal bone, and that helped me to learn it reasonably well.

The benefits of a study wall are similar to those of a poster. The down sides are that it occupies the wall. You can only put it in a private area or else you will be divorced or ostracized. It is a mess to clean up.

Chapter 127.

Always be ready to learn.

"The most natural desire is the desire to learn." - Michel de Montaigne, French writer.

When Dave Schultz was in grade school, he had dyslexia, poor grades in school, he wasn't good at sports and his parents got divorced. He was kind of an unhappy kid.

Then he found wrestling, and he loved the trickery of technique that could be used to defeat larger opponents.

In junior high and high school, he always carried around a backpack with his wrestling gear so that he could take advantage of any opportunity to learn wrestling technique.

He routinely rode over to nearby Stanford university to practice with the college team. He went on to become world champion and the greatest technical wrestler in the world. The Bruce Lee of wrestling.

Likewise, in a lot of situations it is good to carry around a book or flashcards. For example, your parents might make you go visit your grandparents. You can read during the car ride. At the grandparents house, when you are done talking and eating, you might have time to read.

"It may be that people that inherit a high degree of information processing capacity or native intelligence will have a tremendous need for intellectual and cultural stimulation. They will accordingly buy books, subscribe to magazines, visit musuems and galleries, engage in diverse hobbies and do whatever else they need to maintain a mentally active life." - D. K. Simonton, from "Origins of Genius."

Chapter 128.

Condensed notes in med school and residency.

In college, at least in 1980's, there was a limited number of sources of information. These were the teacher, teachers handouts-syllabus, and textbook.

Spiral notebooks worked very well for condensed notes, and that is what I used for classes like organic chemistry. There was a detailed syllabus for the core biology courses and I wrote in the margins of it for biology classes.

In med school there were often several books for a given subject. **For some subjects I used the old college method of using a spiral notebook for condensed notes.**

For other subjects I might have two sources of key notes. For example, in anatomy, one could use an outline text as the base text for written notes and then cross reference it with an atlas that had lots of notes written in the margins.

I would sometimes use adhesive stickers to make tabbed markers to individual chapters. Adhesive stickers are neater and more long lasting for this purpose than are post-its.

Same thing for biochemistry.

In residency, there were even more sources of information which now included journal articles.

An outline format book was used as the base text for written notes and then it was **cross referenced.** One could just reference the article in the condensed notes by writing in the margins the issue and page number, and leaving the article inside the journal.

Another option was to cut the picture out of a journal and to tape it inside another book. Lest you be aghast at this vandalism of a journal, fret not for this method of processing the material led to deeper learning, that obviated needing to go back to the article. The key information was written in the margins adjacent to the cut out image. **The book that received the cut out from the journal functioned as the picture review book for that topic.**

Outline format books with a detailed index work well for condensed notes. The idea is to only write down the key stuff that lets you derive the rest. You do not want to clutter these notes with obvious stuff that you already know well.

These notes are an essential distillation of the stuff that is worth reviewing. They are for you only.

For example, **mnemonics** for a given anatomical region were written in the margin next to that topic in the condensed notes. I made up tons of mnemonics in med school and residency and found them very helpful. So even though it takes a while to make up a mnemonic, the pay off is that retention and comprehension are great.

Information gleaned from review lectures and question books was also written into the condensed notes.

It is good to try to write neatly as you will go back to these notes repeatedly. It is good to write in the margins whatever **word associations** you have made up relative to the topic, if any.

It is good to try to **make these notes as memorable as possible in whatever way seems to help.** In other words, emphasize clear explanations written in active voice. Draw arrows or stars next to key points or circle key words. Whatever works for you.

Condensed notes are condensed. One page in a textbook might be summarized as a single line or two in your condensed notes.

When it was time to study for school exams, the condensed notes were reviewed. This saved time because there was no need to go back to the regular textbooks unless something needed to be looked up.

The great benefits of an **outline format book** are that it tends to be concise, well organized and to have a good index. Just studying this book alone would likely get you a passing grade on an exam.

It is the stuff you add into the margins that makes it more memorable and which enables you to get into the higher percentile scores on exams. Your spiral notebooks or together, your outline book and your margin notes and the atlas with pictures taped into it, should cover just about all the key information that you need to know on the subject.

The reason a med student wants to do well on boards part one is that it helps them to get into the residency of their choice.

Should you type or hand write your notes? It depends. If you are putting them into an outline format book then you will write them by hand.

It is true that the word processing options on a computer are great, but that also limits you to studying on a computer or computer like device. I know some good college students who insist on typing their notes.

However, I like to keep mine portable. I like to be able to walk around with them, take them to the library or to a friend's house.

Chapter 129.

Other ways the internet can help your memory.

You can make **your own website or blog** where you write about whatever it is that you are learning.

This is a convenient way to have the information available without having to carry a book around with you.

You can send **emails to yourself.**

For example, during my neuroradiology fellowship I wrote a training manual of procedures.

During the workday, I would perform a procedure, for example a cerebral arteriogram,

Then I would summarize the procedure in an email to myself.

The benefits are;

It is easiest to write about something immediately after experiencing it, as it is fresh in your mind.

This gave me something to do while waiting for the rush hour traffic to decrease.

Once home, I would just copy and paste the "chapter" into a training manual. It was easy and the approximately 300 page manual, quickly "wrote itself."

Chapter 130.

Big backpack.

"Kids didn't have huge backpacks when I was their age. We didn't have backpacks at all. Now it seemed all the kids had them. You saw little second-graders bent over like sherpas, dragging themselves through school doors under the weight of their packs. Some of the kids had their packs on rollers, hauling them like luggage at the airport. I didn't understand any of this. The world was becoming digital; everything was smaller and lighter. But kids at school lugged more weight than ever." - Michael Crichton.

In med school and residency I always had a big backpack, the kind designed for carrying a large, laptop computer.

These have internal padding to protect your stuff and thick straps to protect your shoulders.

This made it easy to carry around both lunch and books.

Chapter 131.

The greatest secret and Earl Nightingale.

"Watch your thoughts for they become words. Watch your words for they become actions. Watch your actions for they become habits. Watch your habits for they become your character. And watch your character for it becomes your destiny. What we think we become." - Bishop Beckwaith and Frank Outlaw.

"You become what you think about." - Earl Nightingale and Ralph Waldo Emerson and Ralph Waldo Trine and likely others.

"When a boat sets out to sea, it arrives at its destination because it knows where it is going. The captain has a travel plan. Without a travel plan the boat would just drift aimlessly. Make sure that you have a good travel plan to get you to your desired future." - Earl Nightingale

"Successful people focus on positive things. They focus on what they want to achieve. Unsuccessful people focus on negative things. They focus on what they are afraid of." - Earl Nightingale and Brian Tracy

"When you have negative thoughts, you need to talk back to them. You need to defend yourself from them. This can make you more positive and happier. (approximate wording based on memory)**."** - Martin Seligman (famous psychologist), author of several books including "Learned Optimism."

The key point of this chapter is to recommend the advice of the persons from the above quotes. Decide what you want to achieve. Make a plan to achieve it. Make a list of things you need to do from a short term and long term perspective. Start doing these things. Focus on the positive, on what you want to accomplish.

Chapter 132.

Pedagogy versus andragogy.

Ped means child as in pediatrics. Andr means man as in androgen.

Pedagogy refers to learning in kids and andragogy to learning in adults. Kids are like stem cells, lots of potential. School is designed by adults. Adults determine the curriculum and kids mostly take required classes. Kids are taught a wide variety of information.

The kid has to learn a wide variety of things to prepare for standardized tests and to move on up to the next academic level. They have a lot of career options. As they move up to the next level, they become progressively more specialized. For example, college biology student can go in a lot of directions. Medical school student can go into clinical work or research. Clinical medical resident can go into a surgical or nonsurgical field, etc.

After thirty years of age, learning is different. It is more specialized. At this age, there are more distractions and responsibilities like providing for one's own children and maintaining a house, that limit the adult student's time.

The thirty plus, adult student, directs their own education to help them with their personal and/or career goals in a more precisely focused way.

The best time to learn something is just before you need it. This is because your short term memory is best for about two weeks. Also, when you use the information soon after learning it, you are more likely to "push" that information into long term memory storage.

Professor Howard McClusky, psychology PhD., in the 1960's and 1970's developed a **"theory of margin" regarding adult learning** whereby adults had a **load** (personal and financial obligations) and **resources or power** (free time, money, family support, social skills, social network, servants-helpers).

Professor Roger Hiemstra PhD of Syracuse university and Elmira college has also written about the "theory of margin" with the information in this chapter obtained primarily by reading the work of Professor Hiemstra. From personal experience I can say, that this is a good, accurate, concise way to summarize the challenges of a middle age to older adult.

Basically, an adult has "a load to carry" and a certain amount of "power-resources" with which to carry that load. The higher the load the more difficult it was to pursue learning. The higher the resources the easier it was to pursue learning.

The more power-resources a person has relative to the load they carry in life, the higher their margin. The higher the margin, the more freedom the person has to do additional things.

By keeping their load low, Eg. buying a smaller house, the adult has more resources Eg. money available for learning or doing other things.

An adult can also increase their power-resources by increasing their money making skills, money saving skills, social skills, coping skills, physical fitness, etc. Adult learning is an important way for an adult to increase their power-resources.

Chapter 133.

Aging and learning.

"I'm an alpha male on beta blockers." - George Carlin.

"To win back my youth, I would do anything except take exercise, wake up early or be a useful member of the community." - Oscar Wilde.

"Anyone who stops learning is old, whether at twenty or eighty. Anyone who keeps learning stays young. The greatest thing in life is to keep you mind young." - Henry Ford.

"Love, especially unconditional love, also cures people – both those who give it and those who receive it. To receive love is transformational." - George Vaillant MD, author of "Aging Well and of Spiritual Evolution", researcher on several lifetime longitudinal studies at Harvard.

"A primary task in life is to come home to ourselves." - Patricia Berliner, American psychologist and author.

This chapter is for people over 30 years old.

With increasing age, adult humans tend to gain weight and move around less. Staying active is one of the key aspects of retaining one's health and vitality.

There is a great series of paintings called, **"The Voyage of Life"** by Thomas Cole.

You can look them up on the internet or buy the book. It is well worth it to see these paintings as they encompass so much of what it is like to be a man.

A teenager and young adult man in his 20's wants to get his education and start making his way in the world, with a steep upward climb.

In one's 30's and early 40's, one is often very busy with their jobs and perhaps marriage and/or kids.

In the late 40's and early 50's some physical decline becomes noticeable, and one realizes that they have to make physical fitness a priority.

"For a young adult, exercise is recreation, for an older adult it is a necessity." - T. Boone Pickens, author and expert on oil and natural gas.

At these ages one also realizes that a lot of their friends are living in fixed routines whereby they are not challenging their brains anymore, and they are becoming a little dull minded. They also see lots of old people developing vascular dementia, Alzheimer's dementia and other medical problems like obesity, diabetes, heart attacks and strokes.

This is a big motivator to make a person want to optimize their overall body health and brain health.

As a man gets older, he loses a lot. His parents die, his kids grow up and move away. His physical strength starts to decline after 45 years of age.

He also gains a lot. He becomes a lot wiser between the ages of 35 and 55. He knows a lot faster, if something is likely to work, or to be a waste of time. He understands women a lot better than he used to. **High levels of accumulated knowledge, wisdom, judgment and verbal skills are some of the highlights of middle age.**

Women, in my experience, seem to handle middle age better than men. They tend to have better developed social networks. Often a married guy's social network is largely controlled by his wife.

A middle age person needs to keep learning, in order to remain current in a challenging job.

Job knowledge tends to remain strong for a long time. I have seen lots of doctors performing excellent work in their 70's.

The "**cognitive reserve theory" of aging** is that persons who are more learned, are more able to maintain cognitive function in their 70's and 80's. In other words, persons who obtained more education, and who read more are less likely to get Alzheimer's dementia.

The **"Nun study"** provided support for the cognitive reserve theory. A large number of nuns, the Sisters of Notre Dame, agreed to allow their lives to be studied and subsequently to undergo when they died, autopsies. What was found was that even the nuns with normal mental function, had some histological (microscope) evidence of vascular injury and/or Alzheimer's dementia type lesions. The cognitive reserve theory poses that a highly learned brain has more reserve, it can maintain "normal" function with the loss of more neurons than an uneducated brain.

By far, the most common cause of disease in the USA is diet related. High fat, high simple sugar diet leads to obesity and atherosclerosis. The obesity often leads to type 2 diabetes. This type of patient is often treated with cholesterol, triglyceride and diabetes medications.

With obesity the body has to pump blood to a larger body and this often leads to high blood pressure. This is treated with antihypertensive medications. The blood pressure is now better controlled, but one of the possible side effects is impotence. Now a medication like Viagra is added. The obesity can also cause abdominal problems like GERD (GastroEsophageal Reflux Disease) which is treated with another medication.

The **atherosclerosis gradually causes narrowing of the arteries of the heart, the penis and the brain.** Obstruction of a coronary (heart) artery can cause a heart attack (myocardial infarct). Obstruction of an artery in the brain can cause a stroke (ischemic infarct).

Obstruction of an artery to the penis can cause impotence. When a lot of heart muscle is lost, the heart cannot pump adequately leading to congestive heart failure and death. When there is extensive narrowing of multiple brain arteries a person tends to develop MCI (Mild Cognitive Impairment), VCI (Vascular Cognitive Impairment) and eventually vascular dementia.

Ok, ok. I know that that sounds very sad.

Well, here is the good news. It is mostly preventable. Eat healthier, and body weight improves, and the arteries stay open. In this context, a person can be vibrant, energetic and sexually active into their 80's.

To die of natural causes is to die at around 80 to 95 years of age of congestive heart failure. That is what you want to do. To be healthy up into your 80's and then the ticker goes.

I have always had a lot of difficulty attracting women.

"I never had casual sex. I always had to work for it." - Rodney Dangerfield.

I figure, if I can stay healthy, I'll finally be popular with the ladies when I'm at the nursing home.

With increasing age, I have increasing admiration for architects, painters, musicians and comedians. They entertain us and give us things that are lasting, and that improve our lives.

"The capacity for friendship and loving relationships is what matters most in life." - George Vaillant MD.

"Amor Vincit Omnia." Love conquers all.

For persons interested in learning more about lifetime, longitudinal studies on healthy aging, I recommend, "Aging Well" by Harvard physician researcher, George Vaillant.

This book discusses what was learned by following persons over the course of their lifetimes and periodically interviewing them. One of the big insights was the importance of the social aspects of life. Having good social relationships is important for long term job success and for personal happiness. Exercising and being involved in on going learning at the age of 50 were both associated with being healthy at 80.

"Genius lasts longer than beauty." - Oscar Wilde.

"We all have our time machines. Those that take us back are memories...Those that take us forward are dreams." - H. G. Wells.

Chapter 134.

<u>Learning in college versus the outside world.</u>

"Knowledge has to be improved, challenged, and increased constantly, or it vanishes." - Peter Drucker.

College is the best place to learn things that are well known and standardized. For example, biology, chemistry, physics, engineering and math. At the college level these subjects are the same everywhere. Everyone takes the same MCAT.

There are things where college is optional. For example, if you want to learn Spanish, you could do it on your own. It would certainly help to take high school or college classes in Spanish, but there are several ways to learn Spanish with or without involving a school.

There are other topics for which college so far has not been that good at teaching. For example, if you want to start a business, you would be better off learning from entrepreneurs from the outside world. College could be helpful for taking classes in subjects like accounting.

It is not a coincidence that lots of successful entrepreneurs did not go to, or finish college. While the college students were devoting 4 years of life and possibly more including graduate school, to learning academic subjects, the future business owners were living at their parents' houses, developing their businesses.

That is a unique time in life when you can financially live off your parents and experiment with starting a business. This is one of the few "safety nets" in the real world.

There is nothing in life that is without risk.

"The person born with a talent they are meant to use will find their greatest happiness in using it." - Johann Wolfgang von Goethe, German writer.

"If you let fear of poverty control your life, your reward will be that you eat, but you will not live." - George Bernard Shaw, Irish writer.

"In order to be free, you must be able to endure poverty." - Victor Hugo, French writer.

"Self education, I firmly believe, is the only kind of education there is." - Isaac Asimov, famous science and science fiction writer.

Chapter 135.

<u>**Happiness.**</u>

"When you have once seen the glow of happiness on the face of a beloved person, you know that a man can have no vocation but to awaken that light on the faces surrounding him. In the depth of winter, I finally learned tha within me lay an invincible summer. And that makes me happy." - Albert Camus.

Chimpanzees groom each other physically. Humans groom each other verbally.

This next group of chapters focuses on social and financial intelligence which are important for academic and social success. The best students academically are often the ones who most need this information.

"For many years in history, the most common setting that people described as bringing happiness was talking with friends and family while eating.......It was not from buying things." - Geoffrey Miller, author of "Spent: Sex, Evolution and Consumer Behavior." (approximate quote from memory of an interview of the author).

Happiness in a study skills book?

Dear reader, please give me a chance. I shall try to repay your patience with useful information to help you or a loved one.

Studying a lot can be lonely at times. Understanding how to make yourself happier can help to protect you from loneliness, depression and suicide.

When I was at Harvard, one of the three imaging guided surgery (interventional radiology) fellows was a pretty, blond girl from Los Angeles.

The Harvard fellowship environment was a rough place. The basic attitude was, "You are lucky to be here. Shut up and do as you are told. If we tell you to take out the garbage, then you will take out the garbage. Pay your dues and do your job. At the end of the year you will get a graduation certificate and have the word, "Harvard" stamped to your resume for the rest of your life."

The other fellow was a tall, good looking guy whom we will call Joe. He had 4 simultaneous girlfriends, sometimes 5. I was totally jealous of him. I asked out the supply room clerk. She asked me to introduce her to Joe.

The LA woman talked to Joe. She seldom spoke to me. Joe told me that she was upset because the attendings were mean to her. They criticized her and once yelled at her.

She told him that she missed her boyfriend in LA. The hours were brutal. It was routine to be in house (in the hospital) from 6 am until 8 pm. Sometimes I worked from 5 am until 11 pm. Then back in house the next morning at 6 am.

Twice I noticed that her breath smelled funny at work. The first time I wasn't sure what it was. The second time I was sure. She reeked of alcohol.

I thought maybe she was out late last night drinking, or maybe she is an alcoholic. I should have said something to her. But I didn't. I should've said something to Joe, but I didn't. Nobody said or did anything.

She jumped off the roof of her apartment building and committed suicide.

Her mother was too distraught to come to Boston. He father was crying at the wake. He was so sad. It broke my heart. I felt very ashamed that I had not spoke to her about the alcohol. I felt sad that I was so socially incompetent that I had not recognized the intensity of her loneliness.

So that's why I'm writing this chapter.

Humans need to belong to a social network. There is a great book on this topic by Matthew Lieberman (psychologist) called, "Social. Why our brains are wired to connect."

Helping other people makes us happy because reward neurotransmitters and endorphins are released in our brains. This is evolution's way of incentivizing things that promote survival of the human species.

"Those who have a "why" to live can bear with almost any "how." - Viktor Frankl.

"An abnormal reaction to an abnormal situation is normal behavior." - Viktor Frankl.

"Love is the ultimate and highest goal to which man can aspire. Then I grasped the meaning of the greatest secret that human poetry and human thought and belief have to impart: The salvation of man is through love and in love." - Viktor Frankl, from "Man's Search for Meaning.

Laughter makes us happier. It is good to have funny friends and to watch comedies. It is good to try to learn how to be funny.

"The key point of the play by Oscar Wilde, "The Importance of Being Ernest" is the importance of being playful." - James Heffernan, English Professor from thegreatcourses.com.

"Humour is the best antidespair device." - Edward de Bono, from "H Plus."

"Maybe there should be a happiness rating for movies. There could be an HH film or even an HHH film." - Edward de Bono, from his book, "H Plus."

For guaranteed happiness, watch the movie, "The 4th Tenor" starring Rodney Dangerfield.

"My general theory is that happiness is a reward for an animal doing what it should be doing. So if a horse runs, it feels happy." - James Watson.

"The best way to cheer yourself is to try to cheer someone else up."
- Mark Twain.

Spending time with friends brings happiness.

Having a dog increases happiness.

I recently adopted a bull mastiff dog. I am going to breed him with a cocker spaniel to make a new breed called, "MaStiff ____."

I have invented a new and improved version of the Shih Tzu. It Shih Tzu and then it cleans you.

When I take the mastiff for a walk, he is so happy, that he makes me happy.

"That which is essential can only be seen with the heart. It is hidden to the eye." - Antoine de Saint-Exuprey, from "The Little Prince.

"The soul's joy is in doing." - Percy Bysche Shelley.

Getting adequate sleep makes us happier.

"The best things in life make us sweaty." - Edgar Allen Poe.

Of course he was talking about exercise.

Exercise creates happiness from the release of reward neurotransmitters and helps us to sleep better. It also improves our physical appearance.

Pursuing a worthy goal brings happiness. Seeing ourselves improve at something creates happiness. Living in the moment creates happiness.

Don't dwell on the past. Dwelling on sad stuff from the past, just makes you sad. **Better to try to have a laugh in the present moment, try to make someone smile.**

"The world you see is a mirror to what you show to the world." - Earl Nightingale.

Be nice and friendly to other people and they will usually be nice and friendly to you. Try to find what you have in common with people you meet and talk about that. Let them talk more than you. Let them talk about themselves. That will make them happier and like you more.

Avoid talking about negative stuff if possible. Avoid negative people. Try to be around positive people.

"Cultivate your own garden." - Voltaire.

This means do not worry too much about the outside world which is beyond your influence. Instead, focus on yourself and the people around you. Try to be nice to them and to make friends with them.

"Love does not dominate. It cultivates." - Goethe

Develop an attitude of gratitude. Think of all the things that you are grateful for. For example, if you are reading this book, you are a smart, educated person. Be grateful for that. Think about someone who has been kind to you and be grateful for that.

Meditation can help you learn how to better manage your stress according to some persons. I never could do meditation with the chanting and all that stuff, it just seemed too boring to me.

However, I do think the concept of **focusing on your breath** for a while and taking deep breathes is helpful to calm yourself down when stressed out or upset. The idea is that we can really only focus closely on one thing at a time and that by focusing more on our breath, we focus less on the annoying thing and that in so doing, we regain an increased sense of control.

It is important to maintain a social network of family, family friends and other friends. Having an extended family network makes life easier.

There is something called the **"Roseto effect"** which describes the town of Roseto Pensylvannia in the 1900's whereby a lot of Italian families lived surprisingly healthy and long lives in comparison with matched demographic populations.

The Italian families in Roseto tended to have the grandparents and grandchildren living in the same house. If someone was sick or lost their job, they had family members and relatives to take care of them.

The communities were relatively close knit. It is thought that this extended social network led to improved health by reducing the "stress of life's obstacles." Persons in Roseto had fewer heart attacks and better cancer survival than other persons.

Later on, Roseto became more like the rest of America with children moving farther away from their parents in pursuit of job opportunities, and things changed.

There is something about nature that can also make a person happier. It can be uplifting to walk around in a beautiful park.

This sense of nature induced revitalization is beautifully described in the poem "Tintern Abbey" by William Wordsworth.

"Five years have past; five summers, with the length of five long winters! And again I hear these waters, rolling from their mountain springs with a soft inland murmur. Once again do I behold these steep and lofty cliffs, that on a wild secluded scene impress thoughts of ………." - William Wordsworth, "Tintern Abbey."

Chapter 136.

Social skills and envy.

"People are not so much good or evil as charming or tedious." - Oscar Wilde.

If you have good social skills, then you can skip this chapters.

"The more relaxed you are, the better you are at everything. The better you are with your loved ones." - Bill Murray, American actor, comedian.

"He is a fool that cannot conceal his wisdom." - Benjamin Franklin.

"Envy is a weed that should not be watered." - Cosmo Medici.

When he was young, Cosmo was a bit of a show off. Some jealous persons in Florence ran him out of town. Later when he returned to Florence, he was more successful than ever, but he kept a low, public profile and dressed in a humble way in order to not stir up envy.

While some famous people like to show off as a way to advertise themselves, for most people they need to be careful about this.

When Frank Lloyd Wright was told that someone had written that he was the greatest living architect in the United States, he said, **"what do you mean "living"?" "What do you mean "in the United States"." "I'm the greatest architect that ever lived in any country."**

When people are negative towards you, the best thing to do, almost always, is to avoid them.

"Does my speed with numbers mean nothing to you people?" - Martin from the cartoon by Matt Groening and others, "The Simpsons" when the other kids were teasing and bullying him, from the video episode called, "Bart gets an F."

"To be great is to be misunderstood." - Ralph Waldo Emerson.

"Great spirits have always encountered violent opposition from mediocre minds." - Albert Einstein.

"I learned never to humiliate an antagonist and never to desert a friend." - Jack Valenti from his speech, "Lessons learned at the center of power."

"The individual has always had to struggle to keep from being overwhelmed by the group. If you try it, you will be lonely often, and sometimes frightened. But no price is too high to pay for the privilege of owning yourself."
- Friedrich Nietzsche.

"Keep away from people who try to belittle your ambitions. Small people always do that, but the really great make you feel that you, too, can become great." - Mark Twain.

"All your life, people will try to take your accomplishments away from you. Don't you take it away from yourself." - Michael Crichton.

"The purpose of life is to stay alive. Watch any animal in nature-all it tries to do is stay alive…..Whenever any animal's behavior puts it out of touch with its realities, it becomes extinct." - Michael Crichton.

"In the face of criticism, one can neither protest or respond. One can only continue to do good and with time the situation is likely to yield in their favor." - Goethe

"I think I am better than the people that are trying to reform me." - Goethe.

Like attracts like. When you meet people, focus on what you have in common.

It can also be helpful to mirror their body language to some degree. The Greek, Alcibiades is famous for this, albeit in a scandalous way.

"A good way to assess a relationship is laughter. If you laugh often and easily when in the company of another person, that is a good sign." - Brian Tracy.

However, when a person is difficult to read, go by what they do, not what they say. Talk is cheap. What they do is how you can tell what they really think, and whether or not they like you, and have your best interest at heart.

Try to have good posture. This increases your testosterone and makes you look and feel more confident in an attractive way.

Dress well. This makes you feel more confident and attractive and other people tend to treat you better when you are better dressed.

See chapter on "dress for success."

Try to be optimistic and positive in your attitude and conversation.

Try to be a good listener.

"The most important thing in communication is to hear what was not said." - Peter Drucker, Austrian born, American author, business expert.

"It is a wise thing to be polite; consequently, it is a stupid thing to be rude. To make enemies by unnecessary and willful incivility, is ...insane." - Arthur Schopenhauer.

It is almost always best to avoid arguments. It is just not worth it. When dealing with an obnoxious person, if possible, try to just avoid them.

"It is better to give the path to the dog." - Abraham Lincoln. I remember that he then said something like, **"though you might defeat the dog, it may bite you and the wound will take time to heal."**

"How many legs does a dog have if you call the tail a leg. Four! Calling the tail a leg, does not make it a leg." - Abraham Lincoln.

In life there are good days and bad days. There are ups and downs. It is part of life that some days you will feel loved and happy, and on some other day lonely. That is part of life. Even the richest and most beautiful persons in the world have these problems.

You learn from them and move on. That is part of why it is good to enjoy the present. It is good to try to add a little happiness to each day. It can be just simple things like being nicer to your family, peers your pet etc.

"Mostly it is loss which teaches about the worth of things." - Arthur Schopenhauer.

"We seldom think of what we have, but always of what we lack." - Arthur Schopenhauer.

"To remind a man of the good turns you have done him is very much like a reproach." - Demosthenes.

Chapter 137.

Mothers and Fathers.

"If people can just love each other a lttle bit, they can be so happy." - Emile Zola.

"The greatest gift thay you can give others is the gift of unconditional love and acceptance." - Brian Tracy.

When I was in eighth grade, I said to my dad, "I have been having some ideas lately that seem kind of interesting and different. Stuff that other kids don't think about. I think I might be a genius."

Dad, "Are you a math genius?"

Me, "No."

"A science, engineering, architectural, genius? Musical, artistic genius?"

"No."

Dad, "I know what type of genius you are."

Me, "Really! What type?"

Dad, "A bullshit genius."

Everyone knows that moms are great. When I was growing up Mother's day was the biggest holiday of the year in our house.

Nowadays, more so than ever before, fathers are underrated. On TV, fathers are nowadays typically portrayed as dopes. For example on TV shows like "The Simpsons" and "Family Guy."

When I was a kid there was more respect for dads on shows like, "Andy Griffith," "Leave it to Beaver," and "Father knows best."

What I have noticed is that fathers tend to be more demanding of their children, especially the boys.

Dads say stuff like, "you need to study more and develop other skills."

Moms tend to be more nurturing in a gentle, thoughtful way.

If you read about the lives of lots of great persons, you will see that their dads were often a key part of their lives, especially their academic and career lives.

For example, Johnny Von Neumann's dad taught him a ton at mealtimes. At my house, my kids call it "the dad show" whenever I talk "too much" about something academic during mealtime.

Ansel Adams credited his father as the key to his success.

My dad was a great role model for me by reading a lot and being a hard worker, and always fair, but he was never around, always working.

Fathers tend to spend a lot of money on their kids educations, especially for college.

Chapter 138.

Emotional intelligence.

"There's one problem with all psychological knowledge – nobody can apply it to themselves. People can be incredibly astute about the shortcomings of their friends, spouses, children. But they have no insight into themselves at all. The same people who are coldly clear-eyed about the world around them have nothing but fantasies about themselves. Psychological knowledge doesn't work if you look in a mirror. This bizarre fact is, as far as I know, is unexplained." - Michael Crichton.

"In the battle of (modern) existence, talent is the punch and tact is the footwork." - Wilson Mizner, American playwright.

"The most important decision you make is to be in a good mood." - Voltaire.

Emotional intelligence quotient = EIQ.

It is good to try to learn more about your emotions. Emotions are very powerful. Emotions overlap with instincts which are also very powerful.

The more you know about your emotions and instincts, the better you will be able to control them.

Try to be aware of your emotions as you are experiencing them and try to focus on being able to control them.

In the book about power by Robert Greene, he emphasizes the importance of learning how to control one's emotions as being a necessity for increasing your power in the world.

Talleyrand, the great French diplomat also emphasized the importance of being able to control one's emotions.

Emotional intelligence can also refer to getting along well with other people and negotiating well with other people which are discussed elsewhere in this book.

"The way you see people, determines how you treat them. The way you treat them determines what the become to you." - Goethe.

It is best to see every meeting with a new person as an opportunity, a chance to make a new friend.

"When I left the dining room after sitting next to Mr. Gladstone, I thought he was the cleverest man in England. But after sitting next to Mr. Disraeli, i thought I was the cleverest woman in England." - a woman who dined on consecutive nights with two famous British prime ministers in the 1800's.

The frontal lobes are one of the last areas of the brain to become fully myelinated. The frontal lobes are important for executive function, mature, responsible behavior and understanding delayed gratification. This late timing of frontal lobe myelination might partly explain why guys in their late teens and early twenties often do impulsive, crazy things.

It is important to be resilient. There are always going to be ups and downs in life. When you have a setback, try to figure out how you can springboard it into something positive.

Things that tend to cheer up a person include exercise, time with friends and family, pet dog, help someone else and humor. Helping someone is great because it gets your focus on them instead of yourself and it makes both of you happy. Pick up the phone and call a friend. Listening to Brian Tracy, Maxwell Maltz MD and similar types of speakers helps put me into a positive frame of mind.

"The night is darkest before the dawn." - Thomas Fuller, 1650.

"Tough problems don't last, tough people do." - Gregory Peck and Robert H. Schuller.

Another issue that arises is a sense of social responsibility. If you follow the academic guidelines in this book, you are going to be very successful. You will be a leader in some way in whatever field you go into.

Make sure that you are nice to people.

"Always be nice to people. You are going to meet the same people on your way up as on your way down." - Wilson Mizner, American Playwright.

"To be agreeable in society, you must consent to be told many things which you already know." - Charles Maurice de Talleyrand, French diplomat.

"The purpose of speech is for men to conceal their thoughts." - Talleyrand.

Chapter 139.

<u>Pharmaceutical cognitive enhancers and inhibitors.</u>

I spent a long time reading about this.

There is a separate chapter on coffee and caffeine that is grouped with the chapters on diet.

As far as the actual pharmaceuticals that are available today, I do not recommend any of them for persons who are otherwise healthy.

For any medication it is wise to look at the risk benefit ratio.

For healthy persons, at this time, 2014, the potential side effects outweigh the potential benefits.

I could not find evidence of any drug having significant benefits on cognition for healthy, well rested persons. There are a few drugs that have minimal benefits but major side effects.

All drugs have side effects, short term, long term or both. Trust me on that one.

Even a seemingly mild drug can have rare, serious, severe side effects.

Your brain is a delicate thing, a miracle of millions of years of evolution. Do not risk messing it up with a pill.

Sometimes a single use of a drug can lead to addiction.

Some drugs can ruin a person's appreciation of life. For example, cocaine causes such a massive release of dopamine that down regulation of the receptors occurs, such that it now becomes difficult to enjoy other things.

Maybe someday there will be a pill you could take to become smarter, but for now, there is no such thing available to the general, healthy public.

I know your are going to read about stuff on the internet, and you are going to hear rumors amongst college age people.

My advice is don't do it. Do not even think about it. Do not "try it once."

It may injure you, and you may not get a second chance. The human brain is much more fragile than most people think. Don't risk ruining the most valuable thing you have, your brain.

There are drugs that block memory. For example, the benzodiazepines like Valium (diazepam) and Versed (midazolam) can block memory.

Patients often say to me, "can you knock me out for this procedure, I don't want to feel anything. I don't want to remember this."

The point is that patients "want the drugs." They like the idea of a drug that makes them forget.

I'm the opposite. **I would rather have a little discomfort and pain than take a drug that may effect my memory.** It is rare, but some patients have lingering memory problems after anesthesia.

If I had to go for an operation requiring general anesthesia, I would ask the anesthesiologist for whatever drugs were least likely to affect my memory.

It is true that doctors are often the worst patients. They ask a lot of questions and have lots of little annoying requests.

For example, I insisted on being the first patient of the day for my colonoscopy. I wanted that scope to be well cleaned. I started my own IV, but hep-locked it (capped it off), and had no sedation.

Some of my doctor friends teased me about this. "Why would you want to remember your colonoscopy?"

I said, "if the doctor finds something, I want to be able to discuss it with him, and I don't want to have any drug that may effect my memory."

I asked the gastroenterologist his opinion, and he said that when he gets a colonoscopy, he also has it done without sedation.

I just want to share one more medical secret with you. Movers do a lot better. People who soon after surgery, are eager to get moving, and start walking do a lot better.

Chapter 140.

Marriage.

"**Physics is like sex. Sure, it may give some practical results, but that's not why we do it.**" - Richard Feynman.

"**Physics isn't the most important thing. Love is.**" - Richard Feynman.

"**A fool and his money are soon married.**" - Carolyn Wells, American author.

"**I've been divorced twice and married once.**" - Oscar Wilde.

"**Love is like an hourglass with the heart filling up as the mind empties.**" - Jules Renard, French writer.

"**If the double helix was so important, how come you didn't work on it?**" - Linus Pauling's wife to her husband, when the Nobel Prize was awarded to Crick, Watson and Wilkins.

"**The key to a happy marriage is separate bathrooms.**" - Dave Barry, writer, comedian.

What does marriage have to do with academic performance?

Marriage is one of the most important decisions you will ever make in your life. It is right up there with what career to pursue and how to will maintain your health.

Marrying wisely can enrich your life in many ways. Marrying foolishly can cause great pain and suffering.

There ought to be a required class in high school called, "Understanding Marriage."

In the USA it is commonplace to say, "of course one should marry for love."

Well, if love is so great, then why do half of marriages in the USA end in divorce?

"Whoever said talk is cheap, never said, "I do." - Rodney Dangerfield

"What is the difference between an arranged marriage and marrying for love? You can spend the rest of your life blaming your parents instead of yourself." - unknown.

"To marry for a man is to halve his freedoms and double his responsibilities." - Arthur Schopenhauer.

"Marriage is a ceremony in which a ring is put on the finger of the woman and through the nose of the man." - Herbert Spencer.

"If there is such a thing as a good marriage, it is because it resembles friendship rather than love." - Michel de Montaigne.

Intense, romantic, sexual love can last about 3 years. **Friendship can last a lifetime.** Therefore, make sure to focus on friendship when picking a long term partner.

I saw the movie, "Lord of the Rings." At first I thought it was just an interesting fantasy, but then I realized there really was a magic ring with superpowers. My wife has the real one and controls me with it. Unfortunately, mine doesn't work on her.

"Keep your eyes wide open before marriage, half shut afterwards." - Benjamin Franklin.

Chapter 141.

<u>Mentors and playing it smart.</u>

There are all kinds of mentors. First of all, there are **older students.** Someone who just took the class is going to remember it best.

Ask them about which books to read and how to approach the class. Ask them why they recommend a particular thing so you can see if it will be likely to work for you.

Second is your **teacher**. Your teacher is the most important person related to that class. Being a student is a job, and your teacher is basically your "boss" for that class.

In the outside world, a boss rewards the worker by paying them money and by treating them well or at least fairly. In the academic world you are rewarded with grades.

In big classes, you might never meet the teacher. In smaller classes it is especially important to get along with the teacher. If the teacher is wise and kind, they can help guide your academic career. They might help you with recommendation letters and with guidance on who to seek out as advisers for other subjects.

It is wise to try to get along with your teachers as well as possible. They control your grade for that class.

The best way to learn something is to do it out in the real world, under the supervision of an expert mentor. This is how Michelangelo learned sculpture and painting in the house of Medici in Italy in the 1400's.

Competition also inspires improved performance. That's why so many world records are set at the Olympics.

Michelangelo would go around Florence and see the great works of other artists and this inspired him to improve his own work. Competition with other artists such as Leonardo Da Vinci was also a big motivator.

Doctors in residency of course also learn by the apprenticeship method. They start their first year of residency, their internship on July 1st.

That is why it has been truthfully said, the worst day to go to a university hospital is on July 1st. All the interns are running around clueless. The third year internal medicine residents and senior residents from other fields have graduated, and gone off to their post training jobs.

As you go farther along in the academic world, you will be in more and more specialized environments. Especially when starting out, it is wise to keep your eyes and ears open and your mouth shut.

Different places have different ways of doing things. Whatever the pattern is, it took time to establish it. It is usually shaped that way because the powerful people at that location want it that way.

Even if it seems backward and stupid compared to what you saw at your old place, it is better to not say anything. The naive young person thinks, "these people will be glad that I am showing them a better way." Wrong!

The people at the new place have been there longer than you. They usually have a vested interest in the status quo. If you try to change it they will more likely be annoyed with you. Trust me on this one.

If someone famous in your field has been interviewed, then read it. This can give you insights that are otherwise hard to find.

Over the course of your academic career **you will accumulate a paper trail** that includes your grades (transcripts), academic degrees, recommendation letters and potentially your publications.

It is wise to think of these things as being like "passports."

For example, you could be happy at a job and get along well with your boss. Then a new boss is put into place and they don't treat you so well.

You'd be wise to have a developed network of social contacts so that it will be easy for you to get good recommendation letters and job offers somewhere else.

Or better yet, **figure out how you can become the boss** so that you can control things. It is good to be the boss. The boss has more control over how the department is run, work hours, vacation time and more influence over hiring to select people who they respect and like. The boss also usually gets paid more.

Chapter 142a.

Great Teachers.

"When the student is ready, the teacher appears." - Buddhist proverb.

"Good teaching is one fourth preparation and three fourths theater." - Gail Godwin, American novelist.

Actually, it more like 50:50.

In medical school at the University of Illinois, there was a pathology teacher from Illinois Masonic Hospital whose name was Dr. Kirshenbaum. His lectures were very clever, insightful, clear and fun.
He came up with helpful metaphors and expressed them in a memorable, almost theatrical way.

I said to my dad, "Wow! This guy is a great teacher. When he explains a subject, I just know it. He covers the key points in such a clear, concise way, that it is easy to understand and remember."

My dad said, "you will remember him for the rest of your life."

Me, "I don't know about that. I mean, he's a great teacher, but why do you think it's such a big deal?"

Dad, "There are a lot of good teachers, but great teachers are rare. I can count the number of great teachers I had in school (dad is a double boarded doctor) on one hand. Try to learn as much as you can from this guy. If you get a chance, try to do an elective under his supervision."

I wrote down every word that Dr. Kirshenbaum said. I asked him lots of questions. I loved going to that class. I won the award for best student in the subject of pathology at my medical school, the University of Illinois, College of Medicine in Chicago.

Now, what makes for good teaching? Well it goes something like this.

A lousy teacher barely knows the subject and reads out of the book in a monotone way.

An **average teacher** knows the material better, but still reads out of the book, and talks in a monotone way.

An **above average teacher** is more animated, and puts more effort into the class. They provide study questions and they try to explain things in a way that the students will understand.

A really good to excellent teacher, gives clear explanations, makes a clear list of study questions, puts in extra effort like providing a website for the class and FAQ's or online videos etc.

They provide time for the students to ask questions. They are clear about what is going to be on the test. They are fair about grading and give students the benefit of the doubt when something is borderline. They are kind. They are forgiving. They are nurturing. They are friendly.

A great teacher goes even beyond that. Well, you may ask, "How?" How could a teacher be better than that? Isn't that all anyone could expect from an excellent teacher?

Yes. That is all one could expect from an excellent teacher.

But, **a great teacher goes beyond expectations. A great teacher is a little more animated, more theatrical, more emotional, more dynamic. The tone of their voice goes up and down and key points are made with a dramatic emphasis. A great teacher puts on demonstrations such as showing the experiment in real life, acting out interviews with famous persons, bringing props and costumes into the classroom.**

Let me give you an example. The brachial plexus is a complex group of nerves that begins in our cervical spinal cord and then passes out to our arms.

The relationship of the brachial plexus to other structures in the neck is very important for radiology and surgery in this area. You could study this area all day long for a week and still not be sure how to keep it in your long term memory, and how to apply it to clinical practice.

There are some mnemonics to help you such as "C3-4-5 keeps you alive." This is an example of a mnemonic based on "rhyming." Those are the nerves that innervate the diaphragm which you need to breathe. Injury to the cervical spinal cord above this level and the patient ends up on a ventilator.

There's another mnemonic, "DR CUMA." This means Drop wRist Radial nerve, Claw hand Ulnar nerve, Median nerve Ape hand. Ie. This is a mnemonic that uses the first letter of the item to remind you of the rest. This is great, classic, medical student mnemonic.

However, in the real world, this is not enough.

I needed something more, to really understand what was going on with the brachial plexus in the neck. So I figured I would watch a lecture on neck anatomy by Dr. Halliday, a neuroradiologist.

As best I can remember, it went something like this.

Dr. Halliday said,

"Do you remember the names of the Supremes? Diana Ross. Diana, Diana, Diana. She's the only one we remember."

"Well it's the same thing with the scalene muscles. You only have to know the anterior scalene muscle."

"It's the G-spot of the lower neck. The brachial plexus and subclavian artery are just behind it. The phrenic nerve is on top of it. The carotid, jugular and vagus are right in front of that. It's in the middle of everything."

Then like a loving parent he said, "you just find that anterior scalene muscle and then you know where everything is."

"Then you will know everything you need to know, to help the ENT surgeon, the vascular surgeon or the neurosurgeon and to help the patient."

Now, that's great teaching!

Why is it so great?

It is good to ask the question "why?"

When you know "why", then you can more quickly recognize it. Then you can more efficiently seek it out. Then you can try to be that type of teacher yourself.

I knew that I loved the way Dr. Halliday teached. I knew that I learned fast and well from him, and that his words have remained in my mind for years.

As a matter of fact, a very smart person (Mark Brumlich, computer programmer, par excellence) once asked me, "Do you believe in the concept of the "soul."

I said, "Everyone knows that a sole is an important part of a shoe."

Mark said, "no really. Do you think a person continues to live on in some way after their physical body dies?"

I said, "hey man, I don't want to talk about religion."

Mark said, "I'm not talking about religion. I'm talking about the voice in your head."

I said, "hey man, I don't want to talk about psychiatry. Recurrent auditory hallucinations,are suggestive of schizophrenia. I do not have any voices in my head!"

Mark said, "Yes you do!"

A little bit annoyed, yet retaining my composure, I said, "No, I don't!"

Mark, "What about your mother?"

Me, "Don't you talk about my mother or ____."

Mark, "Calm down! I'm talking about hearing the voice of your mother in your head. You can hear it. The things she used to say to you when you were a child. The things she used to say to you over and over, or at special moments in your life. I'll bet you can hear her words in your head right now."

Me, "Wow. You're right. I can remember my mom saying stuff to me like, "Peter, do you know how much I love you? Do you know how much I love you?," with that warm, loving, Motherese (dialect of how a mom talks to her child) tone of voice.

Mark, "that's what I mean. Her voice or perhaps her soul lives on in your mind and when you say or do something based on that, it also lives on in that way."

Me, "I don't know if it is her voice or her soul or just a memory, but it I do know that it makes me happy to think of her and the things she used to say."

That really helped me in life.

Love has power. Love gives hope and strength and courage. Love inspires. Love heals.

When someone knows that they are truly loved, it gives them some protection from the outside world. They have more confidence in themselves. They will not accept being mistreated in a social situation because they know they deserve to be loved.

My mother's voice in my head, gives me these things. The love of her voice in my head makes me a better person, than I would be without it.

Mark, "I rest my case."

Me, "why? Is it tired?"

I think I understand how to articulate it, now. Dr. Halliday's teaching was **great because it was clear, brilliant, correct and created an emotional experience.** The **clarity** made it easy to understand. The **brilliance** made it important to learn. The **theatrical flair, emotionality and humor** made it memorable.

He **understood the audience**, young neuroradiologists like me. We were afraid of screwing up on a difficult neck case. We were afraid of looking stupid in front of our trauma surgery, otolaryngology, vascular surgery and neurosurgery colleagues.

He **understood the context**, whereby the brachial plexus, med school mnemonics were more useful for passing tests than taking care of patients. He acknowledged our fears and showed us how to overcome them.

He was funny and **warm**. The warmth lowers the stress level associated with learning about such a complex subject. It's kind of like **the "Goldilocks Principle" of finding the happy medium.** No stress tends to be mundane and boring. Too much stress tends to be counterproductive and distracting. But a little bit of stress is helpful to focus attention.

I usually watch a lecture once and take notes and memorize these. I almost never watch a lecture twice. I watched Dr. Halliday's lecture three times. I made sure to memorize every word. Whenever I look at an MRI or CT of the lower neck, I think of Dr. Halliday's explanations.

That's why some teachers are able to get outstanding results, because they go beyond expectations.

Chapter 142b.

Great teachers (continued)

There is a great movie about a great teacher called, "Stand and Deliver", starring James Olmos. It shows how the path to academic success is so much more than books and studying.

Now in the modern medical world it is very fashionable and important to try to always be "professional."

Now, I'm not talking about a college or med school classroom. I'm talking about the post med school doctor world of lectures. In this setting, the typical lecture is delivered in an almost monotone way with no jokes or unconventional comments. A whole bunch of powerpoint slides are shown with way too much writing on them. That is considered doing a "good job."

It's the safe thing for a young doctor to do. It's the safe thing for a middle aged doctor to do. It will get you through the event with your academic and career status unchanged. You will have met the expectations of the moment and that is goal of most people.

Well you know what? Many of these lectures are kind of boring. The audience knows this, but it is considered unconventional to criticize. "How could anyone criticize a speaker who is just doing their job, being "professional."

Well, I can, because it is true. All doctors know this, whether they acknowledge it or not. A big part of the reason for this is that another thing all doctors know is that, "you can never get into trouble for being "professional."

Why do doctors where long coats? To cover their asses.

Well, be that as it may, it is also true that the audience loves it when a doctor has the knowledge and personality to lecture like a great teacher.

A routine lecture is followed by 10 seconds of polite clapping and that's it.

A great lecture is different. The audience is more engaged, laughing, makes occasional funny comments like hecklers at a stand up comedy show. At the end the clapping lasts longer. There are more questions and often some fun comments. The highlight moments get talked about at the lunch table.

This speaker gets invited to speak again. The audience wants more of them. Great medical teachers are paid to travel around the USA giving lectures.

To be fair, a medical lecturer can give a great talk just by presenting the material in a great way, with no theatrical flair and no jokes. There is a famous neuroradiologist from New York named Tom Naidich who is as serious as he is brilliant.

I initially thought of him kind like the Mozart quote in the movie Amadeus, **"The Gods (Greek and Roman) are so lofty, it's as if they shit marble."**

I thought he was boring. Then I started to really listen to him carefully, and I bought and read all his books. Now, I really enjoy his lectures. I just had to tune into his teaching style and his personality.

My favorite quote from Dr. Tom Naidich is, "**functional MRI is to the study of the brain, what the microscope is to microbiology**. We are just at the beginning of tremendous discoveries about how the brain works."

Wow!

Good teaching makes a big difference for students. It accelerates the learning curve. It keeps you pointed in the right direction of rapid progress. It can leap frog a student years ahead.

In the book, "Developing Talent in Young People" written in 1985 by Benjamin Bloom, he showed that good teaching led to dramatic improvements in the academic performance of students.

Benjamin Bloom says, **"the most critical step in the transition from being a talented teenage pianist to becoming a professional, performing soloist is moving to a master teacher.......The teachers provided them with role models of the highest order. The teachers already were what the students only dreamed of becoming. The teacher's presence alone motivated, inspired and instructed. The students learned attitudes and habits and ways of working that they often were not even conscious of learning, simply by being in the presence of the master."**

"The master teachers knew much more than how to make music. They knew how to perform."

"The teachers did not tolerate sloppiness or laziness. The teachers valued music above the musician so they were likely to be short and curt with their students. Feelings were not spared."

"The work they assigned required a tremendous amount of time and attention from he pupil. Students were expected to practice anywhere from four to seven hours a day."

"At the great music schools, comradeship with the other young aspiring musicians was both exciting and frightening. They sometimes competed to see who could play the Chopin etudes the fastest. There was also a competitive thing set up when people are practicing: "who can do more?"

These are some of the ingredients of great success. High level motivation. Hard work. Focus on a specific task. Good to great teaching. Competition.

Benjamin Bloom also emphasizes that becoming an "independent learner" is important. Ie. When curious about something, an "independent learner" goes and makes a big effort to find that information.

You will often learn very interesting things when you are on your way to looking something else up.

I believe that the subconscious mind "nudges" the conscious mind. For example, I think that **when you get a whim that it might be interesting to look something up, you should go do it right that moment. Or at least write it down on your list of stuff to look up** so that you will remember. These are fleeting moments of opportunity and when taken often lead to useful insights.

In the book, "the Smartest Kids in the World and how they got that way" by Amanda Ripley, she emphasizes that the most important thing was good teaching. The children from Finland tended to perform better than kids from other countries because they had better teachers. The had better teachers because it was a higher priority in Finland to pay teachers high salaries so that the schools could recruit better teachers and the teachers were given a higher status in society.

Just for a little perspective, I know an excellent, grade school math teacher who made 25,000 dollars a year in 2010. That is not a lot of money for one year in the USA. That is why teachers like this often go into other fields, because they need to make more money for their families.

The teaching point for this chapter is to **seek the best teaching you can find. When really good and great teachers come along, try to learn as much as from them as you can.**

One last thing in this chapter that I would like to talk about is teaching assistants. They are highly variable. Some are great. Some are hard to understand because their English language skills are so limited. **The bottom line is that the student is responsible for their own learning, to make sure they are prepared for the exams.**

You can't count on the teacher or the teaching assistant to be good. You just need to make sure that you do what it takes to learn the material for the class. Anybody who has gone down the premed route has had plenty of classes where they basically had to teach themselves.

Even when the teacher is a famous bigshot, that does not mean the teaching is going to be good. Quite often the bigshot just gives a few lectures and the rest of the class is taught by someone who barely speaks English. Well, tough beans. The only reason I wrote these last few paragraphs is to remind you that you are not alone. It is difficult and frustrating, but sometimes you are given a tough row to hoe and you've just got to ho-ho-ho.

Chapter 143.

Motivation.

An incentive is paying people extra to get them to do what you want them to do.

"True motivation is getting people to do something because they want to do it.....Motivation factors include challenging work, recognition, responsibility, and personal growth." - Clayton Christensen, from "How will you measure your life?"

Each individual has to find their own reasons to be motivated.

It can be for the pure joy of learning, to get better grades, a degree, a job, to impress a potential lover, to help a patient.

Education tends to build on itself. You often have to learn introductory material in order to be able to understand the advanced stuff. You are building up the knowledge base of your mind.

Hands on experience can help you figure out what you want to do. Eg. I learned a lot about orthopedic surgery and cardiology from visiting those clinics because I was considering going into those fields, and wanted to find out more about them.

It is good to dream about becoming an expert in whatever subject you are studying. When I studied bird biology, I dreamed about being an ornithologist.

When I was in chemistry class I dreamed about synthesizing a magic potion that would make women fall in love with me.

Actually, in organic chemistry class, I did have the idea of making a chewing gum that would prevent cavities. I presented it to the professor and he told me it was a stupid idea. He left Stanford a few years later, presumably to live off his new business that makes a chewing gum to prevent cavities.

It is also good to give a class a fun name. Eg. Organic chemistry was referred to as "orgasmic chemistry."

Whenever I studied a new subject in medical school I always tried to fantasize about what it would be like to be a doctor in that field.

It can be helpful to reward yourself by having something specific to do when you finish studying a topic for that study session. Eg. you can reward yourself with exercise, your favorite meal, phone calls, watching a movie etc.

Constructive discontent and anger can be motivators. Try to rechannel your energy towards a positive goal.

For example, a friend of mine once asked me a question about the posterior, lateral corner of the knee on MRI. I did not know the answer. I was so mad at myself, that I read extensively on the subject that weekend. So the frustrating moment was converted into something positive and useful.

Being highly motivated makes you smarter because, you pay closer attention. When you pay closer attention, you learn faster and better. You are also likely to try harder.

There is a good motivational video on You Tube called, "How bad do you want it" as told by Eric Thomas.

Chapter 144.

Calibration.

You need to calibrate your efforts and methods to the level expected to get an A in the class.

You also need to calibrate your efforts and methods based on how much time you have left before a test.

The ability to do this improves with experience.

Initially, it is better to overdo it, for example for midterm exams, and then you will have a better sense on how to prepare for final exams.

In general, I would go by how well I felt I knew the material relative to the teacher's expectations, and how I sensed the other students felt about the class as well as quizzes and midterms etc.

Chapter 145.

Making a schedule.

Make a schedule. It helps you to get organized and to use your time more efficiently.

Make a list for each week of the stuff you have to do for school, and a separate list for the nonschool stuff.

A study schedule can be written on a calendar. This can include class times, when papers are due, the dates for exams and whatever else is relevant.

A study schedule can help you to pace yourself. For example, it can help you to systematically go thru your study materials before a standardized exam.

Chapter 146.

How to make an important, difficult decision.

"Dare to live the life you have dreamed for yourself. Go forward and make your dreams come true." - Ralph Waldo Emerson.

"Whoso would be a man must be a nonconformist." - Ralph Waldo Emerson.

"Don't be pushed by your problems. Be led by your dreams." - Ralph Waldo Emerson.

"Successful people focus on what they want. Unsuccessful people focus on what they are afraid of." - Brian Tracy.

We have all had to make difficult decisions such as choosing where to attend college. There are some strategies that can help you to make good choices.

The first is to **delay the decision as long as possible. At the very least, try to sleep on it at least two nights.** You want to make the decision with a cool head, looking at the long term significance.

Try to talk to someone who has already done it. For example, talk to persons who have already attended college, or better yet, the college in question.

Get out a piece of paper and write everything down, using the Feynman method to expand your working memory.

Make a list of pros and cons.

Talk to your parents, friends, teachers, coaches etc.

Read about it. Look for relevant past parallels.

Ask yourself, what is gained? and what is lost? by making the choice.

How will it affect me academically, socially, financially?

Go visit the place, and competing places.

Chapter 147.

<u>Attention span.</u>

It is easier to read a long article in the form of text from a book than from hypertext on a computer screen.

Nicholas Carr in his book, "The Shallows: How the internet is changing our brains" has suggested this is due to the many distractions on the internet such as hyperlinks, advertisements and email.

Well, what do you do when you are finding it difficult to concentrate?

You could take a study break.

Another trick is to walk and study. This is discussed at length in the chapter on walk and talk.

The purpose of this chapter was simply to mention that I have often found that when I'm distracted while sitting down reading, that I can pick up the book and start walking and then be able to read a lot more.

Just the act of walking while reading improves concentration.

Chapter 148.

"Walk and Talk" learning and self test.

This topic was introduced earlier.

Now we can talk about the details.

This is one of the longest chapters in the book because "walk and talk" is one of the most powerful and versatile learning techniques known to mankind.

It imitates the normal way that prehistoric humans learned, on the move, while foraging.

I have seen students go from "F" to "A" by using "walk and talk with self test."

For example, just this week, I had a prenursing student, who was sad because she had failed her anatomy midterm and was told that she was unlikely to be accepted into nursing school.

I tutored her for 2 hours on the anatomy of the abdomen followed by her repeating all the information in a "walk and talk, self test," and she got an "A" on the retake. She is on her way to nursing school.

The same thing happened with a doctor who had failed his residency certification boards several times. A little bit of "walk and talk with self test and he passed with flying colors."

The reason is that "walk and talk with self test" activates multiple areas of the brain and gets the student to produce the information.

Vocalizing puts a copy of it in that part of the "mind's library." Hearing oneself say the information puts a copy there.

These multiple copies and formats of the information in the mind pay off when it's test time. They make it easier for the conscious mind to quickly find the information.

Being able to verbally produce the information builds familiarity with the material and confidence. It also functions as a self test to confirm that the student knows it.

This is a much deeper level of information processing than just reading over notes. Deeper level processing increases understanding and memory.

This chapter is only for persons really interested in "walk and talk." You can skip this chapter if you want.

It is normal to learn while walking around.

Roger Schank is a famous computer programmer and innovative pioneer in teaching. I have enjoyed reading several of his books. He compared how humans have traditionally learned and how they learn nowadays.

Nowadays they sit in a classroom and a teacher lectures to them about a subject and they read about it.

Contrast this with how humans have learned for hundreds of thousands of years. The adolescent boys walked around with the men, to go forage and hunt in the forest. The lessons taught had immediate impact on survival.

"That plant good to eat. That plant bad. This is how we hunt rabbits."

The **most common type of "walk and talk,"** that I do, is really, **"walk and read."** I walk around in circles inside my house while reading a book. **I always read with a pen and make notes in the margin. If there is something good, I also fold over, the upper, right corner of the page, so I can go back to it later.**
If an idea pops into my head, then I write it down on the inside, back cover of the book. This, by the way, is a very common occurrence.

"All truly great thoughts are conceived while walking." - Friedrich Nietzsche

While you've been walking, the subconscious mind has been busy. It has been searching the "university, library stacks of books in your mind," of your brain's long term data base. It does this subconsciously. That's why it is called the subconscious mind. Then it somehow, "pops" this idea into your conscious awareness.

When this happens, **"YOU MUST WRITE IT DOWN IMMEDIATELY!"**

Otherwise you may forget it, potentially for a long time. It is good to try to be attentive to your subconscious mind. It is your friend.

It is more knowledgeable than your conscious mind. But be careful, it does sometimes come up with ideas that are impractical or quite frankly inappropriate for the modern world. You gotta remember, the whole system was designed to help you walk down a path in a forest and survive.

This walking exercise provides new brain neurons through neurogenesis and the reading puts information on them so that they are more likely to establish synaptic connections that will survive.

The whole process is synergistic as the reading holds my interest so that I can walk longer. On a work day the average walk is 30 to 60 minutes. On a day off, 1.5 to 2.5 hours.

The **2ⁿᵈ type** of "walk and talk" is **"walk and flash."** Now don't get the wrong idea. We're talking about flash cards of course. A pile of flash cards is placed on the table. Then I go through several, each time I walk around the circle.

I look at the flash card briefly and then ask myself, what does this really mean?

The **key is instant recognition** and ideally an **instant mental visualization** of the significance. If I get that automatic, immediate recognition of confident understanding, then I put that flash card in the **"done" pile.**

If I immediately recognize it now, then I will immediately recognize it when taking a test or taking care of a patient. This means the information has been sent from my **"slow, logical, effortful, conscious, thinking brain = system two"** to the **"fast, automatic, subconscious, emotional, autopilot = system one brain."**

That concept of "system one" and "system two" brains is from the book, **"Thinking Fast and Thinking Slow"** by Nobel Prize winner Daniel Kahneman. I highly recommend it.

Also, this concept of a slow, logical **system two** and a fast, autopilot **system one** also relates to attending, physician radiologists. They had to be very studious and logical in order to complete diagnostic radiology residency. But then when they go into clinical practice, they have to transition more and more into the into the fast, automatic mind, so that they can read films quickly.

The ones who have a hard time getting themselves to go into automatic mode, are slower to read their films.

The point is that one has to develop the knowledge and skill, and then learn to trust oneself so that they can do it automatically and quickly.

You just have to trust yourself that you know it, look at the film, dictate the words that come into your head (just trust them and don't overanalyze them), sign off the report and get on to the next patient.

On the other hand, if I look at the card and kind of only "half" get it, or there is a delay, then I put it into a **"needs work pile."**

This is an indicator that one is familiar with the material, but it have not yet learned it well enough. In order to ensure long term retention, it should be automatic and fast.

The **3rd type** of "walk and talk" is actually **"walk and talk (read out loud)."** This is mostly for **learning a foreign language (L2)**. The goal is to get in the habit of speaking the language out loud. I just walk indoors in circles and read the book out loud. Eg. I'll start out with easier books like fairy tales and work up to more complex books.

Fairy tales are great for learning foreign languages because the stories are familiar, illustrations are readily available and the vocabulary is mostly relevant eg. family, etc.

By reading out loud, one gets practice reading, speaking and hearing oneself speak. The **brain likes stories.** The brain pays attention to stories.

The brain learns faster from stories, a lot faster than it does from random lists of vocabulary words.

You can increase your memory of it even more by adding some theatrical flair. Vary your vocal intonation. Act as if you were reading the story to an interested audience. This adds to the sensory and emotional aspects of the memory.

The **4th type** of "walk and talk" is **"walk and talk and shout."** This is the same as the 3rd type, except the reader "shouts the words". Actually, **I just say them a little louder**. It takes too much effort in an unpleasant sort of way to really shout the words. Now, why is this even being talked about?

Well, Alexander Arguelles once recommended it and I thought I would try it. Also, I must confess that I almost never do this. I don't enjoy it that much. However, there is something very interesting about it.

On fMRI (functional MRI) it was shown that when people go from subvocalize to speak, to shout, more effort is required and **more neurons are recruited for the task**. This implies that the task is then stored on more neurons. Ie. more brain "real estate" is devoted to the task and theoretically at least the task is faster learned and "better" remembered.

The **5th type** of "walk and talk" is to actually **shadow**, which is also for learning L2. Alexander Arguelles likes to do this with earphones from an audiotape/CD/mp3 player. I like to just use a big CD player on a table while I walk around in circles indoors. This is something that I actually do like to do when studying L2. If the material is relatively new, I do it with the book in hand. If the material is well known, then it can be done without the book.

One can also buy a **variable speed CD player** to slow down L2 when the material is relatively new and to speed it up for a challenge later.

The company CaliFone makes a variable speed CD player that lets you speed up audio play by 15%. There is also software on computers to play things at variable speeds. I like the VLC player for playing audio CD's speeded up. It is a downloadable program for the computer that has a great variable speed player. It lets you speed up three fold.

The **6th type** of "walk and talk" is **to play an English language CD** and to **go through** the related **course booklet**. This is good for some audio CD books and for audio CD courses, eg. From "the Great Courses". **"The Great Courses"** are audio CD, download and DVD courses from the website great courses.com. I especially like their history courses. This is a fun way to walk, and it is very easy to walk for 1.5 to 2 hours while listening to these courses and periodically looking at the booklet that goes with it. I carry a pen and make notes in the book.

The **7th way** to "walk and talk" is **to walk with another person and talk to them**. I do this when tutoring students.

The **8th way** to "walk and talk" is to **"self test."** Eg. after having read about something or viewed a lecture on something, I will walk around in circles indoors and try to say out loud as much of it as I can.

Eg. lets take a topic like the circulation of blood. The conversation with myself will go something like this, "the IVC is on the right side of the abdomen. The IVC returns blood to the right atrium which pumps it through the tricuspid valve and into the right ventricle, etc."

The point of self test is **to prove to yourself** that **you know the material** and **to rehearse** what you know so that you will remember it better.

Now, lets say, I remembered that the left atrium pumps blood to the left ventricle, but could not remember the name of the valve. Well, I would put a copy of an anatomy atlas on the table, so that I could look up stuff quickly. Pop open the book to pictures of the heart and, "oh yes, the valve between the left atrium and the left ventricle is called the mitral valve."

This having stumbled on trying to recollect the "mitral valve", and then looking it up, is a great way to learn.

"Nothing is so firmly fixed in our memory as that which we have blundered." - Winston Churchill.

Once you know you missed it, and you had to look it up, that information tends to be easy to remember after that. That is because this experience of having failed on that question during a "self test" creates an **emotional experience** and this emotional moment releases epinephrine from your adrenal gland which then stimulates your amygdala and hippocampus to better remember the information.

Self test is a great thing to do. You are taking the material from a **phase of "recognition"** by reading to a **higher level** of **spontaneous production, oratory** by saying it out loud. And you are **rehearsing** it and repetition helps memory. The challenge of the self test adds an emotional component and also benefits memory.

The **9th way** to "walk and talk" is on the **basketball court**. I walk in a circle on the basketball court and shoot a lay up or something similar with each circle around the court. With each circle, one self test item is spoken out loud. The dribbling and shooting of the basketball makes it more fun. Do this when it is sunny and you also get your vitamin D for the day.

The **10th way** to walk and talk is on a **treadmill**.

There it is. Ten ways to do a "walk and talk." Of course you can modify it any way that works well for you. The key is to just get moving and to make it a habit.

Chapter 149.

Diet and carbohydrates.

Protein "perks." Carbohydrates "calm." This is true in my experience.

If I drink skim milk, (high protein meal), my mental sharpness stays good.

If I eat a box of organic cereal, (high in complex carbohydrates meal), I often feel sleepy an hour or so later.

Simple sugars (used interchangeably here with simple carbohydrates) are sugars without significant fiber. For example a cereal for young children will often have lots of sugar added. I avoid these like the plague.

Complex sugars (used interchangeably here with complex carbohydrates or STARCHES) are sugars associated with intrinsic fiber. By intrinsic, it is meant that the fiber is part of the foodstuff. Therefore in order to absorb the sugar into one's bloodstream, the fiber has to be peeled off by the digestive enzymes of the small bowel such that the glucose molecule can be set free for absorption into the bloodstream.

This is important. Here's why.

Glucose is the energy of life. The equation of photosynthesis is how plants produce glucose and oxygen from water, carbon dioxide and sun light. The near opposite equation is that of human metabolism whereby glucose is consumed and burned for energy with the release of carbon dioxide.

When you eat a kiddy cereal with lots of added simple sugars and almost no fiber, the glucose is very rapidly absorbed. This can lead to an upward "spike" in your blood glucose level.

People have variable sensitivities to upward spikes in blood glucose level and this sensitivity can change over time. For example, I became more sensitive to it as I got older, Eg. Over 30 years old.

The problem is **rebound hypoglycemia.**

In response to glucose being absorbed from the intestinal tract into the blood stream, the pancreas secretes the hormone called insulin.

Insulin "pushes" the glucose into muscle cells, brain cells and other cells. When insulin release from the pancreas is properly "titrated", everything works well. You are in the **"ZONE OF OPTIMAL FUNCTION."**

The blood glucose remains in a normal range and we feel good. Our energy level is high, mental clarity is high, and we are not hungry. The brain wants glucose. The brain wants a normal blood glucose level, not a big upward spike and not hypoglycemia (low blood glucose).

However, meals with excess simple sugars and the resultant upward spike in blood glucose can cause in many people, an overcompensation of the pancreas whereby too much insulin is secreted. This excess of insulin "pushes" the glucose out of the blood too rapidly.

This leads to a rapid fall in the blood glucose level which is experienced as a sense of unease, blurred vision, queasiness and most of all, ravishing hunger.

This is called **REBOUND HYPOGLYCEMIA** (low blood glucose). At this moment, a person will eat anything. Typically, they will run to the "coffee table," snarf down some caffeinated coffee and then pound down a couple of handfuls of sweets such as cookies and donuts.

This little snack is of course is loaded with simple sugars and the process repeats itself. This leads to repeated cycles of hyperglycemia (high blood glucose) and rebound hypoglycemia leading to a **blood glucose curve that looks like a roller coaster.**

Over time, this leads to weight gain, and can lead to obesity.

Far better to eat a meal with **intrinsic fiber** such as a cereal with minimal if any sugar added and with naturally occurring fiber. For example, I routinely eat organic cereals with 4 or fewer grams of sugar per serving.

In addition to cereals, other sources of complex carbohydrates include potatoes, sweet potatoes, wheat, corn, rice, some spaghettis, whole grain breads etc.

These types of meals provide a gentle, gradual rise in blood glucose that is well handled by the pancreas and insulin. You don't feel that hungry. You just eat whenever it is most convenient, and the best food is available.

It is worth your while to learn more about food, because it is the source material to build your body including your brain. Food is also the fuel to energize your body. Just as you want the best fuel for your car, even more so, you should want the best fuel for your body.

I told my kids the "three little pigs story" with the emphasis that their "body" was the "house" they were building to live in. I thought this was a great way to bring the point across. They responded with the expected, "dad, why are you bugging us?"

It is difficult for a short, average build, bald guy like myself to tell my 6 foot tall, muscle bound, 16 year old son with hair like Elvis that junk food will make him short and weak. The answer to why kids are taller nowadays, but not healthier can be partly found in the book called, "Missing Microbes" by Martin Blaser.

Here's a conversation with my daughter when she was 9 years old.

"Daddy, do fruits and vegetables really make you grow tall?"

Me, "Yes."

"Then why are you so short?"

Chapter 150

Diet and protein.

"There's a Drosophila melanogaster in my soup." - Gary Larson, American cartoonist, (this is a caption from a cartoon where a biologist has a fly in his soup).

If I drink skim milk (a high protein meal), for lunch, my energy level and mental clarity are good. If I eat a box of cereal for lunch, I feel sleepy in the afternoon.

The box of cereal does not have that much of a sleep inducing effect if it is for breakfast.

The smart move for you is to pay attention to the affect that different foods have on you. Try to figure out what type of eating pattern helps you to function at your best.

It is helpful to write this down on a calendar to keep track of it for a few months. Time yourself after eating breakfast and lunch to see how soon you get hungry. Also keep track of how mentally sharp you feel with the different types of meals.

Chapter 151.

Diet and fat.

"French fries kill more people than sharks and guns, but no one is afraid of French fries." - Robert Kiyosaki.

A little bit of fat in the diet is ok.

At parties and celebrations and family holidays it is normal to splurge a little bit.

However, it is wise to limit your fat intake on a daily basis.

Oxygen is delivered to tissues when red blood cells (RBC's) pass thru capillaries (very small blood vessels that connect the arteries to the veins). The average red blood cell (oxygen carrying cell) and the average capillary are both in the ballpark of 7 microns.

Sometimes the capillary is smaller and the red blood cell needs to deform itself, bend-fold upon itself, in order to squeeze thru the capillary.

The bottom line is that it is a tight fit under good circumstances.

Well, what has that got to do with fat you may ask?

Excess fat intake during a meal can cause aggregation of RBC's, they stack up like a roll of coins, high viscosity, such that they travel slower thru capillaries.

Excessive amount of fat can prevent the arterial lining cells (endothelial cells) from releasing a vasodilator called, nitrous oxide.

The lack of nitrous oxide results in narrowing of arterial diameter (not a good thing).

This is called vasoconstriction.

Habitual eating of excess saturated fat predisposes to chronic and acute problems.

The chronic problem is the buildup of atherosclerotic plaque in the arteries of the heart, the brain, the penis and elsewhere. This narrows arterial diameter on a chronic basis.

Chronic high fat intake is also associated with weight gain which predisposes to high blood pressure. In order to pump blood to a bigger body, blood pressure is often increased.

Then excessive saturated fat intake during a meal can have the superimposed effect of arterial vasoconstriction and RBC rouleaux formation. This increases the risk of a heart attack (myocardial infarction, MI).

Trans fats also have harmful effects on arteries.

A diet high in saturated fats and/or trans fats is associated with increased risk of Alzheimer's disease (dementia).

The bottom line is that chronic, high saturated fat and trans fat intake is detrimental.

Now there is some talk about omega 3 supplementation. The problem is purification.

I used to take them, but they are kind of expensive, and I wasn't sure that the brand I was taking was purified well enough.

The word on the street is that the conversion of plant omega 3's to the type of omega 3's in the human brain, DHA and EPA occurs at a relatively low rate. However, other knowledgeable authors think that the conversion rate is adequate.

I have read a lot about it. I am still not sure what is the best thing to do. Food is a surprisingly complex subject and it can be difficult to sort out factual information from advertisements.

For myself, I currently do not take omega 3 supplements. I just eat a lot of plant foods and hope that adequate amounts will be converted to DHA and EPA.

I was impressed by the book, "Power Foods for the Brain" by Dr. Neal Barnard which suggested that conversion from plant foods appears to provide adequate amounts of omega 3 fats.

Omega 3 fats are thought to be beneficial by means of fluidizing neuronal cell membranes. The rationale is that cold water fish have increased amounts of omega 3 fats in order to keep their cell membranes fluidized in near freezing temperatures.

For example, saturated fat is typically solid at room temperature. When you first get a pizza, it is hot and you can see the liquid oil on it. The next day, sitting on the countertop, this same oil is now cooled to room temperature and is solid.

In comparison, omega 3 fats are liquid at room temperature. Within a cell membrane the concept is that the double bonds in the omega three fatty acids cause a "bend" in the fatty acid. Fatty acids have a standard nomemclature whereby one end is called the "omega" end. Omega 3 means that there is a double bond at the carbon number 3 position.

This "bend" "pushes" away the adjacent cell membrane, phospholipid, fatty acid tail and thus "fluidizes" the cell membrane to speed up membrane activities. A phospholipid is a phosphate connected to two fatty acid "tails." In drawings of a cell membrane, the phospholipid looks like a sperm with two tails.

Cell membrane fatty acids also serve as the substrate for other chemicals. Omega three fatty acid conversion tends to lead to antiinflammatory chemicals.

Whereas, some other types of fatty acids are converted to proinflammatory chemicals, (not good).

The key point of this chapter is that most Americans should be eating a lot more plant foods. I recommend to eat organic when possible.

Chapter 152.

<u>Diet and plants.</u>

Here's a helpful little trick. **Always eat the least palatable, healthy thing first for dinner. That's when you are hungriest.**

Typically I'll start out with the cauliflower or broccoli and then the split peas and if there is still room, save the other entree or cereal for last.

Then clean the occlusive surfaces of the teeth by eating a carrot. This is all chased down with water. Then floss and rinse again with water. I only brush my teeth in the morning before work.

Plants are the best thing to eat. Humans and other animals coevolved with plants. They make glucose as well as almost all the vitamins.

We eat the plants and then our feces serve as a fertilizer.

Imagine yourself in the middle of a open field on a hot, sunny day, 90 degrees Fahrenheit. What would you do?

Most likely you would walk over to the shade of a tree or better yet go inside an air conditioned building.

Well a plant can't do that. It can't walk. It has to defend itself from the sun by using chemicals. Plants are geniuses with chemicals. The plant makes antioxidants to protect itself.

When animals eat the plant, they absorb the antioxidants. You can't get them from eating animal foods, because the animal has already used up the antioxidants.

Plants have intrinsic fiber which has multiple benefits. The fiber slows down the rate at which glucose is absorbed from our gastrointestinal tract (GIT) which is a good thing.

The fiber binds water and thus softens our stools which is a good thing. Eg. Your poop should be somewhere along the spectrum from a "cow pattie to soft little logs".

Meat eaters have slower GIT transit time which allows more water to be absorbed from the food. This dries out the stool and makes it hard. Normally stool should be relatively liquified in the right side of the colon. When it is hard, it can obstruct the appendix and cause appendicitis. Appendicitis is more common in persons who eat a lot of meat.

This dry, hard stool leads to straining at defecation and the backpressure causes diverticulosis (outpouchings of the sigmoid colon) which is extremely common.

These diverticuli can occasionally "pop" and cause inflammation of the adjacent abdominal (mesenteric) fat which is very painful and called diverticulitis.

The high fat content of meat leads to increased secretion of bile from the gallbladder. This increased bile load combined with slow transit time and meat related carcinogens leads to increased risk of colon cancer in persons who eat lots of meat.

The straining at the stool can also cause hemorrhoids.

In addition, the straining increases intraabdominal pressure and can cause hiatal hernia (when the top of the stomach herniates upward into the chest) which is associated with GERD (gastroesophageal reflux disease), reflux of stomach acid into the esophagus and "heartburn" type pain. On a chronic basis, this is also associated with increased risk of esophageal carcinoma.

This whole concept of high meat intake related straining at the stool and the related problems is called **the abdominal pressure theory, and was pioneered by an Irish surgeon named Dr. Denis Burkitt.** He was a very clever fellow and he wrote a nice little book about this.

His nickname was the "fiber man."

Another genius of nutrition with a fascinating life was Nathan Pritikin. He found out that he had heart disease, coronary artery atherosclerosis with an abnormal EKG (electrocardiogram) when he was in his forties.

He was independently wealthy from his engineering inventions and businesses. This provided him with time to read. He decided to learn all there was to know about nutrition, and everything else related to the prevention and treatment of coronary disease.

He noticed that in countries where less meat was eaten during WW2, there were fewer heart attacks. He learned that low fat diets are cardioprotective. He started his own health center which emphasized a low fat diet and walking, and his patients did well.

His books and the videos of him on the internet are interesting. He was the mentor to Dr. McDougall who is another nutrition expert who promotes a predominantly vegetarian diet.

Dr. McDougall helped me to lose weight when I went thru a 4 year fat phase in my life. There is a, "Star McDougaller" article about it on his website, drmcdougall.com.

When I was in college, med school and residency I ate lots of cereal and peanut butter and jelly sandwiches. When meat was available, I usually ate it. I did not care about diet other than for convenience.

So the truth of the matter is that the hormonal excellence of youth is more important than diet. At those young ages of 18 to 34 years old, people tend to be mentally sharp even if their diet is not so good. However, it seems wise to optimize diet at all ages.

I did not switch to being an organic only, lacto-ovo-vegetarian until I was in my late 30's. Lacto means milk, and ovo means eggs. Milk is liquid meat. I only eat eggs about twice a month.

As you get older, past 35 years of age, you see more and more people getting fat, developing hypertension (HTN), diabetes, coronary artery disease and impotence. That's why people over 35 who want to optimize their health start taking diet a lot more seriously.

"If all the nutritionists in the world were gathered together into a stadium, the only thing that they would all agree on is that people should eat more vegetables." - Kevin Hannon PhD, Purdue university.

According to Dr. Neal Barnard, the best foods for your brain are vegetables, fruits, beans and whole grains (as long as you don't have gluten sensitivity or related conditions).

"An ounce of prevention is worth a pound of cure." - Benjamin Franklin

"I'm not afraid of a salad bar. I'm not afraid of the vegetable table. I'm afraid of the operating table." - Peter Rogers MD.

The bottom line is that if you eat a predominantly vegetarian diet, you will most likely maintain a normal total cholesterol level, less than 150, and never develop significant coronary artery disease. With this diet you will likely maintain a healthy body weight and have markedly decreased risk of hypertension, diabetes and impotence.

It's a good deal!

Humans are omnivores, but are predominantly herbivores.

I learned the following information on evolutionary evidence of humans being herbivores from a lecture and book by Dr. Mcdougall. For more information you can go to his website or read his books. He is an expert on nutrition and although I don't agree with everything he says, I have learned a tremendous amount from him.

According to Dr. McDougall, the following are approximate quotes based on memory of a lecture and book from years ago.

"The tip of our tongue has carbohydrate taste receptors. Our teeth are designed for grinding plants. Our nearest animal ancestor, the chimpanzee, is predominantly vegetarian. Our gastrointestinal tract is designed for a predominantly vegetarian diet."

"In contrast, cats are obligate carnivores. The tip of their tongue has amino acid (protein) taste receptors. Their teeth include fangs for grasping and tearing meat. Their intestinal tract is also designed for meat."

"When you see a plate of fruits and vegetables you salivate for them, just for them."

"When you are driving down the road and you see a cow at pasture. You might say to yourself, "gee, I could really go for a hamburger with some lettuce, tomatoes, cheese, ketchup, soft buns etc." You don't say to yourself, "gee, I'd like to run over there and take a bite out of that cow's ass," like an obligate carnivore would." (my phrasing on the last three sentences).

Starches (complex carbohydrates) are your sources of sustained energy. For example, I can eat a box of Mesa Sunrise cereal at 5:00 am and then work straight thru until 8 pm with no lunch except a cup of coffee.

Vegetables and fruits are your sources of nutrients. Only vitamins D (sunlight) and B12 (meat etc.) are predominantly from other sources. I eat broccoli, cauliflower, split green peas and carrots to obtain nutrients, antioxidants and to decrease my risk of cancer or heart disease.

I also occasionally eat almonds. When eating out I eat a much wider variety of foods. I like the whole foods grocery store, and sometimes go to the salad bar there.

Maintaining your body is like maintaining a car. However, your body is a lot more important than a car.

You can buy a new car. You can't buy a new body (plastic surgery, cosmetic alterations excepted). You have to maintain your body so that it lasts for life, approximately 85 years.

"If I had known I was going to live this long, I would've taken better care of myself." - George Burns.

Vegetables are relatively alkaline. That is good.

Vegetables are anti-inflammatory. That is also good.

It is worth the effort to figure a way to get more vegetables into your diet.

Chapter 153.

Diet and caffeine.

Caffeine has benefits, but it also has significant downsides.

Caffeine inhibits adenosine receptors in your brain, which then facilitates increased activity of acetylcholine neurons along with increased wakefulness.

Caffeine mimics the acute stress response to a mild degree. This makes you more awake and more alert. This can save your life if you are driving a car.

Caffeine has also become a social thing. It is common to see doctors walking around with a cup of coffee.

The biggest downside is that once you start drinking it everyday, it becomes an addiction with withdrawal symptoms.

Caffeine causes vasoconstriction of some arteries. When you miss your daily dose of caffeine, you may have withdrawal headaches or other symptoms.

Coffee can cost a lot of money if you buy it everyday at work. It is cheaper to make it at home.

I recommend that you limit your coffee intake to two cups per day or less. Increased caffeine intake can lead to heart palpitations, atrial fibrillation, nausea, insomnia. At higher doses, caffeine can even increase your risk of a heart attack or a seizure.

Caffeine from soda pop increases your risk of cavities from both the sticky sugars and the acid. If you add sugar to coffee, then that can increase your risk of cavities.

I started drinking coffee because one day, post call, after being up most of the night, I fell asleep driving, and my car tapped into another car, that was stopped in front of me, at a red light.

Luckily that car was there, or I would have drifted into the intersection, and probably been killed.

Coffee prevents me from falling asleep in the car when driving late in the day.

My favorite brand is Mount Hagen, Instant Organic coffee.

Chapter 154.

The walking meal.

Sometimes I like to walk while eating. This is especially the case if I spent a lot of the day in the seated position for studying or for work.

Lots of things can be eaten while standing. Our ancestors probably ate a lot while walking around foraging. That way they wouldn't have to carry so much.

A typical "walking meal" may include a box of Mesa Sunrise cereal, some broccoli, some almonds and then carrots to clean off the teeth and some water to chase it down.

This is followed by flossing, also done while walking as long as no one else is around.

For some reason, unbeknownst to me, my wife thinks that flossing in front of other people is near the top of the list for disgusting behavior.

She was not impressed by my rebuttal that there is saliva on all the plates in the sink and that the dogs roll around in the yard in dog crap and then she allows them onto the couch and the bed. Go figure.

That kind of reminds me of how my mom used to go bananas if I rinsed my mouth in the kitchen sink after brushing my teeth. My mother, the kindest, gentlest woman in the world said, "Peter if you do that again, I'm going to kill you."

One last topic of eternal kitchen fuss between men and women is the wastebasket. Usually the woman controls the kitchen with a totalitarian dictatorship, and the wastebasket is small and it slides under a drawer next to the sink. Then it gets filled up every day and gets stuck a lot with piled up junk and you gotta take out the garbage every day.

For years to no avail I have recommended putting a larger wastebasket in the kitchen, like the one outside which holds approximately one million gallons and has one foot diameter wheels. Then you would only have to roll it outside once a week. For some reason, the women in my life have never agreed to this.

Anyways, the whole walking meal tends to take 30 to 60 minutes and if no one is home, then I will often listen to an audio CD during the process.

Simultaneously, I've gotten in 30 to 60 minutes of walking exercise, eaten a healthy meal, maintained dental hygiene and perhaps even listened to one or two audio CD lectures.

Chapter 155.

Teeth.

The reason for this chapter about teeth is that part of being successful in life comes from focusing your energy on your goals.

It is helpful to simplify the rest of your life when possible. I know people who spend thousands of dollars on dental problems every year, because they don't take care of their teeth.

If you take care of your teeth, you will save a lot of time and money and will improve your overall health.

The two main things that cause cavities are sugar and acid. If you avoid eating foods with excess sugar and acid, your teeth will be better off.

After eating food, it is good to first rinse your mouth with water, and then to floss and rinse your mouth again with water.

Flossing is more important than brushing.

I only brush my teeth when I want my breath to smell better, such as in the morning before work.

Overnight, the anaerobic bacteria in the gingival crevice (between teeth and gums) proliferate because we are primarily nose breathers at night with resultant lower oral cavity oxygen level.

When we open our mouths in the morning, many of these anaerobic bacteria die and release smelly byproducts. That's why we get morning, "doggy" breath.

Chapter 156.

Trauma.

You should try to avoid head trauma.

Gee, isn't that obvious.

"It takes an unusual mind to think about the obvious." - Alfred North Whitehead

"Nothing is more difficult to see than that which is right before our faces." - Goethe

"The hardest thing to explain is the glaringly obvious which everyone has decided not to see." - Ayn Rand.

Ask yourself this question. Am I doing anything that involves getting hit in the head?

If you are, then consider to stop doing that activity.

Head trauma is bad for the brain. The brain is a delicate "computer" like organ. Although it has a hard skull to protect it, head trauma can significantly impair cognitive function.

Repeated head trauma can lead to something called CTE (chronic traumatic encephalopathy).

If you are curious, there is a lot more information about this on the internet.

Chapter 157.

The Yin and Yang of life.

Lots of things in life are binary, such as day and night.

In humans, our nervous system has a binary system called the autonomic nervous system. It has been likened to a car with the sympathetic component being the accelerator and the parasympathetic being the brake.

The sympathetic autonomic nervous system (SANS) is for fight or flight. When you are fighting a wild beast or running from it, your body is concerned with survival, not growth and repair.

The parasympathetic autonomic nervous system (PANS) is for feeding, digestion, relaxation and sleep. **During this time your body repairs itself, heals itself and grows in positive ways, such as myelinating brain neurons to make them faster.**

Just as there is a spectrum of transition between day and night, there is also a spectrum from "full go" of SANS, a real fight or flight moment to full go of PANS (sleeping while a meal is being digested by your intestinal tract).

The point is that persons in the modern world have a tendency to spend too much time in SANS. It is good to try to keep a balance in your life with adequate time for PANS, for reading, contemplation, family, friends, relaxation and sleep.

Chapter 158.

Goal setting.

"Don't talk about your goals. Pursue them." - Sylvester Stallone, actor and author of "Sly Moves."

Brian Tracy is famous for writing about goal setting and achievement.

"The ability to set goals and to make plans for their accomplishment is the master skill of success....Success equals goals. Everything else is commentary." - Brian Tracy from "Maximum Achievement."

Having clearly defined short term and long term goals helps you to achieve more.

Research has shown that goals are "contagious." That is why it is good to hang around with people who have similar goals. You will motivate each other.

One day, frustrated by what rebellious, little brats my kids were, I asked my dad, "how do you get a kid to do what you want them to do?"

He said, **"children will rebel against their parents and make themselves a slave to their peers."** (I could not find this as a quote on the internet).

He continued, "encourage them to hang around with nice kids that are doing what you want your kids to do."

Chapter 159.

Brain Toxins.

It is wise to avoid things that are toxic to the brain or potentially toxic to the brain.

For example, some pesticides are also toxic to humans. Try to avoid them.

There is controversy about **aluminum** being potentially neurotoxic and associated with Alzheimer's dementia. There is a lot of stuff like this, where do you don't know if it is really true. My aunt, Irma was a brilliant doctor and she cooked in aluminum pots everyday. However, I now avoid them.

Lead is a neurotoxin. Some older houses have lead based paint. Some houses have lead solder in their water pipes. Consider buying a filter or at least letting the water run for a while before drinking it. Some children's toys were inadvertently painted with lead paint. Working with radiators can cause lead exposure. Metal wicked candles sometimes contain lead.

I prefer clear glass cups, plates and water kettles.

Some organic solvents are neurotoxic and/or carcinogenic. These are often found in **things that rapidly transition from liquid to solid such as glues and paints.**

Avoid diesel exhaust. When I see a truck or bus about to drive by, I walk in the opposite direction and/or hold my breath to avoid breathing the diesel exhaust. Diesel exhaust is neurotoxic.

If your car has been sitting in the hot sun all day, then open the doors and trunk for a moment before you get in to let it "outgas" a little bit. Hot temperatures cause increased outgassing from the car's interior. This is especially the case with a newer car.

If you like fishing, try to fish at a location where the water is relatively unpolluted.

Be careful about burning wood if it may have been coated with arsenic, the smoke may be toxic.

Be careful about detergents and cleaning chemicals. Make sure the area is well ventilated. Open the window or door and consider a fan.

If you are going to paint your house, then do it at a time when you can open the windows or better yet when most persons are on vacation and consider using a fast drying paint.

Make sure to replace the furnace air filters in your house periodically.

Consider having your water tested to determine if you would benefit from some sort of a water filter.

Some things are good for some persons, but bad for others. For example, if you have **iron** deficiency anemia, then it could be good to increase iron intake. However, if you are a man with normal iron levels, then excess iron intake might be harmful, might have an oxidant, neurotoxic effect.

Toxins can also be **inhalational**. For example, it is best to avoid living next to a factory or other business with a lot of fumes.

Toxins can be **transdermal**. I have a lot of friends and relatives that are constantly putting lotions and chemicals on themselves for all kinds of reasons. Whenever I comment on it, they get annoyed with me.

I use the simplest shampoo possible, a type of baby shampoo.

Chapter 160.

Exiles and foreigners.

Exiles and foreigners often write great books. The regular persons are busy working and living their lives. They don't want to make any waves, to annoy their bosses or their peers.

Machiavelli was a brilliant guy and had some fascinating insights about human behavior that remain highly relevant today. He was an exile in later life from the leadership in Florence. This gave him time to write about all he had learned of human nature and leadership.

Other persons who were sort of exiled or separated from the usual career paths include Voltaire (in England), Steve Jobs etc.

"Truth is what your contemporaries let you get away with." - Richard Rorty, American philosopher.

"Philosophers get attention only when they appear to be doing something sinister, corrupting the youth, undermining the foundations of civilization, sneering at all we hold dear. The rest of the time everybody assumes that they are hard at work somewhere down in the sub-basement, keeping those foundations in good repair. Nobody much cares what brand of intellectual duct tape is being used." - Richard Rorty.

The exile has already lost their job and social connections, and is trying to reconnect.
The foreigner is "above the fray" to some extent, and has a wide perspective that might be more objective. They are trying to distinguish themselves, and displaying unique insights is one way to do that.

One other group that should be added to exiles and foreigners is independently wealthy persons such as Benjamin Franklin and Nathan Pritikin. After they had built up their wealth, they had time to pursue their interests.

It takes a lot of time to really read in depth about something and to perform experiments on it.

Chapter 161.

Better grades in math.

Attitude has a huge effect on how someone does in math. My senior year of high school, I had an injury that prevented me from wrestling and I did not like the math teacher who was also an assistant wrestling coach. I felt that he had pressured me to come back before my collar bone injury was healed, and that this was detrimental to me.

It was a statistics class. Despite having an overall high school GPA (grade point average) of around 3.68, I was failing the class. In my own childish way I didn't want to work in that class. I resented having to take the class. I was too immature to see the benefits of learning statistics, and I thought the teacher was a poor lecturer. These by the way are all red flags for academic problems.

In early December, I was informed that it looked like I was going to fail the class. In order to avoid the "F" grade, I had to do lots of homework over the Winter holidays and I changed to a "Pass versus No Credit" grading system. I passed by the skin of my teeth. Not a pretty site.

Now the typical ignorant assessment in this setting would be to say, "well that kid (me) stinks at math."

"Attitude" is the most important word in the world." - Earl Nightingale

Some people fear math because they had a difficult time with it during a grade school or a high school class.

The key is to make up your mind that you want to do as well as you can in math.
Then you need to do the things that will help you to improve.
Great courses.com offers DVD courses with syllabi that walk you thru grade school, high school and college level math.

Khan academy.org has lots of free videos on math topics. In his book, "The One World Schoolhouse," Salman Khan, creator of KhanAcademy.org, writes about how the videos are usually around 10 to 15 minutes in duration to correspond to many student's attention spans. The student can watch the video as many times as they want at home, until they are comfortable with the material.

He also writes about the benefits of a "flipped classroom" whereby the students watch the lectures on their own time, for example at home, and then in the classroom they focus on completing practice problems in the presence of teachers-tutors who are available when the students need help. Thus this is flipped in comparison with a traditional classroom where the teacher lectures in class and the students do the "homework" problems at home.

Mr. Khan also emphasizes the benefits of "mastery learning" whereby the students demonstrate that they are solid on the basic concepts before moving on to more complex topics.

Arthur Benjamin has written books about developing math skills, and has also made DVD courses.

There are books out there like "Speed Mathematics" by Bill Handley.

Using an abacus can be a good way to help kids learn math. There is a video of kids that were trained on an abacus taking a math test, where they were not allowed to use the abacus. They were counting imaginary beads in the air and sliding them over.

There are other DVD courses for math tutoring out there to help you.

The turning point for me in math, was a question of self identity. Up until my wrestling injury as a junior in high school, I viewed myself as an athlete first, and the student component was a distant second. I tried to get good grades in school because I enjoyed learning and I wanted to please or appease my parents.

For example, a typical high school conversation with the "rentals" (teen slang at that time for parents).

Me, "Mom, can I stay out until 11:30?"

Mom, "No. That's too late. You have the SAT test tomorrow. Also, your father has to work tomorrow and I don't want you to wake him up."

Me, "C'mon Mom! I've got good grades. You've seen my report card." Etc.

Once I realized that I might never achieve greatness in wrestling, I gradually decided to focus more on academics. The summer between high school and college, I took calculus at the **local junior college** called Triton college.

Surprise number one. The teacher was great. Surprise number two, I later took other classes at Triton and the other teachers were also great.

Surprise number three. It was fun. In the summer, that was my only class. There was plenty of time to just enjoy learning something new. Summer time is a good time to experiment with taking a difficult class. The class will also likely be less difficult at a junior college than at a university with a room full of red hot premeds.

I went from being afraid of calculus to enjoying it and to crushing the class with an easy A. I think I got an A plus.

Another benefit of summer school is that their is time to fix your deficiencies. Going into the class, I was not that good at math. I had just nearly failed an introduction to statistics class and I had never been that good at the whole algebra, geometry, trigonometry series. In the summer there is a lot of time to "fill in your skill gaps" and to look stuff up, etc.

The key point was that I made up my mind that I was going to do the best I could in math, and that since calculus was a required part of a biology major at Stanford, I was going to have to learn it. I also knew that I might really need to use this knowledge someday.

If you say to yourself, "I'm not good at math, then you are likely to perform in that way."

If you say to yourself, "lots of people have taken this math class and done well. If they can do it, then why can't I?" Then you are likely to do well.

Mnemonic for Biochemistry

For biochem, the two keys were prereading and mnemonics. I converted biochem cycles into concise mnemonics, the minimal information from which the rest could be derived.

I would have about 4 books out on the table with diagrams of a biochem cycle and then ask, "How can this be summarized as concisely as possible?" for example, the key to memorizing glycolysis is to just note the position of the phosphates.

The phosphate changes position about the same number of times as there are digits in a phone number. So I just made it into a phone number that represented glycolysis.

This can be locked into memory in an even more memorable way by converting it into a word with the letter number alphabet.

Mnemonics for most medical subjects.

Basic mnemonics work well for this type of material.

The way to write these is to just list the related items, and then look at the first letter of each word. To facilitate the process, a synonym or substitute word can be used, for example to obtain more vowels to help make the mnemonic.

The time devoted to making the mnemonic is part of the learning process. Once I write a mnemonic and review it a few times, that material is confidently stored long term.

Memorizing tables of data.

The human brain was not made to memorize classification systems and tables of data. The secret of memorizing them is to convert them to a mnemonic or to make up a story using parts of the table in sequential order.

For example to memorize the DNA virus families here is an old mnemonic I made up in medical school. DNA viruses are HAPP(Y) families. More precisely H2APP2(Y).

H – Herpes
H – Hepadna
A – Adeno
P – Papova
P – Parvo
P – Pox
(Y) – (filler to make mnemonic into a word)

The mnemonic gives you a "scaffold" for rehearsal. That is the hardest part of the whole process. The mnemonic makes it easy to memorize the family names. Now it is relatively easy to add in the other details such as clinical subtypes etc.

Medical school topics and flash cards.

Any med school subject can be effectively studied with flash cards. However, pharmacology and microbiology are perfect for flash cards.

Mnemonics for radiology residency.

I just wrote them into an outline format review book which was used as the foundation for condensed notes.

Music suggestions

For lifting weights; Kayne West (Amazing), CIU (put it on the line), Devil makes three (Bullet), Iron Maiden (the Trooper), AC DC (High voltage, Back in black), Motley Crew (Kickstart my heart), Eminem (Lose yourself, Rabbit run, Love the way you lie),

All of the above (Maino), Bob Marley (Exodus and Jamming), Blondie (Call me, I'm always touched by your presence, hanging on the telephone, One way or another), Tupac (California love), Fort Minor (Remember the name), Thin Lizzy (Whisky a jar), Bruce Springsteen (Thunder road, Candy's room), Cindy Lauper (Drive all night), Doors (Love her madly), R. Kelly (Down low, Ignition), Enrique Iglesias (tonight I'm loving you), TI (What you know about that), Ted Nugent (Baby please don't go, Stranglehold), Guess Who (American woman), Roxette (She's got the look), Carly Simon (Nobody does it better), Cheryl Crow (Strong enough), Kool Mo Dee (Wild, wild west, How you like me now), Bon Jovi (Runaway), LL Cool J (I'm the kind of guy), Whitesnake (Give me all your love tonight), 50 cent (Ready for war), Rainbow (16th century Greensleeves and Kill the king live versions, Run with the wolf, Mistreated), Hank Williams Jr. (Country boy can survive), Lynyrd Skynyrd (Simple Man), Queen (We will rock you, We are the champions), Daddy Yankee is like acoustic testosterone (Que tengo que hacer, Gasolina, Lo que paso, paso, Pata boom), Shakira (Hips don't lie, Tortura)

Romantic music; Johnny Cash (Thanksgiving song, Hurt, Ring of fire, I walk the line), ELP (Still you turn me on), Alicia Keys, (No one), Always (Bon Jovi), I will always love you (Dolly), Crazy Love (Van Morrison), Only You (Yaz), Silver Springs (Fleetwood Mac), Rainbow eyes (Rainbow), Change of time (Josh Ritter), That's all I need to know (Sam Cooke), Have I told you lately that I love you (Rod Stewart), How I don't love you (Jamey Johnson), Angel Eyes (Ace of Base), Celine Dion (Falling into you album, seduces me), Violent Femmes (Violent Femmes album), Ace of Base (the Bridge album).

Bummed out about a breakup; Jim Croce, Edith Piaf, Chris Isaaks (Forever blue), Thelma Houston (Don't leave me this way), Scorpions (Lonely nights), Rainbow (Still I'm sad).

Music of hope; Brand new day (Van Morrison), Don't give up (Peter Gabriel), I dreamed a dream (Les Mis or Susan Boyle version), Beautiful life (Ace of Base), I won't back down and running down a dream (Tom Petty), Today (Smashing Pumpkins), Don't worry be happy (Bobby McFerrin).

About the author.

Dr. Rogers started out at Stanford as one of the worst students in his classes and went on to become one of the best, with A+ grades in organic chemistry and biology as well as winning the Student Athlete of the Year Award (Block "S" Honors award) at Stanford.

He then went on to medical school where he earned a 99% national boards part one score, the highest in his class of 333 students.

In residency he also earned a 99% on his diagnostic radiology, written boards and went on to fellowship in imaging guided surgery (interventional radiology) at Harvard and neuroradiology at Rush Medical Center. He taught himself Spanish and he loves Spanish music.

Dedication.

This book is dedicated to my beautiful wife Teresa and our children.

Copyright August 2014.

CPSIA information can be obtained at www.ICGtesting.com
Printed in the USA
BVOW03s2201101214

378883BV00011B/196/P